DOODLE Fantasy Worlds

LEARN TO DRAW WITH 200+
EASY MAGICAL DESIGNS

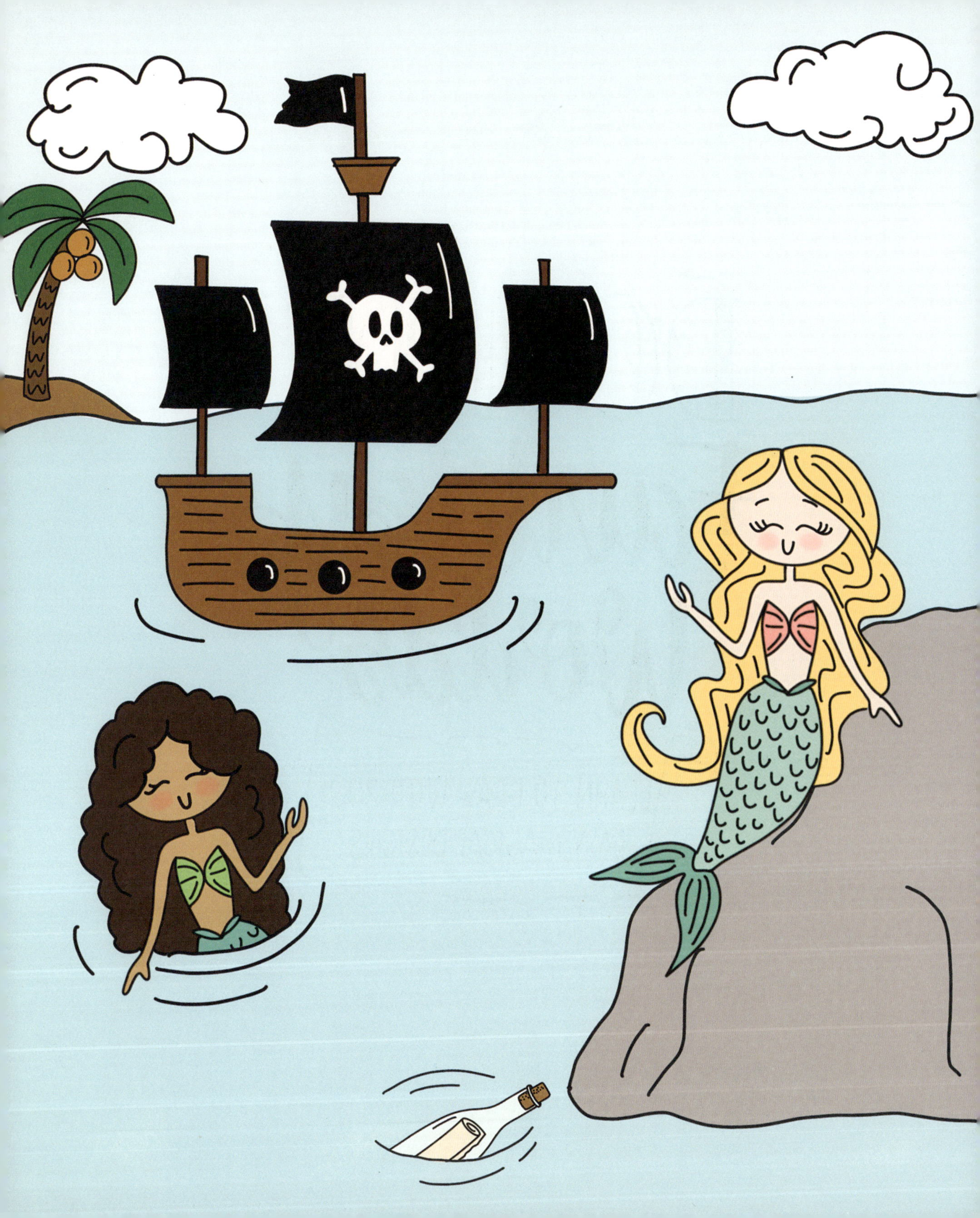

DOODLE Fantasy Worlds

LEARN TO DRAW WITH 200+
EASY MAGICAL DESIGNS

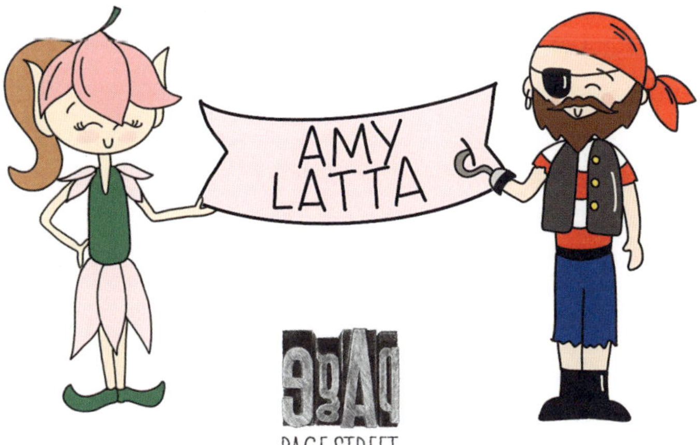

PAGE STREET
PUBLISHING CO.

First published in 2025 by

Page Street Publishing Co.

27 Congress Street, Suite 1511

Salem, MA 01970

www.pagestreetpublishing.com

Distributed by Macmillan, sales in Canada by The Canadian Manda Group.

29 28 27 26 25 1 2 3 4 5

ISBN-13: 979-8-89003-190-7

Library of Congress Control Number: 2024933710

Edited by Sarah Monroe
Cover and book design by Meg Baskis for Page Street Publishing Co.

Illustrations by Amy Latta

Printed and bound in China

Page Street Publishing protects our planet by donating to nonprofits like The Trustees, which focuses on local land conservation.

FOR SARAH MONROE,

WHO WANTED TO DOODLE DRAGONS
AND ELVES. YOUR IMAGINATION INSPIRED MINE,
AND YOUR IDEAS TURNED THIS BOOK INTO A
REALITY. I AM FOREVER GRATEFUL.

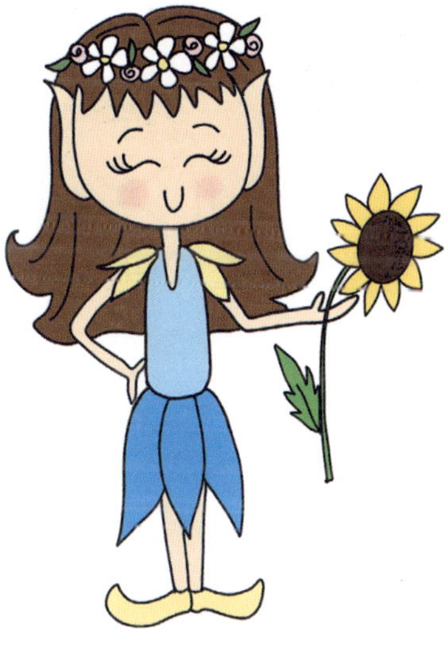

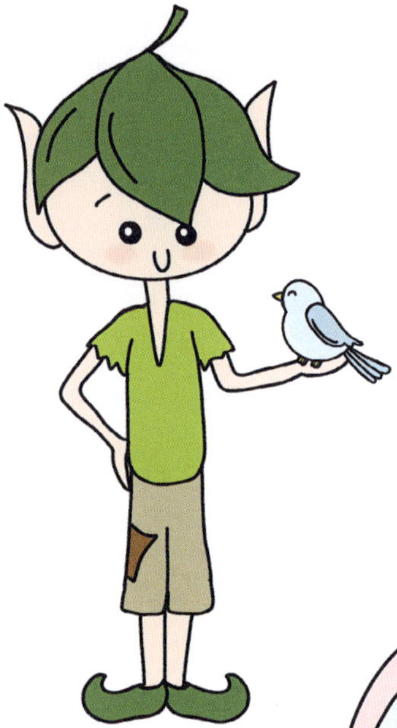
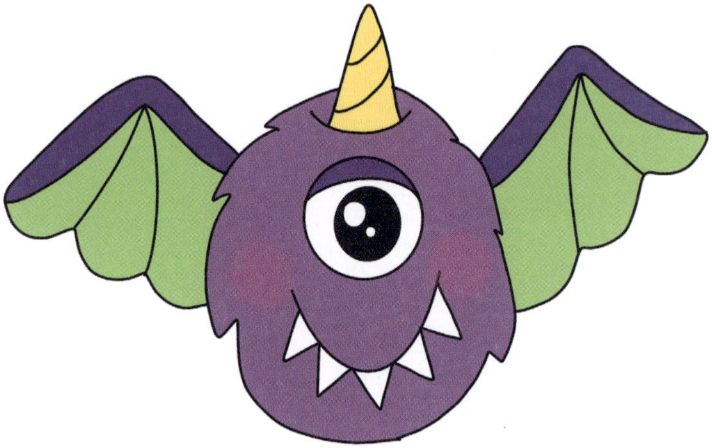
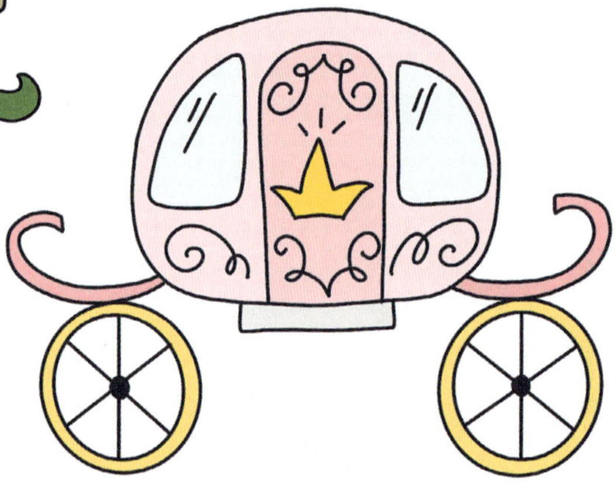
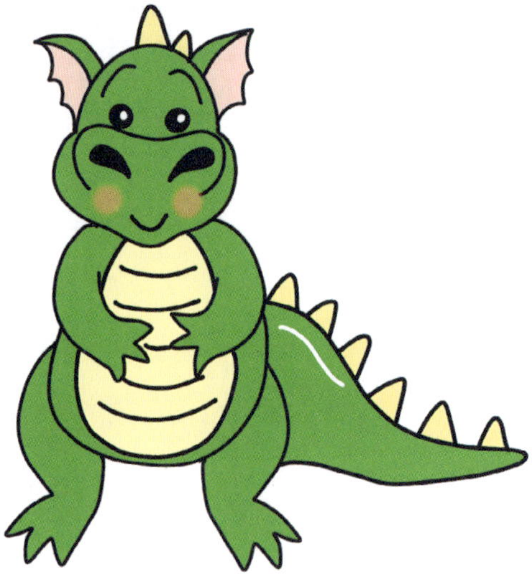
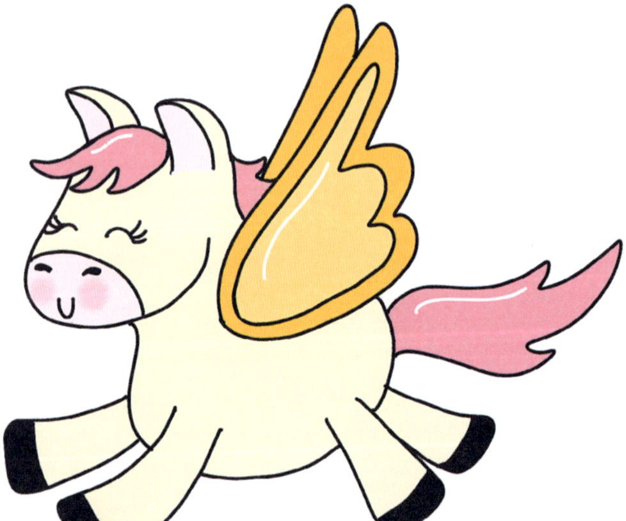
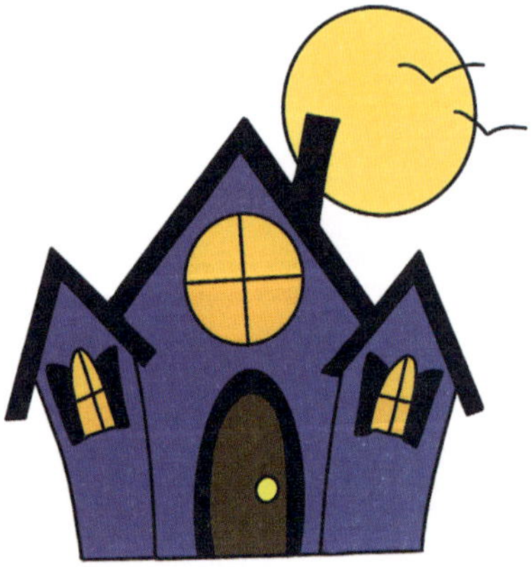

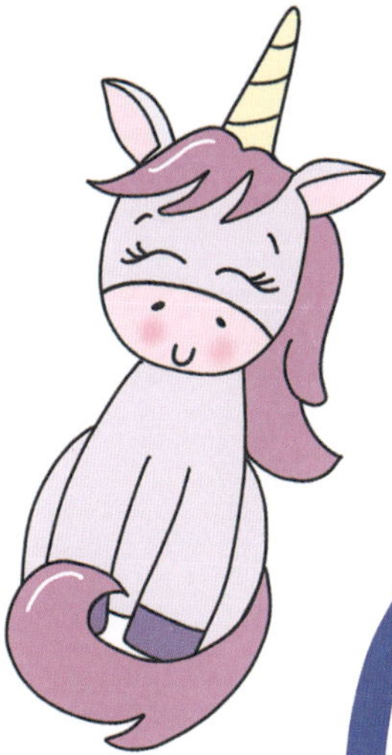
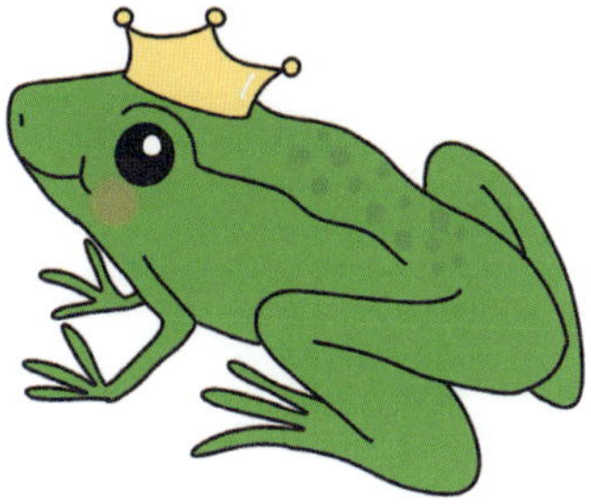
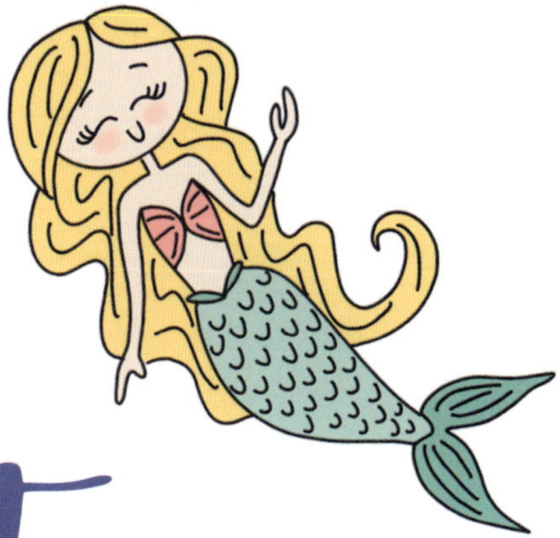

Contents

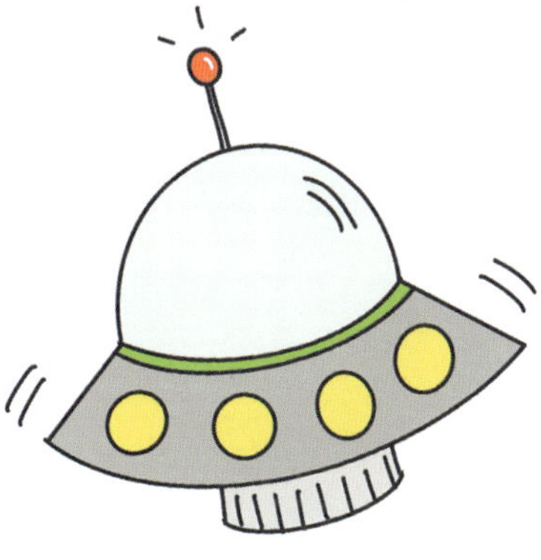
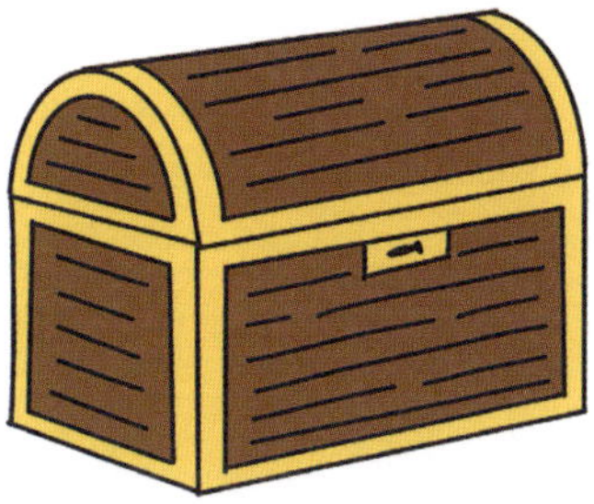
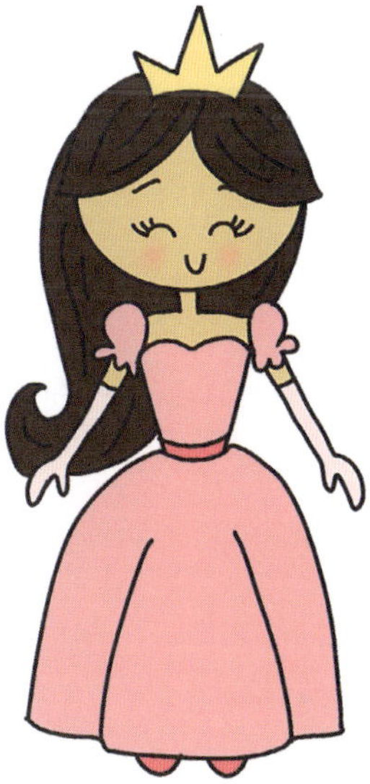

INTRODUCTION

My family likes to joke about the fact that my hands are never still. They're right, especially when I have a pen in my hand. When I'm in a meeting or a class, it typically looks like I'm not paying attention, because my papers quickly become covered in doodles. The reality, though, is that drawing helps me to relax and, believe it or not, to focus on what I'm hearing. Whether I'm sketching flowers, drawing a tiny fairy or creating an elaborate fairy-tale scene, the act of doodling is therapeutic for me.

And if you're reading this book, I'm guessing the same is true for you. Perhaps you find yourself doodling in the margins of your notebooks or around the edges of your grocery list. You may sketch on whatever is handy while you talk on the phone. Like me, you might find that it's calming, or maybe for you it's just plain fun.

No matter how, where or why you do it, doodling is a great form of art because it doesn't require perfection. You don't need any special skills or training to doodle; it's all about creating whimsical little pictures that you enjoy. The pressure is off, so let the fun begin!

No matter what you think your artistic ability may (or may not) be, as long as you can draw simple shapes and lines, you can create all kinds of doodles. My goal as an author and a teacher is always to break down each image into simple, doable steps so that everyone from ages 6 to 106 can be successful. There are visual instructions, as well as written ones, for every image, so no matter what kind of learner you are, you can follow along. You may even surprise yourself by what you are able to create! My husband and my teenage son will tell you they don't consider themselves to be artistic, but they've both been so proud of some of their doodles that we had to immediately go to the store and buy frames for them.

There's no limit to what you can doodle, but in this book, we're specifically going to focus on drawing fantasy worlds. From fairy-tale kingdoms to enchanted forests and outer space, each chapter will take you through a magical place filled with unique characters. We'll draw knights and dragons, monsters, aliens, pirates, mermaids, unicorns and much more. You can use the doodles on their own, or combine them to create entire scenes from your imagination.

Another wonderful thing about doodling is that it requires very few supplies. Even if all you have is a pencil and a piece of scrap paper, you've got everything you need to get started. With that in mind, there are a few things you may want to have on hand as you practice, especially if you want to add color to your drawings.

First, you'll want a pencil and a good eraser (I recommend the Tombow MONO Eraser) to do your basic sketching. For many of the doodles, you'll be erasing as you go in the areas where your later lines overlap earlier ones, so I recommend drawing with pencil first. Next, you'll want a fine-tip monoline black marker like the Tombow MONO Drawing Pen to trace over your pencil doodle. These markers come in lots of tip sizes, ranging from 005 to 08, so you can choose between them depending on if you prefer a thicker or a thinner outline. The higher the number, the thicker the lines will be.

Another good supply to have is a good pack of colored pencils or markers to make your doodles pop. Some of the drawings have white highlights or entire sections that are colored white, so you may want to invest in a white gel pen like the Sakura Gelly Roll® or a white paint pen, especially if you plan to doodle on darker backgrounds. When it comes to paper, this book is specifically designed as a workbook with smooth, heavy pages that are perfect for you to draw on. There are practice spaces provided throughout each chapter so you can doodle right here in the book itself. When you're ready to work outside the book, I recommend a smooth, medium-weight (65 to 80 pound) sketch pad. Bristol board is also a nice surface for doodling, especially if you want to frame your work.

Hands down, one of my favorite things as an author is to see all of the incredible artwork that readers create using my books. When you draw something, I'd love for you to share it with me. You can tag me in your posts on social media @amylattacreations, or post your pictures in my Facebook group, Amy Latta & Friends. I'd also love for you to visit www.amylattacreations.com for more inspiration and project ideas. Let's stay in touch!

Now, I don't know about you, friend, but I'm ready to get started! Let's dive into these magical places and explore all of the fun doodles we can create together.

Amy Latta

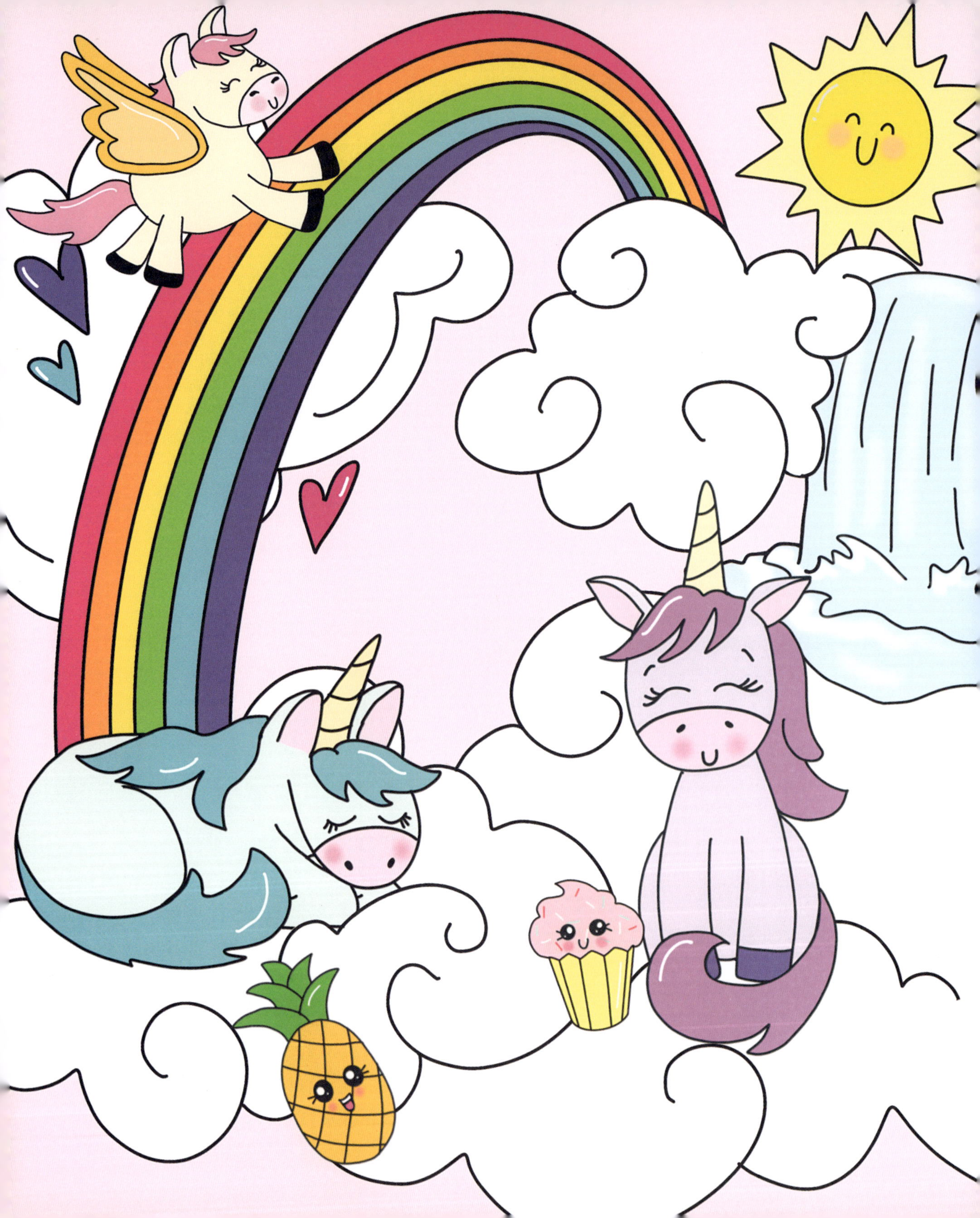

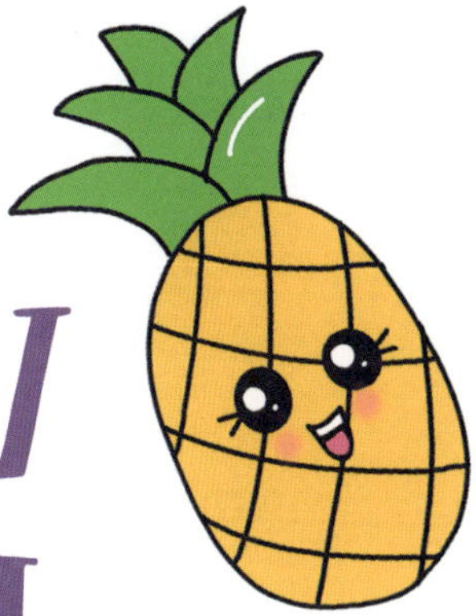

RAINBOW UNICORN *World*

Imagine a beautiful place where unicorns run and play among a carpet of clouds and slide down giant rainbows. In addition to the unicorns themselves, I think this magical world would be filled with waterfalls, cheerful flowers and smiling sweet treats. The sky's the limit—literally!—so let your imagination run wild. Happy donuts, sleepy raindrops and laughing daisies are just a few of the whimsical things you'll learn to draw in this chapter. And, of course, we'll doodle several variations of unicorns and Pegasi so that you can draw them sitting, standing, flying and even sleeping. Grab a pencil and a sketchbook, and let's start creating!

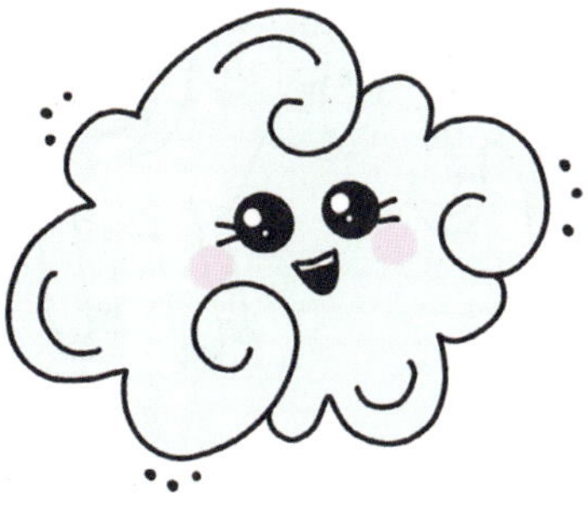

STANDING UNICORN

Unicorns have been one of the most popular mythical creatures throughout history. Drawing one is very similar to doodling a horse, but with a few special variations—like their beautiful horn.

The first step is to sketch the shape of the head and add a pair of ears that point forward. Divide the inner parts of the ears from the outer parts, then sketch a tuft of hair on the forehead. Next, draw the chest and a pair of front legs. Add a curving line for the back and a pair of back legs. Connect the front and back legs to form the belly. Draw a line near the bottom of each leg to indicate the hoof.

Sketch a curving tail, then add a mane going down the back of the neck. Give your unicorn a long, pointed horn in the center of the forehead. Erase any areas in the mane and around the horn where you have overlapping lines. Add detail lines to the horn, mane and tail. Draw eyes and nostrils to give your unicorn a face. I also gave my unicorn a heart on the rear of the body, near the tail. Color your drawing in any way you like to make it unique.

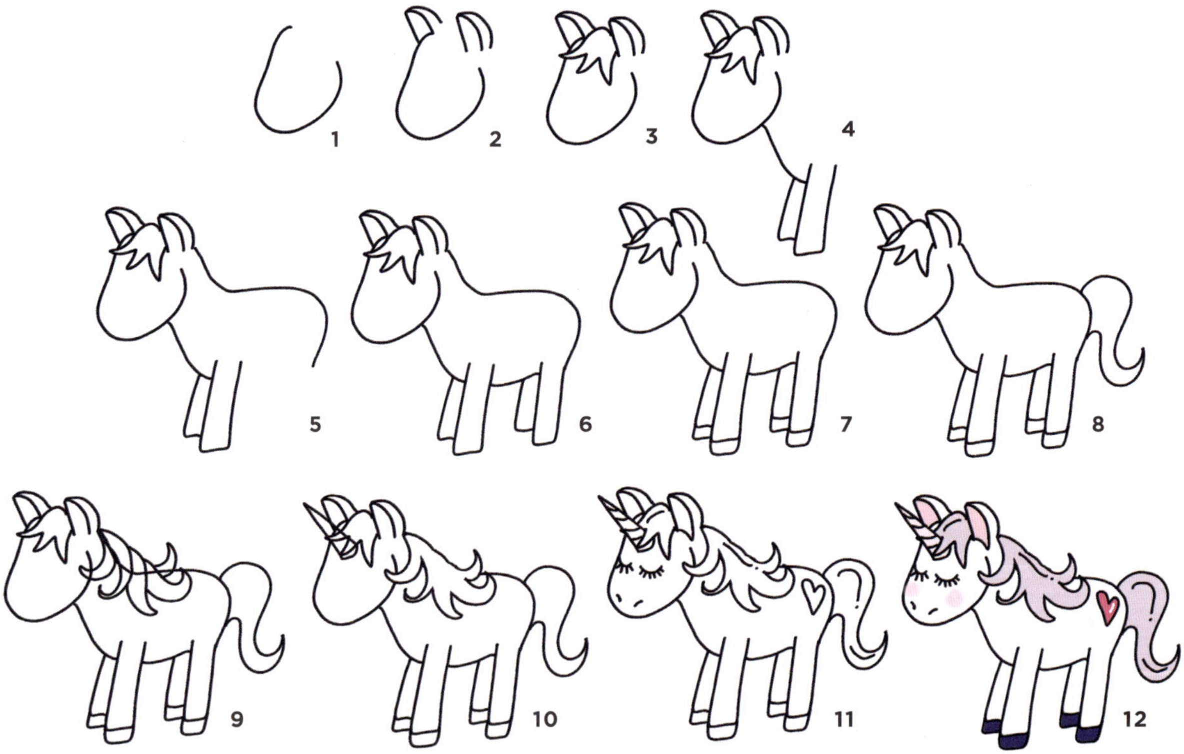

SITTING UNICORN

Let's draw a cute unicorn relaxing in a sitting position. Start this doodle with a "u" shape for the head, and then add an ear on each side. Divide the ears into inner and outer sections. Sketch a horn with diagonal lines inside. Draw a patch of mane to complete the top of the head, erasing any areas where it overlaps your previous lines.

Add two front legs extending down from the head. Draw lines near the bottom of each leg for the hooves, and then connect the legs to complete the front of the body. Sketch a curving line on each side for the back legs, and then draw a curling tail that wraps around the front of the body, erasing any overlapping lines. Give your unicorn the rest of its mane and a face. I divided out the bottom section of the head with a curving line, then added eyes, eyebrows, nostrils and a smile. Finally, add color to complete your doodle.

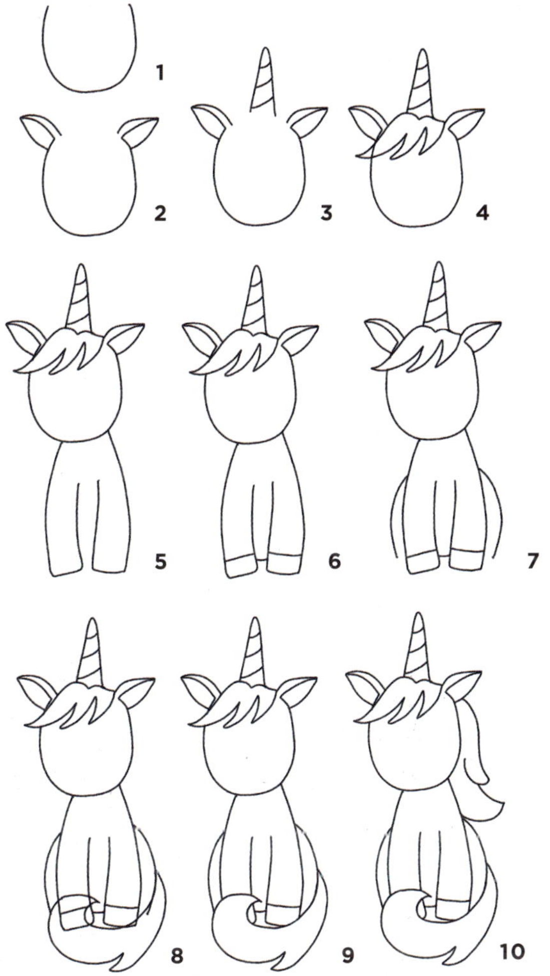

practice here

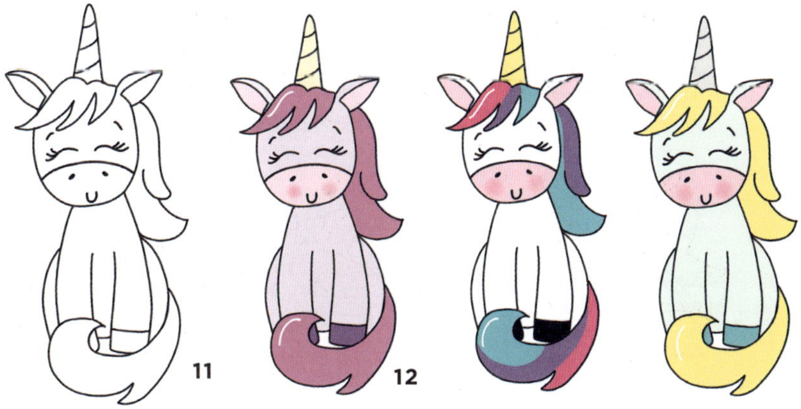

SLEEPING UNICORN

To doodle a cozy, sleeping unicorn, start with a "u"-shaped head and a pair of ears that point forward. Divide the ears into outer and inner sections. Add a horn that's decorated with detail lines between the ears. Sketch a patch of hair on the forehead and erase any areas where it overlaps the horn or face. Draw a long, curving line for the unicorn's back. Add a "c" shape for the top of the back leg and connect it to the head to form the rest of the body. Give your unicorn a mane, erasing the lines where it overlaps the body. Draw a tail that curls around the body, once again erasing extra lines. Sketch two rounded "v" shapes for front legs that are folded under the unicorn. Add a face, then color your sleepy friend.

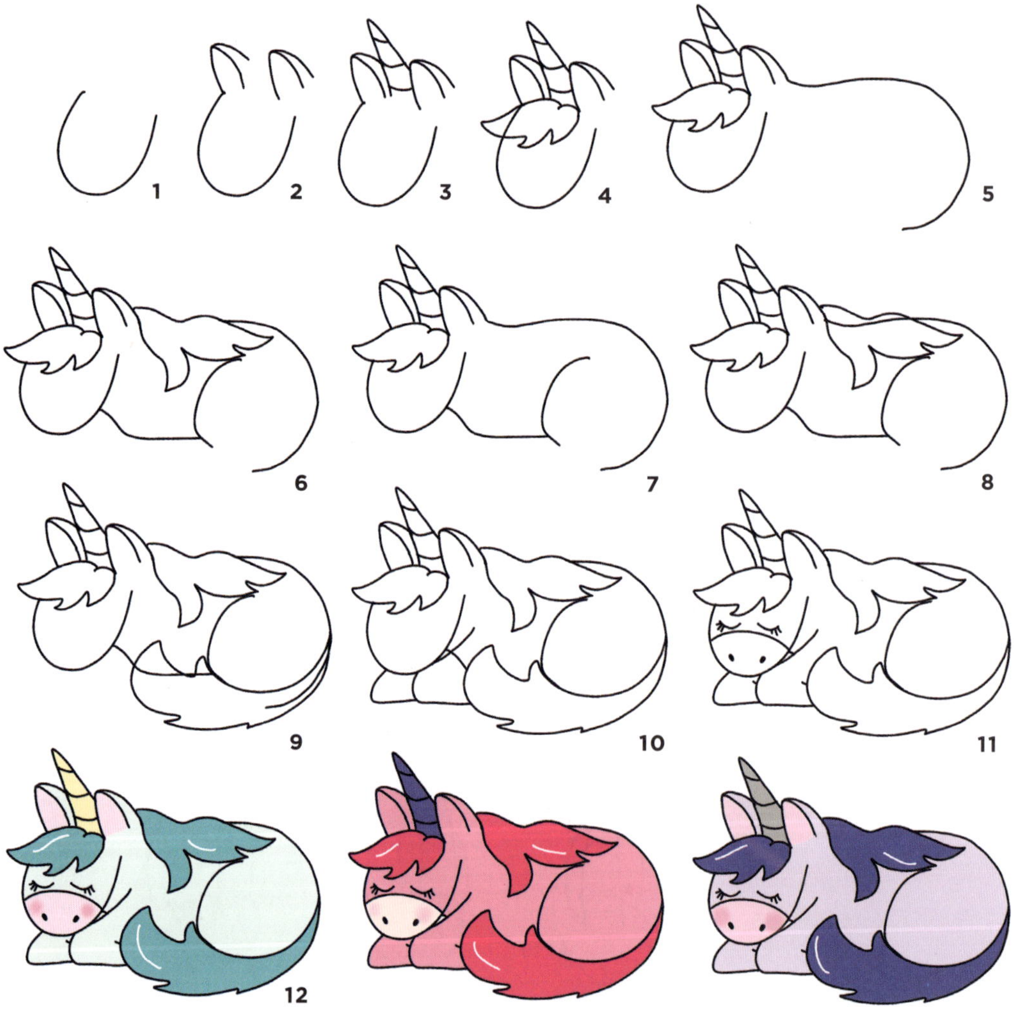

PEGASUS

Another beautiful mythical creature is the Pegasus—a horse with wings! To doodle your Pegasus, we're going to start just like the sitting unicorn on page 13, with the "u"-shaped head and a pair of pointed ears divided into inner and outer sections. Next, add hair on top of the head, and erase overlapping lines. Sketch the front legs, dividing out the hooves. Add a curving line on each side of the body for the back legs.

Draw the rest of the mane, and divide the lower part of the face from the rest of the head with a curving line. Sketch a tail that wraps around the front, then draw a wing shape on each side of the body. Draw a second wing shape inside the first to add detail and dimension. Give your Pegasus a face with eyes, eyebrows, nostrils and a smile. Color your doodle in any way you can imagine.

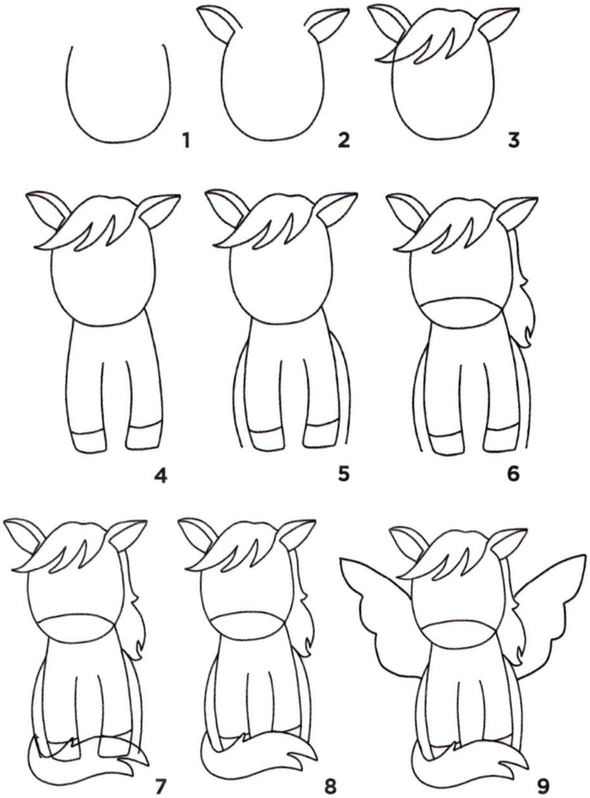

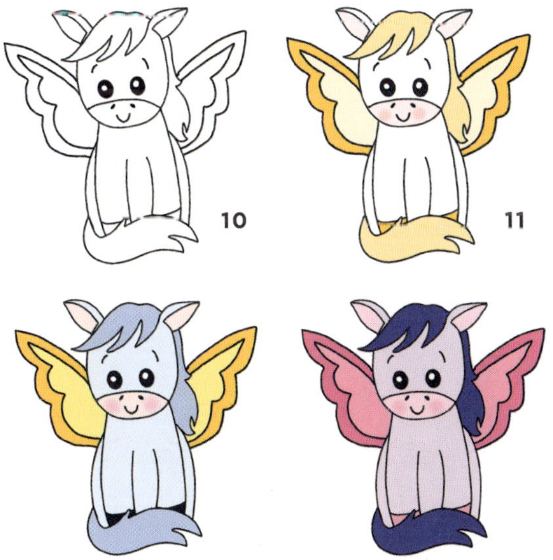

practice here

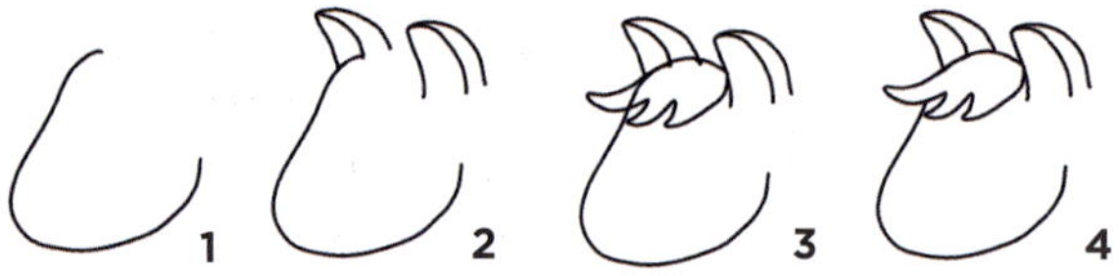

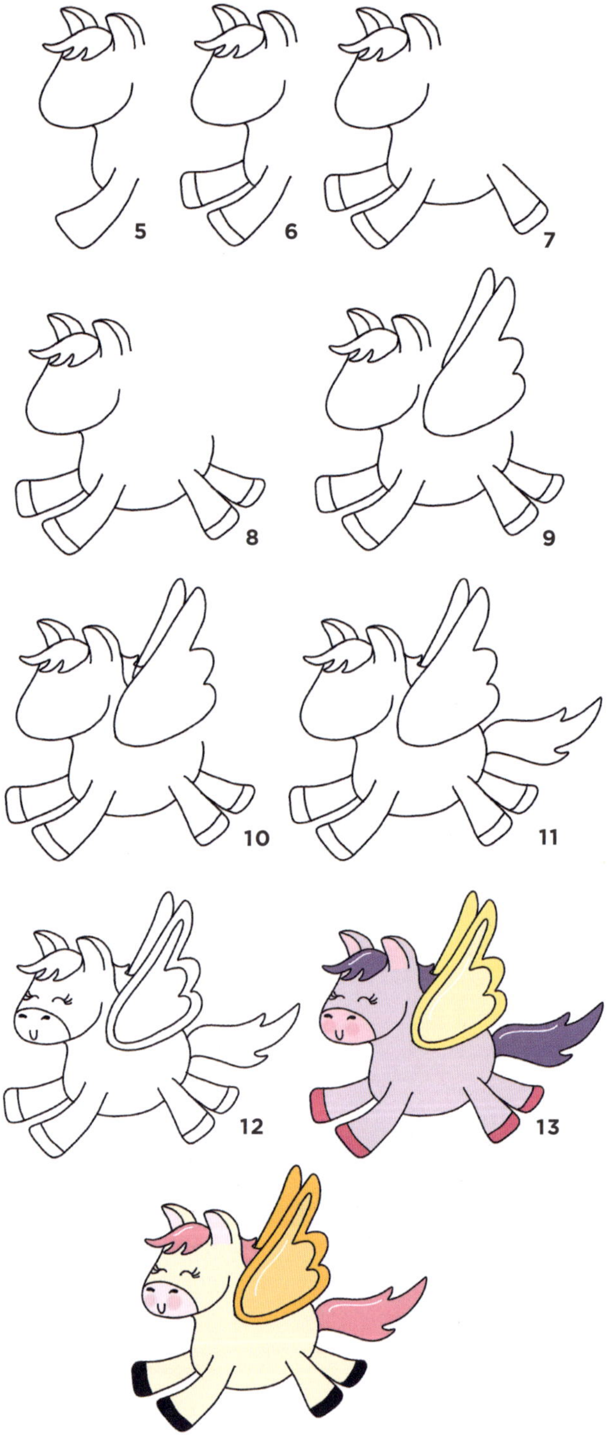

FLYING PEGASUS

Of course, a horse with wings needs to fly, so let's draw our Pegasus soaring through the sky! First, sketch a curving line for the face, then add a pair of pointed ears that tilt forward. Divide the ears into inner and outer sections. Draw a patch of hair between the ears and erase any areas where the lines overlap.

Next, sketch a curving line for the chest, and a leg that extends out to the front. Add a second leg, and draw a line near the bottom of each leg to indicate a hoof. Make a curve for the belly, and then add a pair of back legs with hooves. Draw a wing shape, as well as a line to indicate a second wing behind the first one. Connect the body to the wings, and add a tail and a mane. Give your Pegasus a face, and then add color to complete your doodle.

practice here

CLOUD

Let's doodle some cute clouds for our unicorns' magical world. I like to think of clouds as a series of spirals and bumps put together to make an ovalish shape. Start by drawing a little spiral, and then add a little bump and another spiral on the right of the first one. On the left, make a small bump, a larger bump and one more spiral to form the left side of the cloud. Then, connect the open space that's left with a series of bumps in alternating sizes.

Add details like dots and little curving lines to make your cloud more whimsical. If you like, you can even add a face! This is one example of a cloud, but each one you draw can be unique in the way you arrange your bumps and spirals, just like every cloud in the sky is different from the others. You can leave your drawing as is so that you have a white cloud, or you can color it in a very light shade of blue, gray or maybe even some pretty colors like pastel pink or purple.

practice here

RAINBOW

Of course, our unicorn world needs lots of rainbows! Here I'll show you how to draw this simple doodle with some variations. Start your rainbow by drawing an arch shape. Then, draw a series of increasingly smaller arches inside it, leaving space between each one. You can draw as many or as few arches as you like. Sketch a cloud at the bottom of each end of the rainbow. Feel free to add details like dots and small curving lines to the clouds. Finally, the most important step is to add color.

One option is to color the arches in the traditional "ROY-G-BIV" order: red, orange, yellow, green, blue, indigo and violet. Or, feel free to use whatever combination of colors you like to fill the skies of this magical world.

For a slight variation, you can make one side of the rainbow higher than the other, rather than a perfect arch. As with all of the doodles, the rainbow can be drawn in any size. You can use it as a tiny decoration off in the distance, or fill a whole page with it so that it becomes a slide for your unicorn friends!

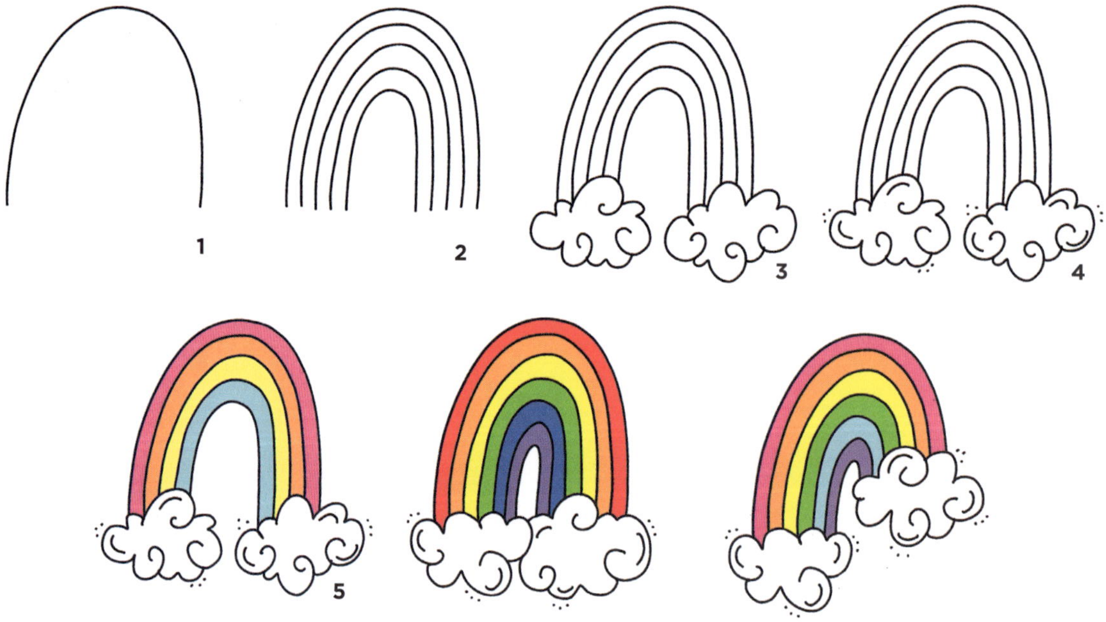

SUNSHINE

The first step in drawing a sweet shining sun is to sketch a circle. Then, make a series of "v" shapes around it, alternating between large and small. Since this is a magical world, we're going to add a cheerful face to our sunshine: a pair of little arches for eyes and a "u"-shaped smile. To finish the doodle, color the sun yellow. I like to use two different shades of yellow, one for the circle itself and another for the sun's rays. To add some extra personality, give your sunshine rosy cheeks on either side of the smile.

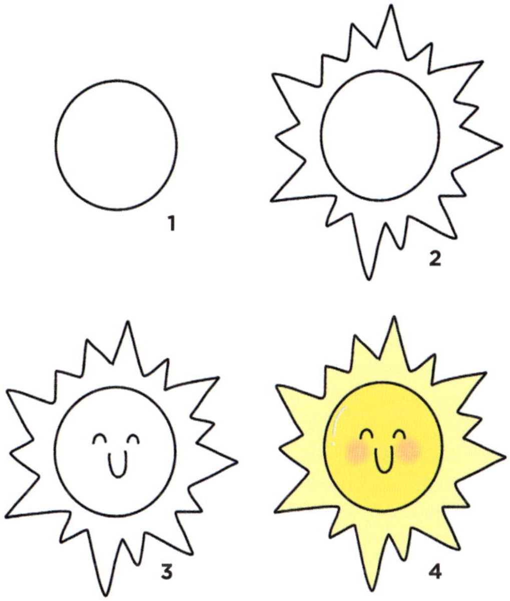

RAINDROP

The raindrops falling from our cloud are small and simple, but you can also draw a raindrop with some personality. Start by sketching the basic teardrop/raindrop shape. Then, add an expressive face inside. I chose to make mine sleepy, with closed "u"-shaped eyes and a colored-in circle to represent a yawn. However, you can add any sort of facial expression you like. Try experimenting with circles, arches or "v" shapes to create different eyes, and then pair them with a frown, a smile or a mouth with its tongue sticking out! Finally, color your raindrop blue and add a pair of rosy cheeks.

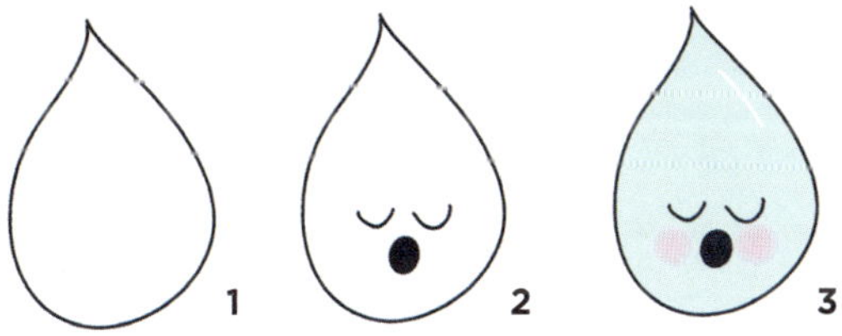

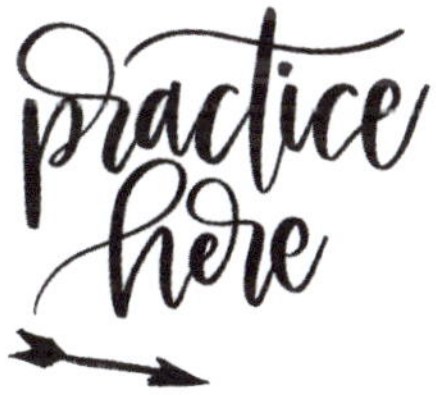

RAIN CLOUD

To make the rain cloud seem a little less whimsical than our cheerful, fluffy clouds, we're going to doodle it by using all bumps and no swirls. Draw a series of "u" shapes that vary in size from small to large, and connect the first and last ones to form a rounded cloud. Then, add a face inside that consists of two "v"-shaped eyes and a little frown. Sketch a few curving detail lines for texture, then draw a group of raindrop shapes falling from the cloud. Finish your drawing by coloring the cloud gray and giving the raindrops a blue tint.

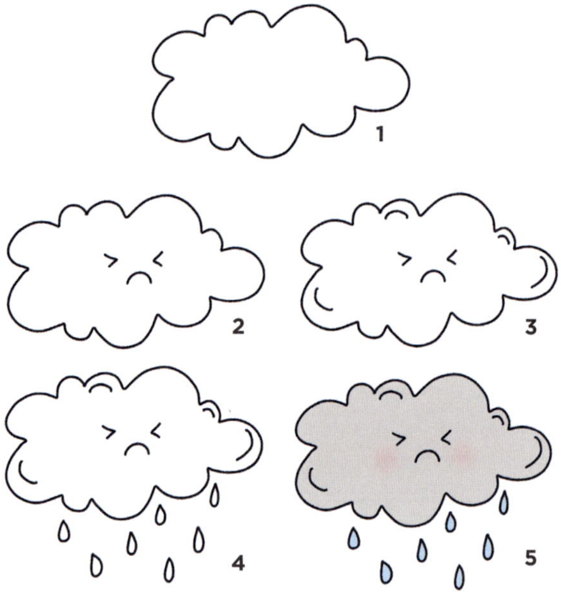

UMBRELLA

Where raindrops appear, so do umbrellas! Let's sketch one, starting with an arch that has a long, thin "j" shape extending down through the center. Double the "j" shape to form the handle. Draw a scalloped line connecting one end of the arch to the other. Erase the part of the handle that overlaps with the umbrella top. Sketch a curving line from the top center of the umbrella down to each of the scallops to divide it into sections. Then, add color to finish your drawing.

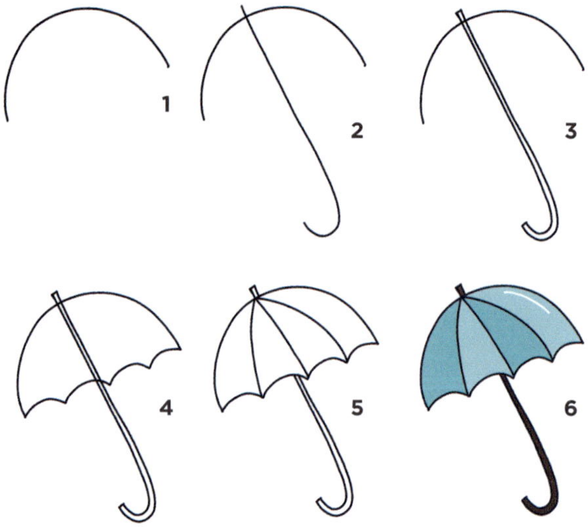

WATERFALL

There is something mystical about a waterfall, isn't there? To draw one, start by sketching a slightly curving vertical line for the left side. Then, draw a curving line to form the top and right side of the column of water. Add some curving squiggly lines around the base to show the splashes where the falling water hits the lake or river below. Draw a series of lines inside the waterfall to indicate motion.

On either side of the waterfall, sketch a bumpy, irregular shape to represent large rock formations. Add texture lines inside the rocks. Finally, draw a wavy semicircle around the base of the waterfall for the still water below. Color your waterfall, adding some white highlights to the blue water if possible. An alternative to this doodle is to draw the waterfall with large clouds on the sides in place of the rocks, as I did in the scene at the beginning of this chapter.

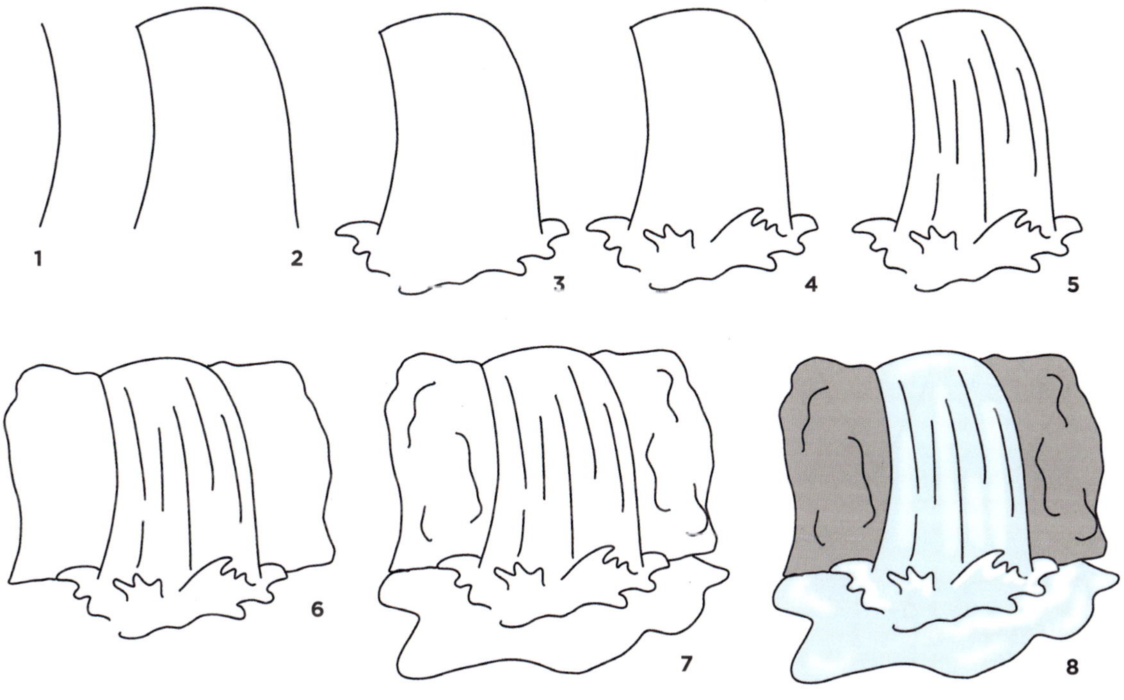

HEARTS

All of us are familiar with how to draw a basic heart shape. However, there are tons of fun variations and embellishments you can try that will help you put your own spin on this doodle. First, try simply extending or squishing your heart shape so that it's either tall and thin or short and wide. Then, add color, and voila!

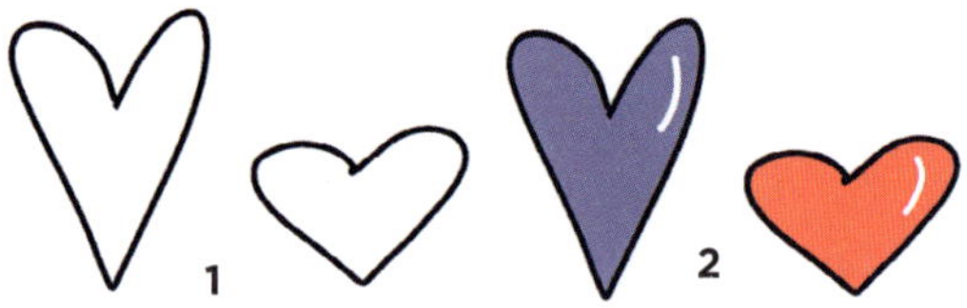

Next, we're going to doodle an asymmetrical heart. Draw one half of the image, and then draw the other half, extending the top half noticeably higher. This adds a fun, playful touch to your drawing.

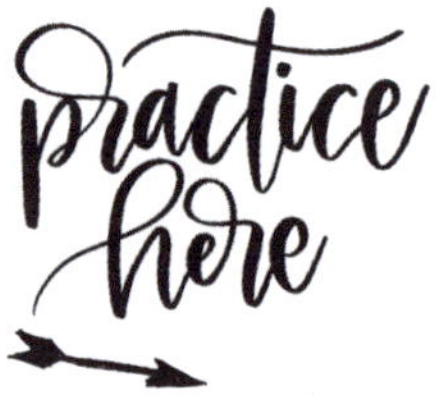

For our next heart, start with a small spiral, and then continue to form the left half of the heart. Make an even larger spiral on the right, and then complete the sketch, connecting your lines at the bottom. This elegant-style heart can be left as a simple outline, or you can choose to add color.

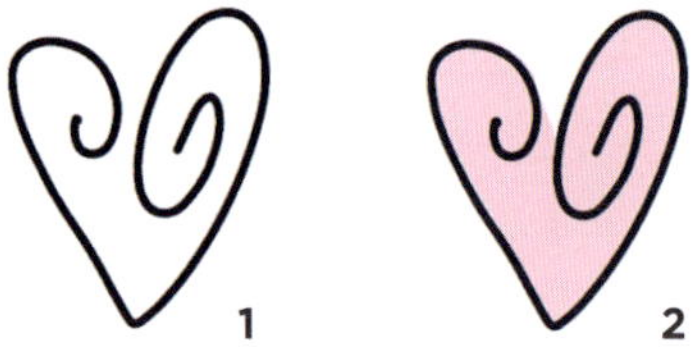

Try sketching a basic heart, then drawing a series of scallops all around it to represent a lacy border. This variation always makes me think of Valentine's Day, but you can use it year-round when you're feeling fancy. I like to color the heart and leave the lace part white; however, you can color yours any way you prefer.

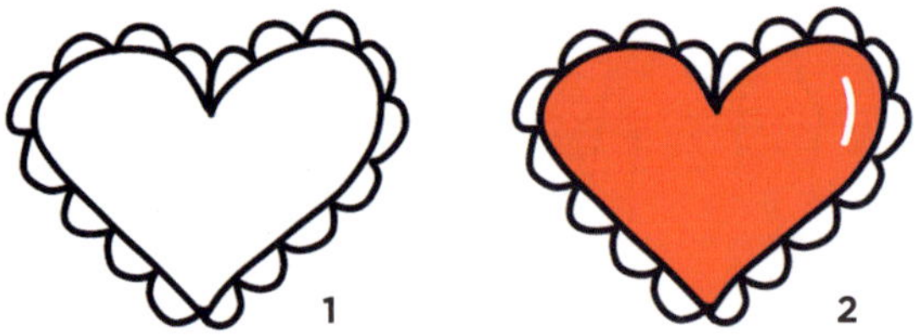

Another very easy heart doodle is simply to draw a large heart shape with a smaller one inside. Then, use two different colors to fill in your drawing.

Try sketching two heart shapes next to one another, slightly overlapping. Erase the lines where the shapes overlap, and then add color.

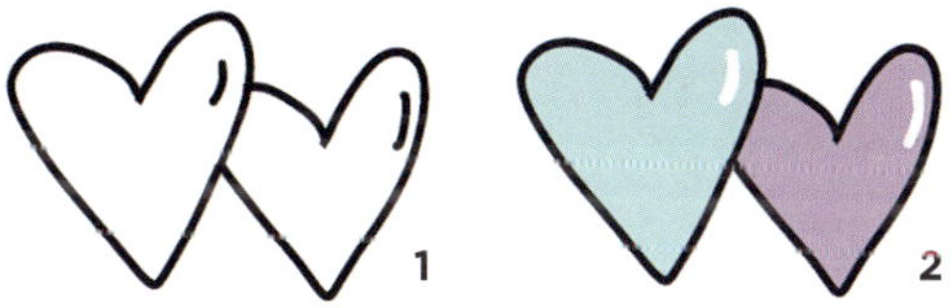

practice here

Elevate any heart drawing by adding a pattern inside, like polka dots or lines going in any direction. Have fun trying lots of different variations to make each one unique.

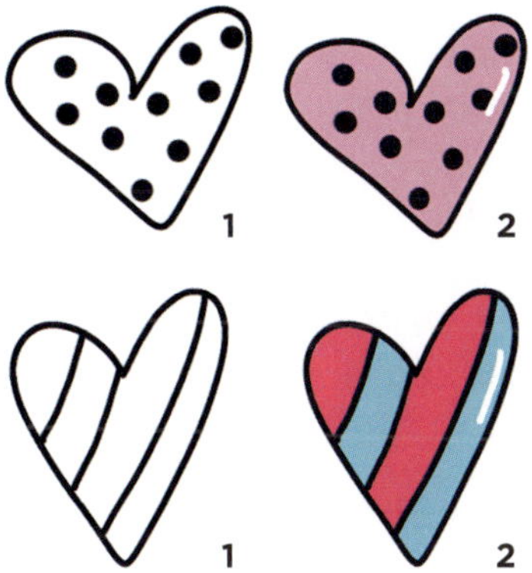

There are lots of other ways to put your own spin on drawing hearts. What other ideas can you imagine?

BOW

Add a fun accessory to your unicorn, Pegasus or anything else in your Rainbow Unicorn World. To draw a bow, start with a pair of parentheses, and then connect them at the top and bottom to form the knot. Draw a wide, rounded triangular shape on each side for the loops of the bow. Add long, thin teardrop shapes near the top of each loop to show dimension. Create streamers by drawing long, triangular shapes that connect back to the knot. Finally, add detail lines and color your bow. I like to color the centers of the loops darker than the rest of the bow for contrast.

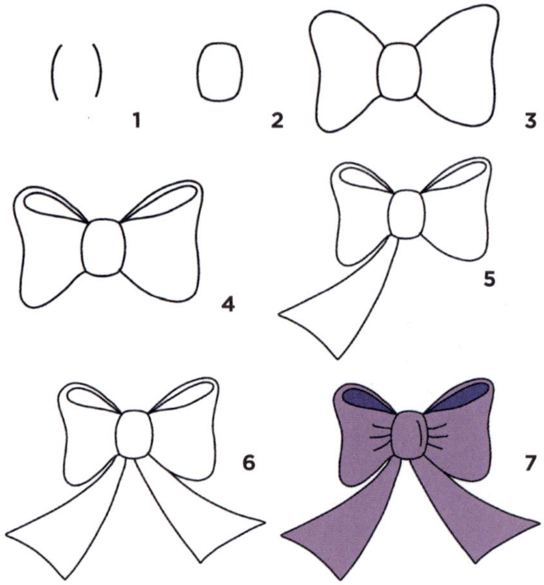

DAISY

Of course, flowers would be a part of the unicorns' world, and since it's such a magical place, we can take our floral doodles a step further by giving them unique faces and personalities. To begin drawing an upturned daisy, start with a "u" shape and connect it at the top. Add four large petals across the top, and then draw a long, wavy line for the flower stem. Sketch two pointed leaf shapes at the bottom of the stem. Add detail lines inside the petals and leaves. Then, draw eyes and a smile inside the center area of the flower. Use whatever colors you like to bring your daisy doodle to life.

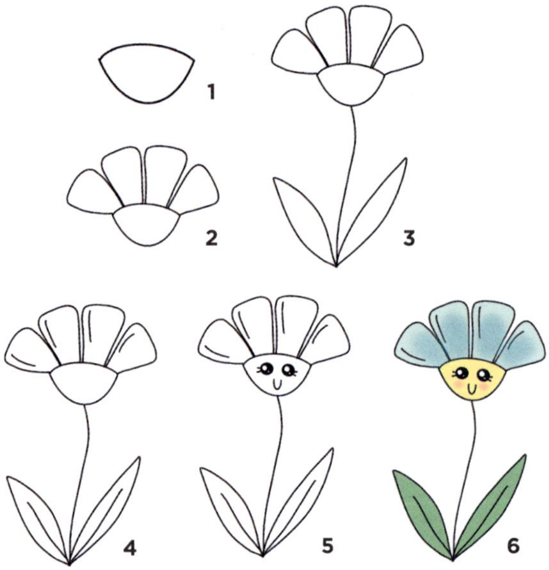

TULIP

To draw a lovely little tulip, start with a "u" shape, and then draw two "v" shapes across the top. Next, add three short vertical lines with circles on the end extending out from the top of the flower. Draw a curving line for the stem, and two long, thin pointed leaf shapes. Add any facial expression you like inside the flower. I chose circle eyes with eyelashes and a small "u"-shaped smile. Finish your tulip doodle by adding color.

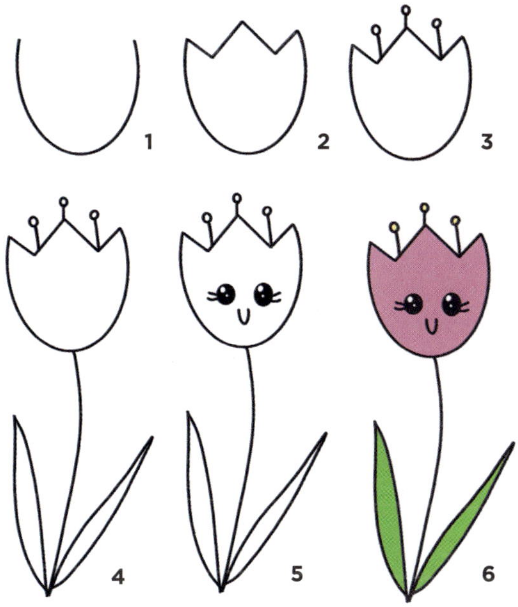

POPPY

The first step in drawing a poppy is to create the center petal, which is basically a "u" shape with a wavy line across the top. Draw a second petal on the left, tucked behind the first one. Then, add a third petal on the right. Draw a wavy line for the stem and a small pair of leaves. Add any kind of facial expression you like on the center petal. I chose a pair of rounded eyes with eyelashes and a simple smile. Finally, color your poppy red with green leaves.

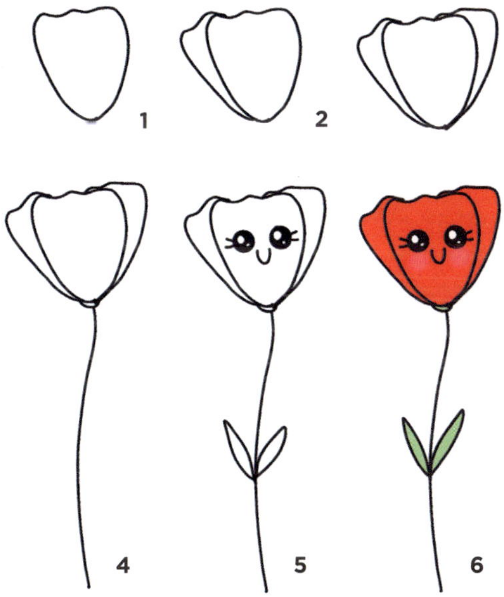

SUNFLOWER

To draw a sunny sunflower, start with a large oval shape for the center. Draw 11 thin, slightly pointed petals around the oval, leaving space in between each one. Then, add a second row of petals in between the first set by making curved "v" shapes. Add two vertical lines to create a long stem, and draw a few large leaves. Give your flower a cheerful face toward the top of the oval, so that it's smiling up at the sun. Finally, color the center brown and the petals yellow to finish your doodle.

practice here

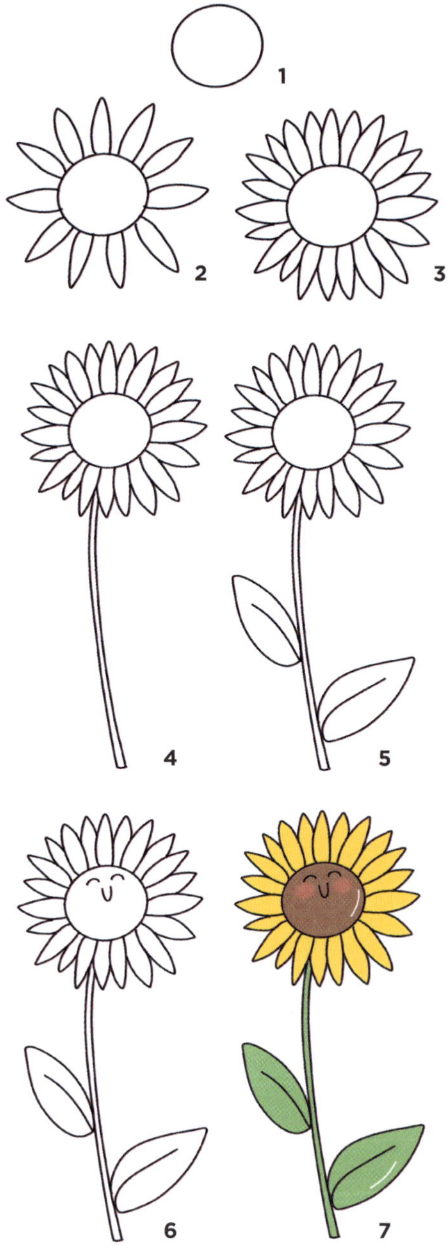

PETALED FLOWER

Start this fun floral doodle with a large circle for the center. Then, add six "u"-shaped petals all around it. Draw a curving line for the stem and a pair of leaves at the bottom. Now, it's time to add some details. Draw a vein inside each leaf, and add a second "u" shape inside each petal. Give your flower a cheerful face inside the center circle. I used small arches for eyes, and a little smile, but you can also choose your own unique expression. Finally, color your flower.

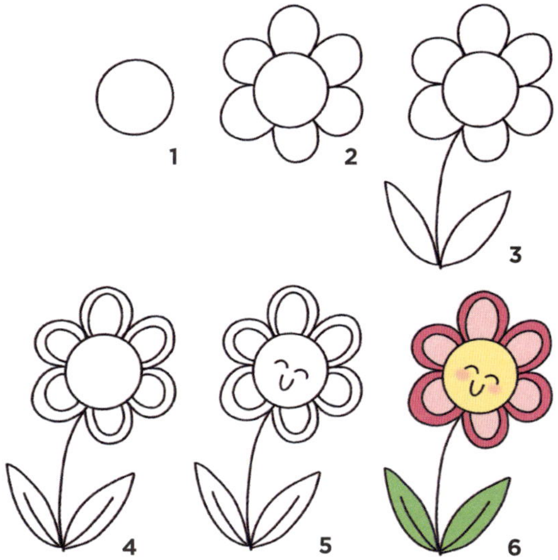

CUPCAKE

Now, let's learn to draw some sweet treats to add to our magical unicorn world, starting with a yummy cupcake! Draw two slanted lines that are closer together at the bottom than the top to form the base of this dessert. Connect the lines with a curve at the bottom and a zigzag line across the top. Draw a line from the base of each zigzag to the bottom of the cupcake for the pleated wrapper.

Next, sketch a small wave shape for the top of the frosting, and add a few bumps on each side that connect it to the wrapper. Finally, add any details you'd like, such as sprinkles or a face. Color your cupcake to make it even more fun.

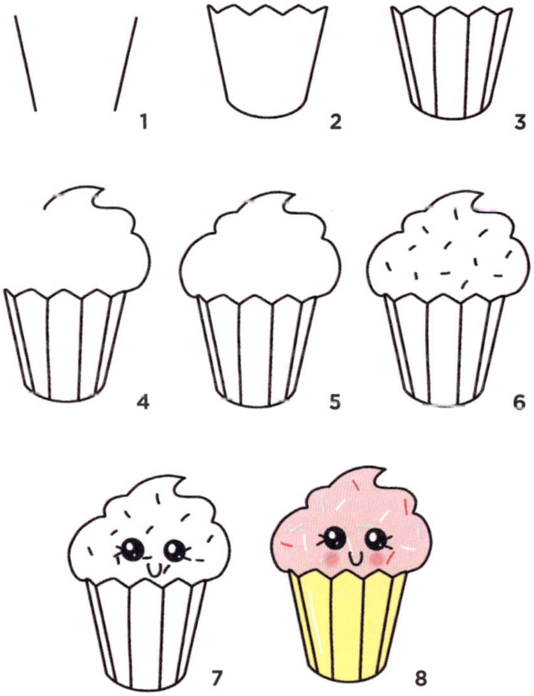

ICE CREAM CONE

To create this doodle, start with a semicircle for the round part of the ice cream scoop. Connect the ends with a bumpy line. Now, draw a "v" under the ice cream to form the cone. Fill in the cone with intersecting diagonal lines for texture. Finally, add a small detail line to your scoop and give it a funny face.

To create a double (or triple) scoop cone, just repeat the same process, drawing multiple ice cream scoop shapes stacked on top of each other. Erase any areas where the lines overlap, and then continue with the rest of the steps for the cone and details. I like to give each scoop its own unique face.

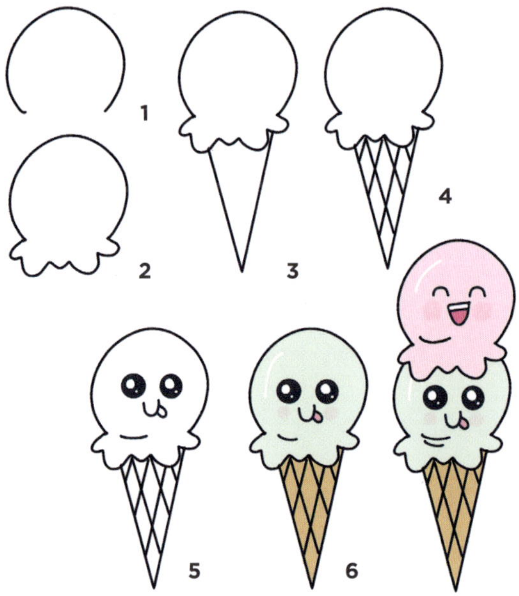

POPSICLE

A popsicle doodle is really just a bunch of "u" shapes put together in a specific way! First, start with a large, wide upside-down "u" that's connected at the bottom to form the basic shape of the dessert. The next step is to draw a long, thin "u" extending below it for the stick. To add texture to the popsicle, make two long, thin upside-down "u"s inside. Finally, give your drawing a whimsical face, and then color it to complete your masterpiece.

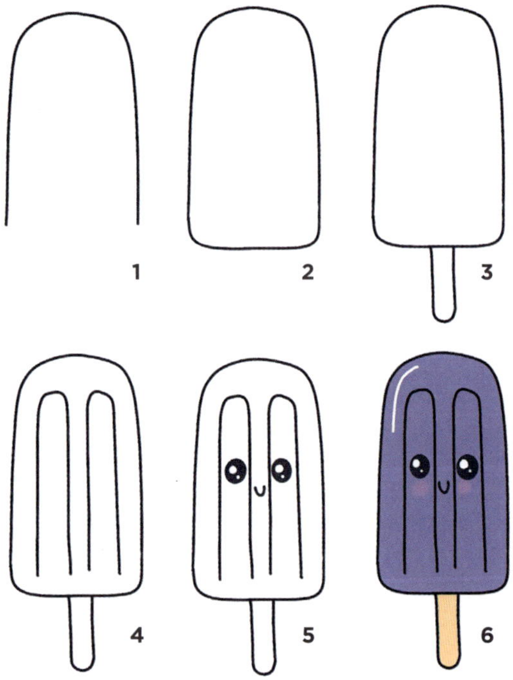

LOLLIPOP

Doodle a lollipop by drawing a circle, and then sketching a slightly rounded rectangle across the center of it. Erase the areas where the shapes overlap. Add a long, very thin rectangle for the stick, and then draw a face on your lollipop. I positioned mine on the center band, but you can put yours anywhere on the surface of the lollipop. Finally, add color to complete the picture.

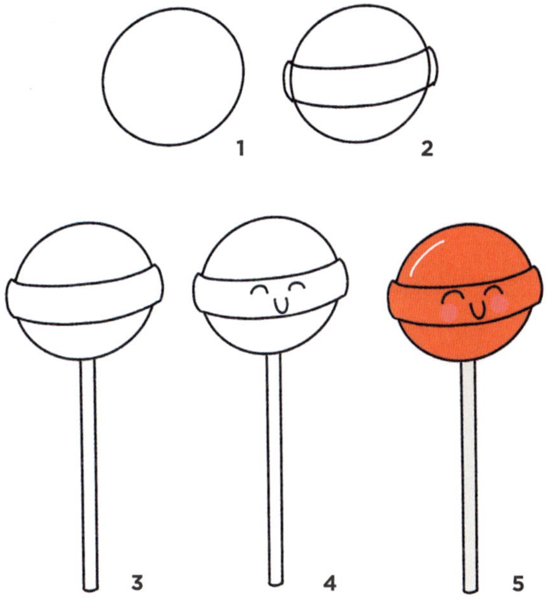

DONUT

Who doesn't love a donut? To doodle this cute confection, start with a large circle and draw a second, smaller circle inside for the hole. Next, sketch a wavy circle in between to show where the frosting is. All that's left to do is add details, like sprinkles and a smiling face. Or, if you choose, you can leave your donut plain. Add color to complete your drawing.

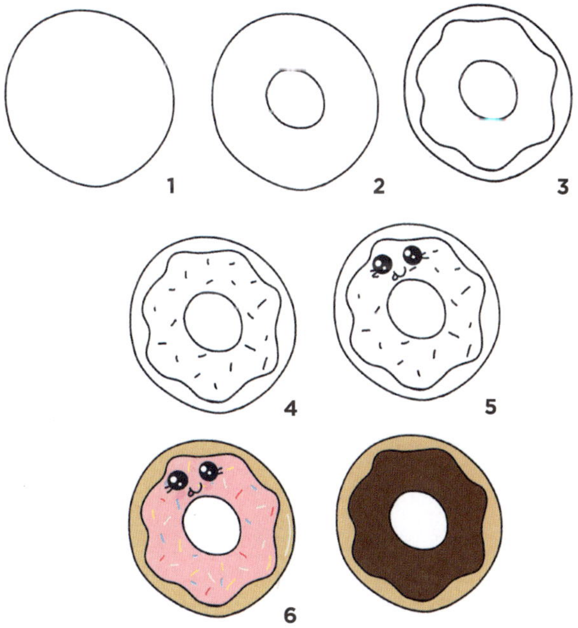

HARD CANDY

Drawing a piece of wrapped candy is easier than it might seem. First, sketch a pair of horizontal lines for the top and bottom of the candy, and connect them on the right side with a curving line. On the left side, connect them with an oval. Draw two lines extending out from the right side and connect them with zigzags. Do the same on the left side, erasing the area where this overlaps your candy. Draw detail lines inside these areas of the wrapper, and divide the main part of the candy into three sections. Add eyes and a smile, and then color your candy in any way you like.

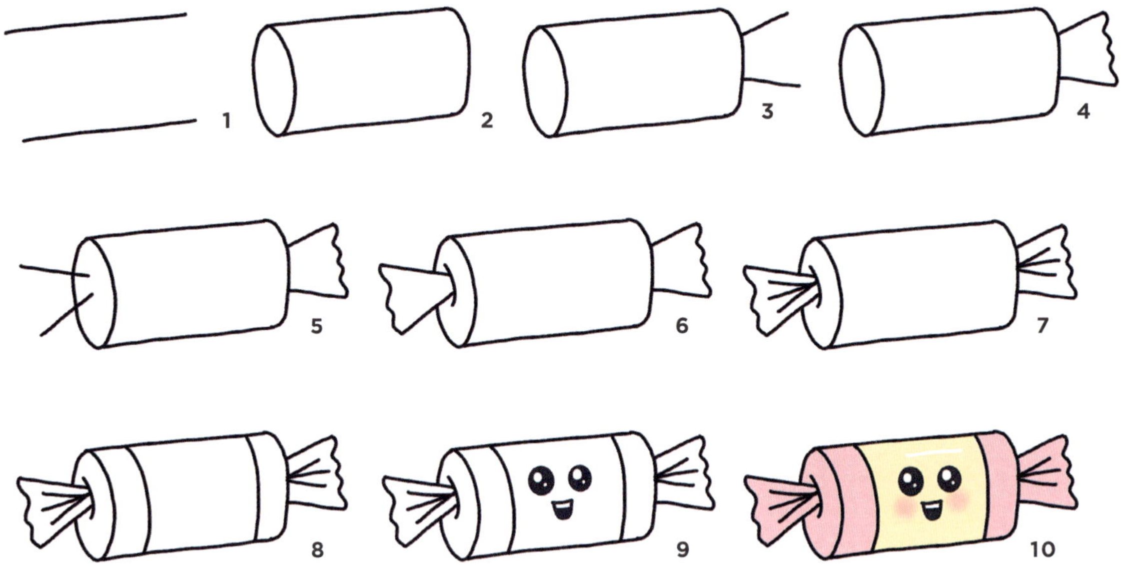

practice here

CHERRIES

Cherries are an easy fruit to draw. First, form the basic shape by sketching two partial circles with a slight dip across the top. Draw a large, curving "v" shape for the stems, and sketch a short, curving line on each end where it meets the cherries. Next, make a pair of pointed leaves at the top of the stems, and draw veins inside each one. Give each cherry its own unique expression, and then color your doodle.

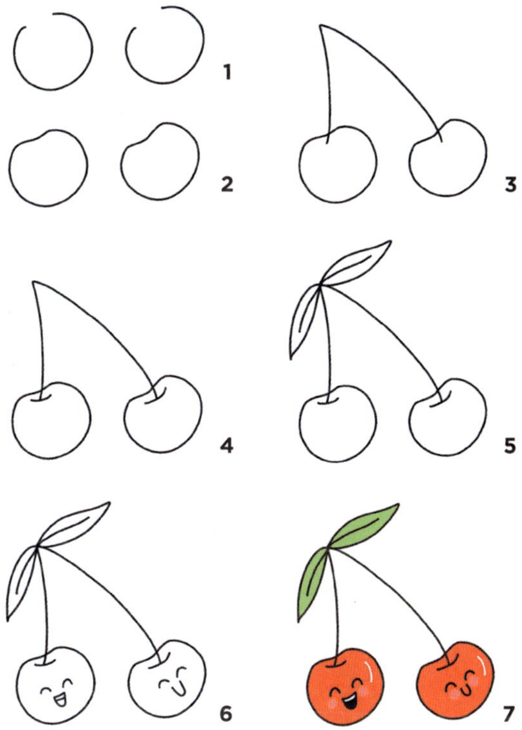

PINEAPPLE

A pineapple doodle starts with an oval for the basic shape of the fruit. Next, add two "v" shapes on top that curve in opposite directions. Repeat the same step with two slightly smaller "v"s in between the previous pair. Sketch one more little "v" shape to complete the pineapple's crown. Fill in the body of the pineapple with intersecting diagonal lines to show texture, and then add eyes and a smile. Finish your doodle by adding color.

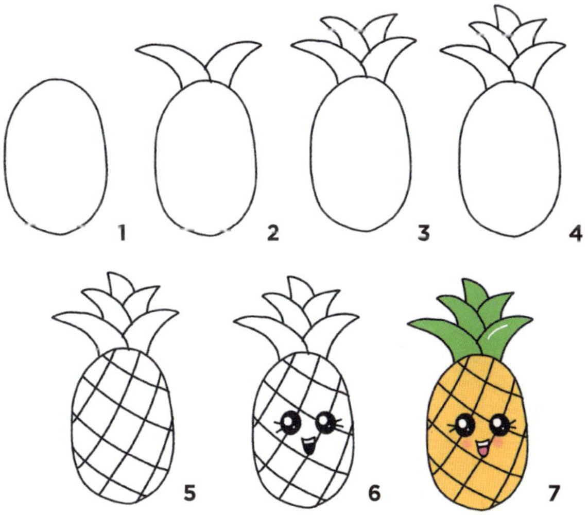

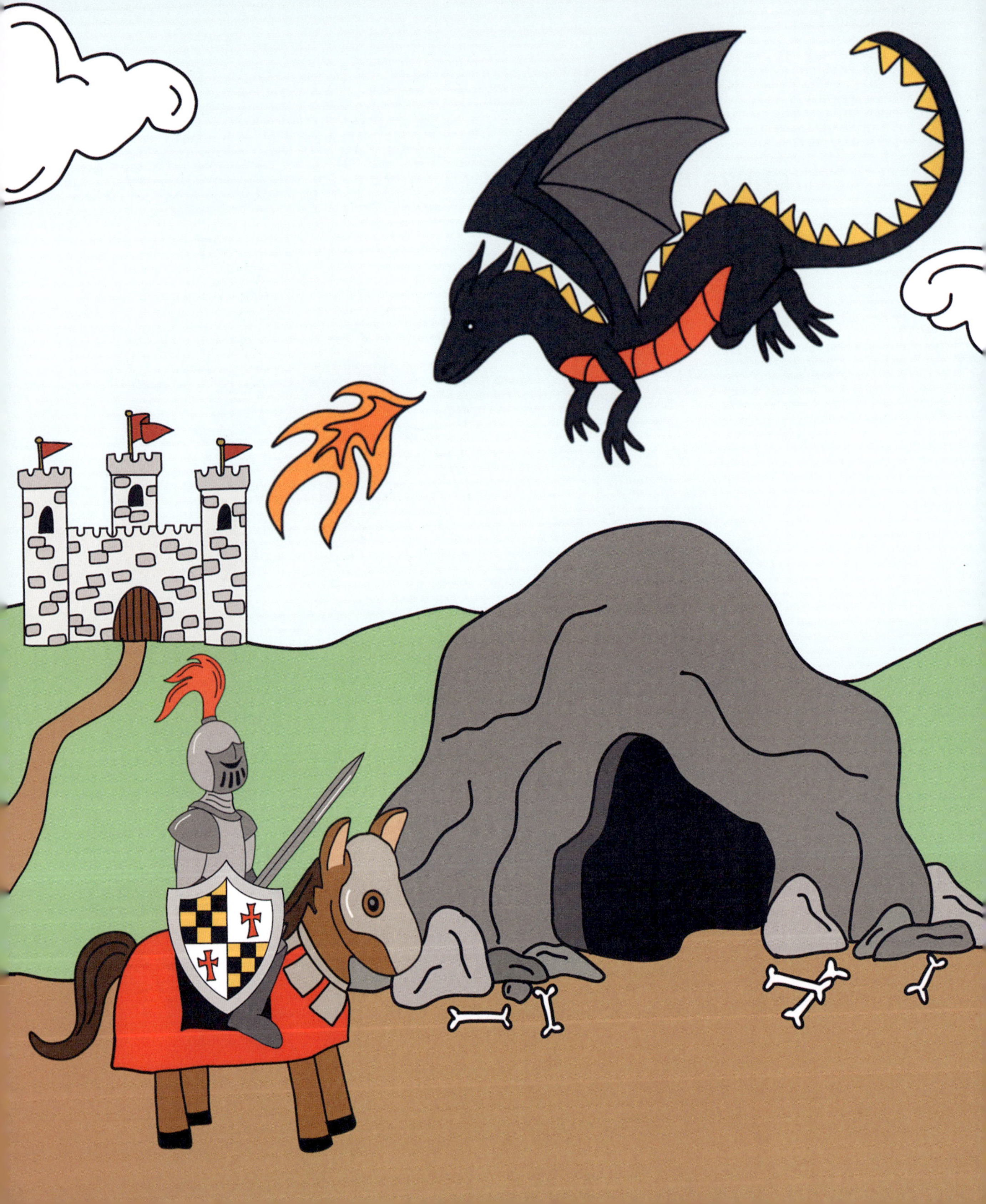

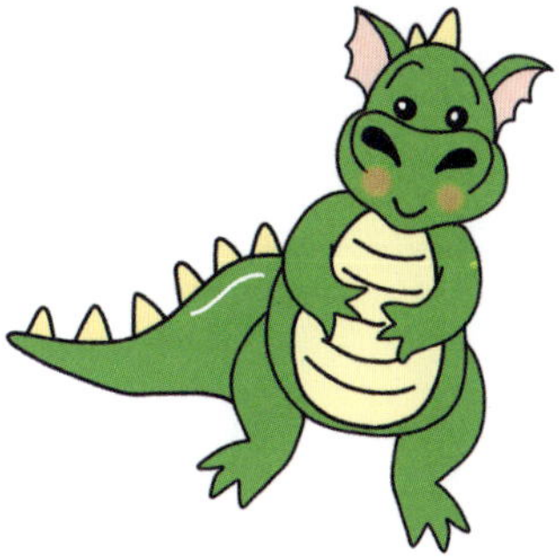

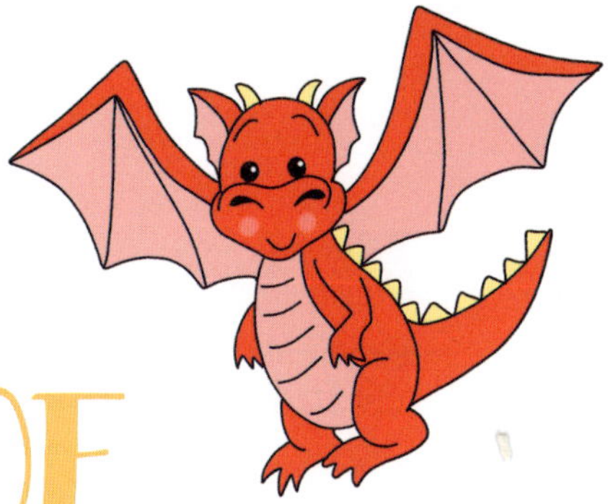

LAND OF KNIGHTS AND Dragons

Tales of heroic knights in shining armor go back as far as the twelfth century, and they still capture our imagination today. Although we often find them in fairy tales and legends, knights were very real—the superheroes of the medieval time period. They wore suits of armor and wielded a variety of dangerous weapons, both in times of war and in exciting public competitions where they tested their jousting, fencing and fighting skills against one another. Their legendary nemeses, dragons, on the other hand, are fantasy creatures that were used in stories to represent humankind's physical or spiritual enemies. We're going to learn to doodle several different dragons, as well as knights, their armor, and some of their weapons. You'll be able to combine some of these doodles to create your own personalized shields and coats of arms, as well as drawing some epic medieval scenes. Grab your pencil and let's get started!

DRAGON

To sketch a basic dragon, start by drawing an arch for the top of the head. Then, draw a semicircle for the lower part of the face, with a slight bump for the chin. Add a curving line for the snout and a pair of nostrils. Give your dragon rounded eyes and a pair of arched eyebrows, and then draw a pair of pointed ears with scalloped lines across the bottoms. Divide the top part of the ears from the inner area.

Now let's move on to the body. Sketch a pear shape, and give your dragon rounded legs with pointy-toed feet. Draw a pair of short, curving arms with pointed fingers at the ends. Erase the areas where the arms overlap the body shape. Separate the chest/stomach area from the rest of the body, and add slightly curving lines to show texture. Draw a thick, pointed tail, and add spikes to the tail and the top of the head. Finally, color your dragon. Mine is green with yellow spikes and a yellow belly, but you can use any color combination to make your dragon unique.

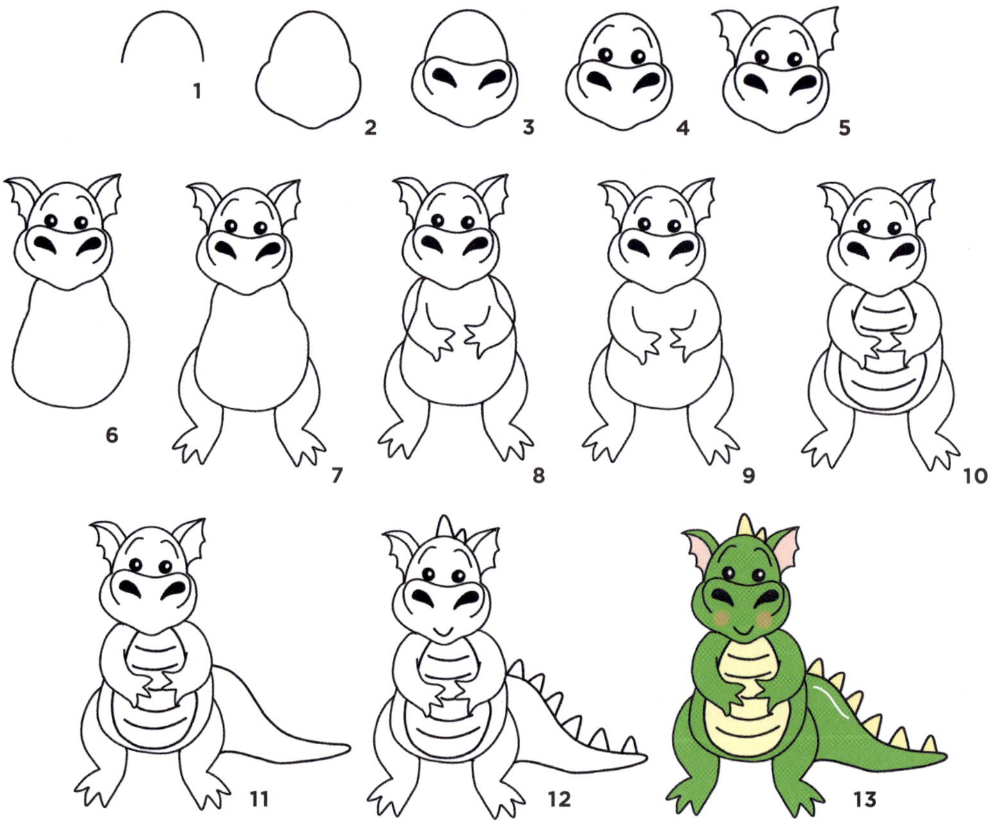

DRAGON WITH WINGS

Our next dragon has a pair of large, pointed wings. Start this sketch in the same way as the basic dragon, drawing the arched head, lower face, snout with nostrils, eyes and eyebrows. Add the same pointed ears with scalloped lines, and then draw a pair of short horns on top of the head. Add a pair of curving lines for the pear-shaped body, and a pair of short arms with pointed fingers.

This time, our view is from the side, so you'll sketch the full front arm, and just part of the back one. Next, draw a "c" shape for the front leg, and add a foot with pointed toes. Draw a second leg and foot slightly behind the front one. Separate the chest/belly from the rest of the body with a curving line, and add texture lines.

Sketch a pair of pointed wings with scallops along the bottom. Outline the top part of each wing, and then draw a line connecting the top point with each scallop. Finally, draw a thick triangular tail, and a series of small triangles along the back and tail. All that's left to do is color your dragon in any combination of colors you like. Here's a look at the same dragon colored two different ways; what a difference a color choice makes!

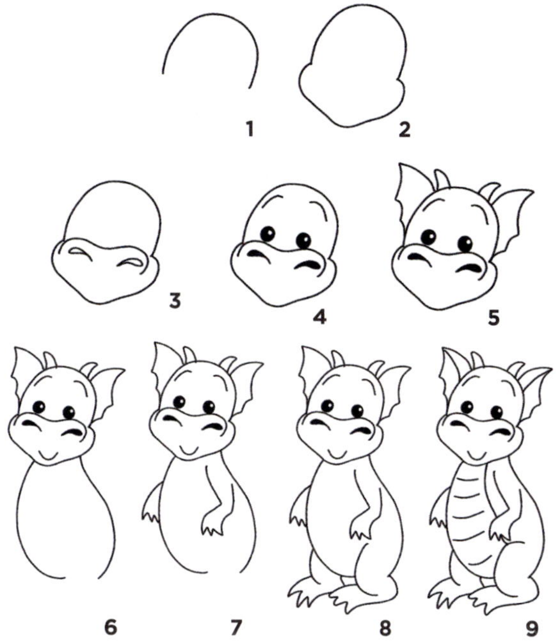

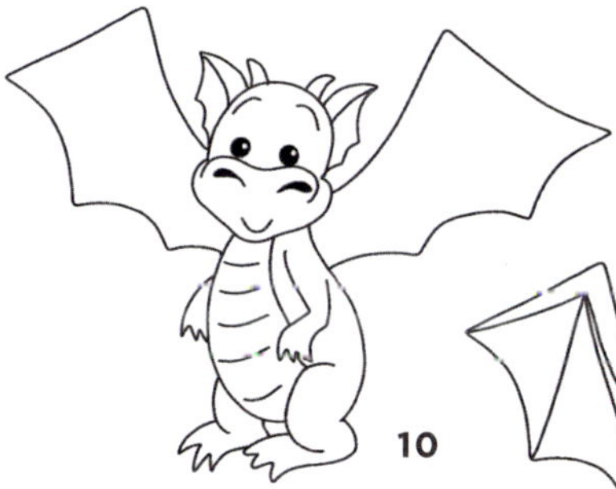
10

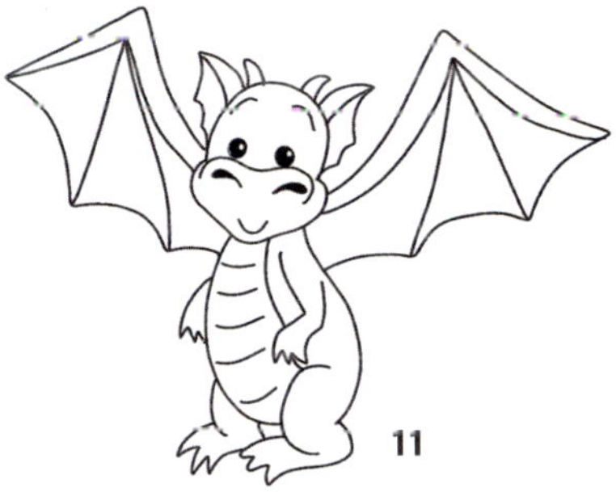
11

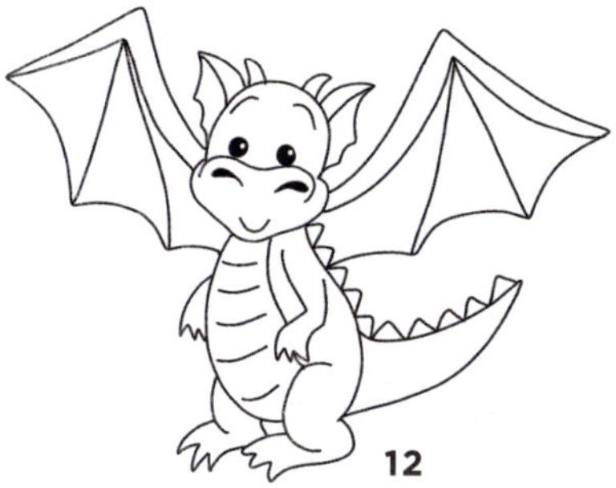
12

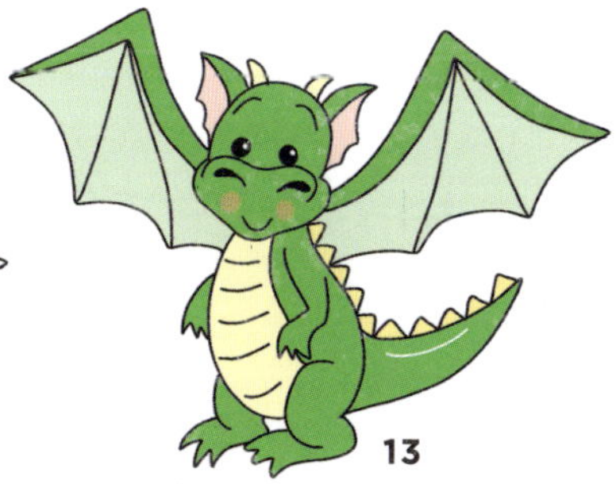
13

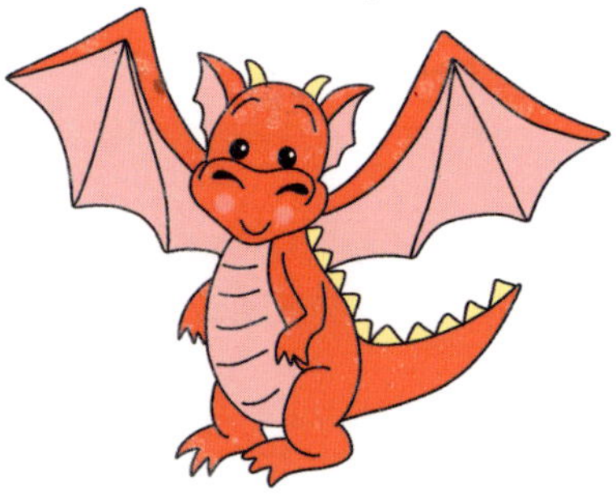

FLYING DRAGON

Let's put our dragon's wings to use and draw it soaring through the sky! First, sketch a long, thin "c" shape for the face. Add a curving line for the lower jaw and neck. Next, draw a pair of pointed horns, and a curving line to finish the neck. Draw a pair of short arms with pointed fingers. Sketch a pointed wing with a second, matching line below it. Add scallops across the bottom of the wing, and draw lines to connect each scallop to the top point.

Draw a curving line for the dragon's back, and then add a back leg and foot. Sketch a second leg and foot behind the first one. Make a long, pointed tail, and then add an eye and nostril on the dragon's face. Separate the front part of the body from the rest, adding texture lines. Finish your sketch by drawing triangular points along the back of the head, the back and the tail. Color the dragon to complete your doodle.

Make your dragon truly fearsome by drawing a flame as if it's breathing fire! Just sketch a shape with five curving points, and then a smaller pointed shape inside of it. Color the flame orange and yellow. Watch out, knights!

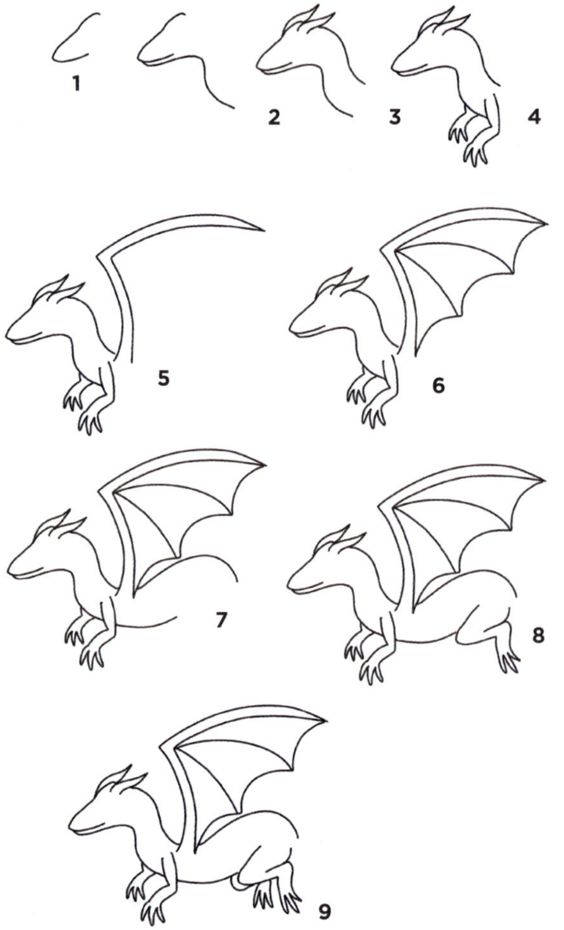

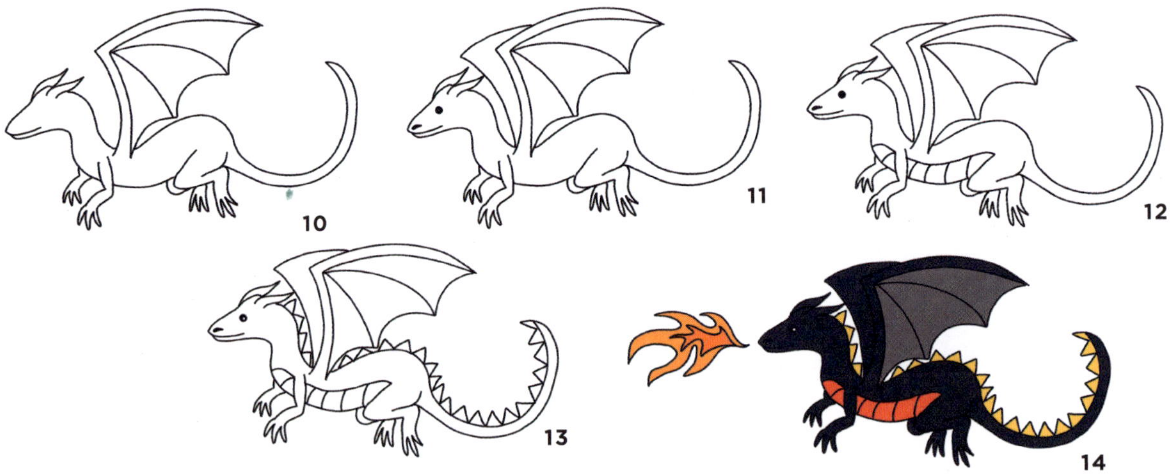

TORCH

In the world of knights and dragons, there was no electricity, so torches played an important role. To draw a torch that will help your knight see in the darkness, start by drawing a "u" shape, and then draw two long, thin "u" shapes inside it. Draw three, short horizontal lines across the top of the torch frame so that it looks like a "w." Add two curving lines to create a thin band across the "w," erasing the areas where the lines overlap. Draw a handle, and add lines to show a twisted texture. Finally, add the flame by sketching a series of four to five wavy points, with the center one taller than the others. Draw a smaller pointed shape inside to show the hottest area of the flame. Color your torch (I used dark gray to represent iron) and the flame.

practice here

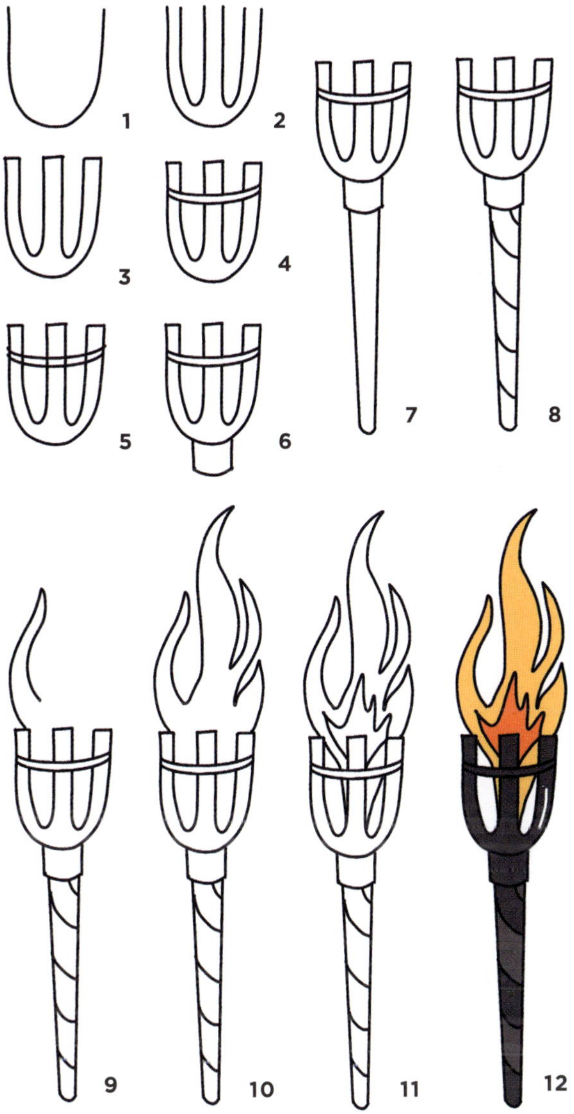

CAVE

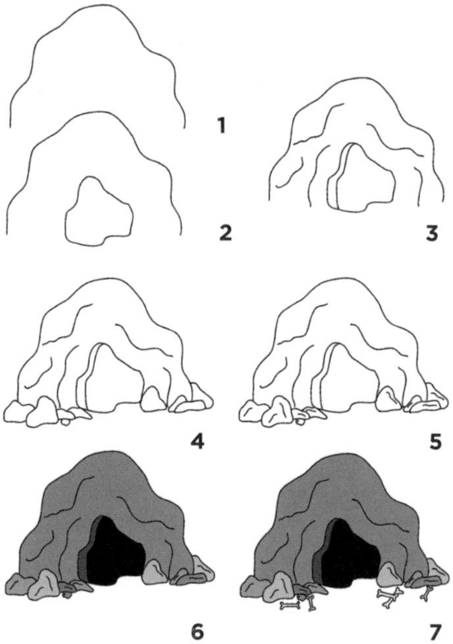

Dragons were said to live in a variety of dark and solitary places, including forests, abandoned castles and caves. To doodle a cave, start by drawing an arch with a few bumps. Inside the arch, draw a bumpy shape for the opening, and then draw a second line on one side of the opening to show dimension. Add wavy lines all around the opening to give the cave a rocky texture. Draw several rocks overlapping each other on either side of the entrance. Color your cave and rocks gray, and the opening black.

To make your cave look like a dangerous dragon lives inside, sketch a few bones around the entrance! Bones are just long, thin rectangles with a heart shape on each end.

CROSS POTENT/ JERUSALEM CROSS

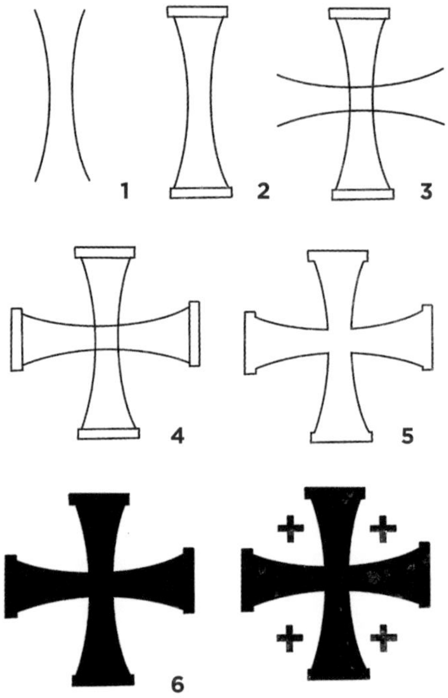

Crosses were another very common symbol used in heraldry. Besides the standard Christian cross, there were variations like the cross potent, which features two lines of equal length that intersect at a center point and have crossbars on the four ends. To doodle this symbol, start by sketching two lines that curve away from each other. Draw rectangles at the top and bottom of the lines. Then, sketch a second pair of curving lines going across the center of the first pair. Add rectangles on each end. Erase the areas where your lines overlap, and then color your cross.

A slight variation on this is called the Jerusalem cross, which adds four smaller Greek crosses around the large cross potent. This became incredibly popular among the royal houses of Europe during the late medieval period.

FLEUR-DE-LIS

One of the ways that knights differentiated themselves from one another was by the coats of arms they wore and the patterns and symbols on their armor and flags. We're going to learn to doodle a few of the most popular symbols so that you can use them to create personalized doodles for your knights. The fleur-de-lis is a symbol that represents a lily and is often associated with France.

To sketch one, start by drawing an arch with a point at the top. Next, add a spiral on each side that curves away from the center. Draw a second, smaller set of spirals inside the first pair. Draw a rounded "v" shape in the center to form the bottom of the symbol, connecting it to the arch from step 1. Add a band across the center and erase the overlapping lines. You can stop here for a simple fleur-de-lis, or add detail lines to give your symbol some extra dimension. Finally, add color to complete your doodle.

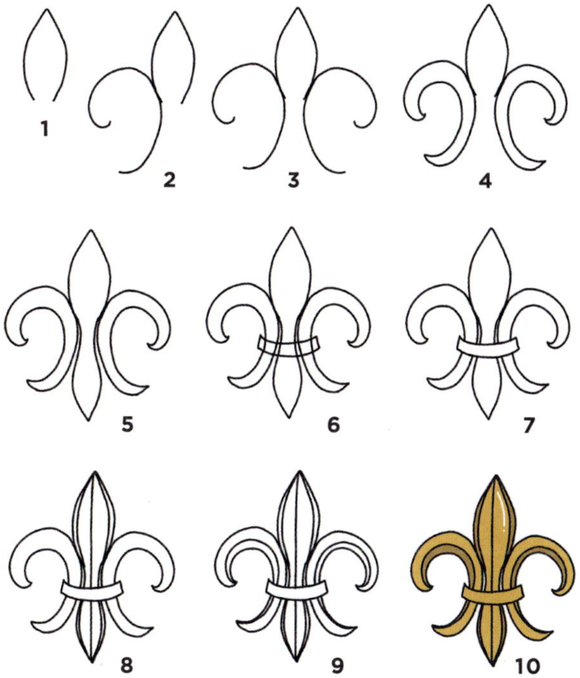

HELMET

Let's draw a helmet together, starting with a "c" shape. Sketch the visor by making a scalloped line and two more curving lines. Draw a curving trapezoid with a curving rectangle below it to cover the neck. Add a small rectangle on top of the helmet. Sketch detail lines inside the neck area, and a small vertical line in the top center of the visor. Add a crescent and some rounded rectangles to the visor area, and color them in to show the areas where there's no metal. Draw a large plume extending from the top of the helmet with several feathery points. Sketch a few detail lines inside the plume to show texture, and then color your helmet.

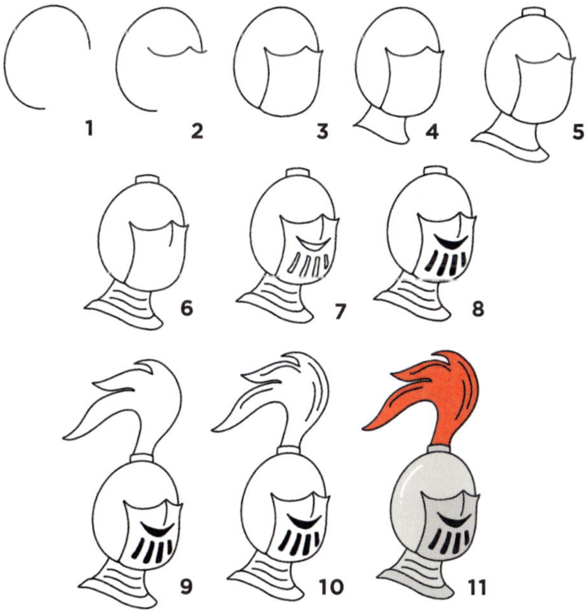

TRUMPET WITH FLAG

Announce your knights' presence by doodling them a trumpet! First, draw two lines that start out parallel, and then curve out in opposite directions at the ends. Draw two curving lines to connect the ends and form the bell of the trumpet. On the opposite end of the trumpet, sketch a small mouthpiece. Add a rounded rectangle shape that overlaps the parallel lines on the left sides, and draw a second rounded rectangle inside of it. Erase the area where the lines overlap.

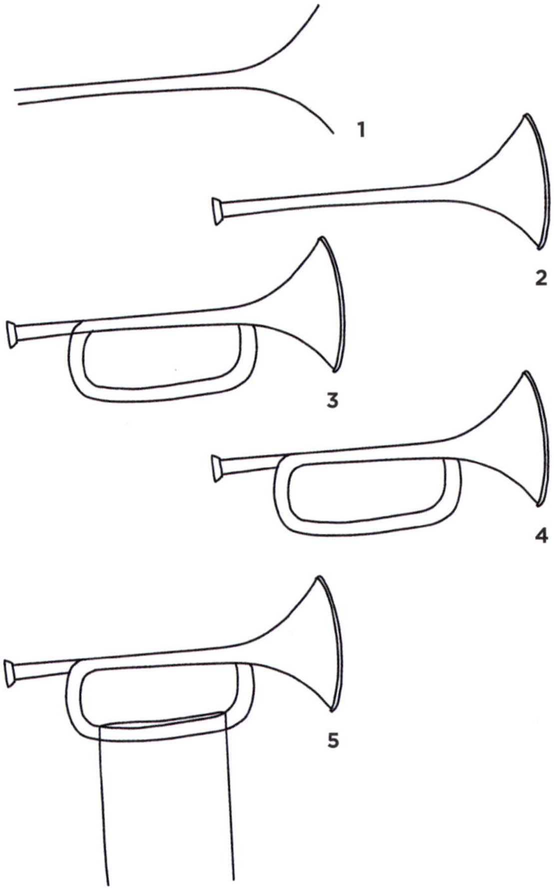

For the flag, draw a horizontal line and two vertical lines extending from the bottom of the rounded rectangle, erasing the spots where they overlap. Add an upside-down "v" shape at the bottom. Sketch a second, smaller flag shape inside the one you just drew. Then, add a symbol like the fleur-de-lis or a cross to complete your doodle. Color your trumpet gold or yellow, and use whatever colors represent your knight to finish the flag.

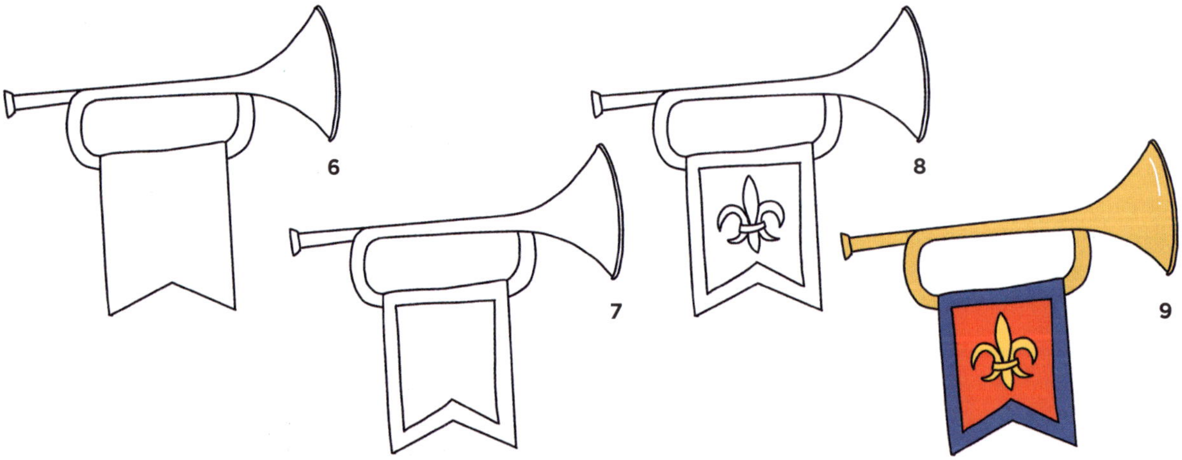

SHIELD

Protect your knight in battle by drawing him a shield. This first variation starts with a horizontal line that has a small, curving line on each end. Connect the curving lines with a large rounded "v" to form the basic outline of the shield. Draw a second, slightly smaller shield shape inside, and then divide it into four sections. Then, draw a third shield shape in the center. Erase the area inside the smallest shape, and then draw a symbol inside, such as a crown, a cross or a fleur-de-lis. Finally, add color to complete your doodle.

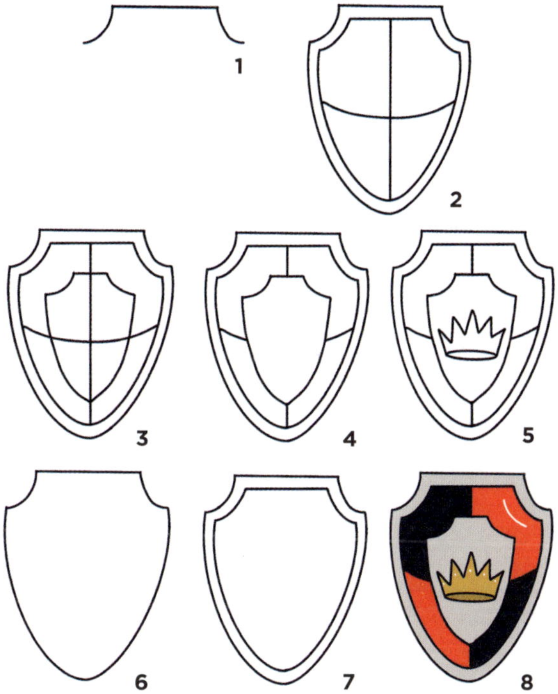

This shield variation has a slightly different shape. To doodle it, start with two curving lines that join to form a point. Connect the ends of the lines with a large "v" to create the outline of the shield. Draw the same shape, just slightly smaller, inside the outline. Draw a pair of intersecting lines inside the smaller shape to divide it into four sections.

Finish the shield by adding a pattern and/or symbol in each section. I chose to draw a checkerboard pattern in two of the sections and a cross in the other two, but you can use any heraldic symbols or patterns you prefer. When your drawing is finished, color the outer part of the shield gray, and use your knight's favorite colors for the inside.

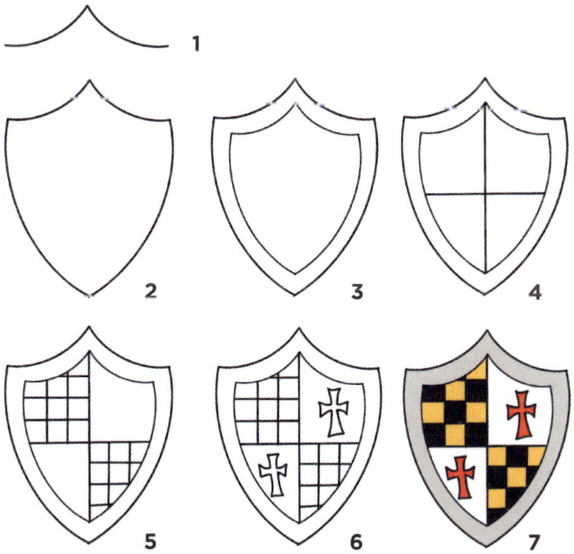

LAURELS

To create a fabulous-looking coat of arms, all you need to do is draw a shield framed by laurels. For the laurels, sketch a pair of curving lines that intersect at the bottom to form a rounded "v." Add a small leaf shape at the top of each line, and then continue down the line, drawing pairs of leaves until you reach the bottom. Color the leaves, and then add your shield doodle in the space formed by the laurels.

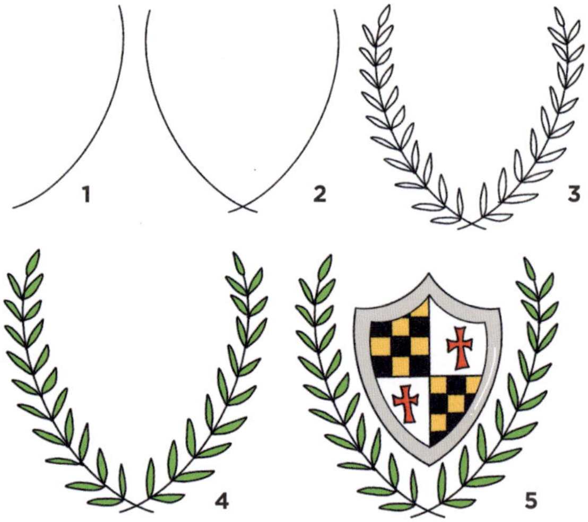

SWORD

Now that our knight can defend himself with a shield, let's learn to draw some weapons for him, starting with a basic sword. To doodle this, begin by sketching a pair of parallel vertical lines. Connect these lines at the top with a "v" shape for the point of the blade. At the base of the blade, draw two curving lines that form a wide "w" shape. Draw a bracket shape below and connect it to the "w" to form the guard. Next, sketch two vertical lines for the grip, with a circle below for the pommel.

Finish your drawing by adding details, like a vertical line through the center of the blade, a decorative line on the guard, curving lines on the handle and a smaller circle inside the pommel. Color your sword to complete the doodle.

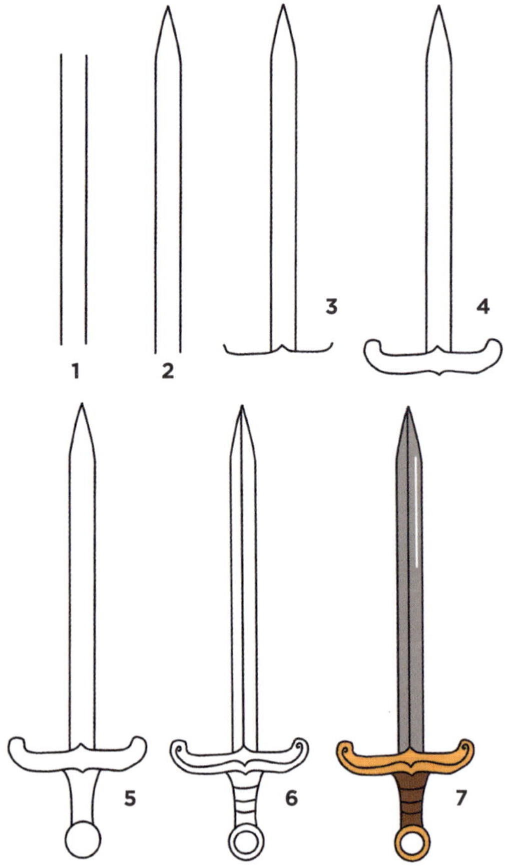

RAPIER

A rapier is a long, thin sword primarily used for dueling. To draw one, start with two vertical lines that get closer together toward the top. Sketch a small "v"-shaped point to connect them. At the other end, draw an arch with a scalloped line below that resembles an umbrella. This creates the rapier's guard. Below the guard, draw a thin, rounded "v" shape for the grip and a small circle under it for the pommel.

Add details to the guard by doubling the scallop shape and drawing small curving lines from the top center of the shape down to each scallop. To create the knuckle guard/loop, make an "s" shape that starts at the top of the grip and ends at the bottom. Double the shape and erase any overlapping lines. Finish your drawing by coloring it any way you like.

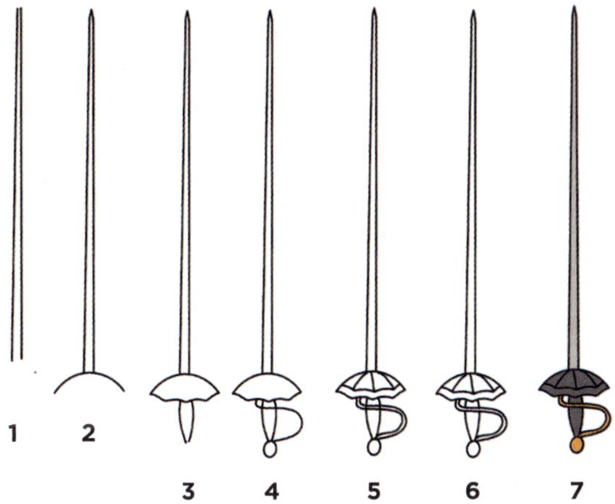

LANCE

The lance is a long thrusting spear that was most useful for a mounted knight. It was not only used in warfare and combat, but for entertainment purposes in jousting tournaments. To draw a lance, start with two parallel vertical lines that are joined at the top with a small, rounded "v." At the bottom, sketch a pair of lines that curve outward, and connect the bottom of these lines with a wide "u" shape. Draw a rectangular grip below, and then sketch a series of decorative curving lines all along the lance. Finish your doodle by filling it in with your knight's favorite colors.

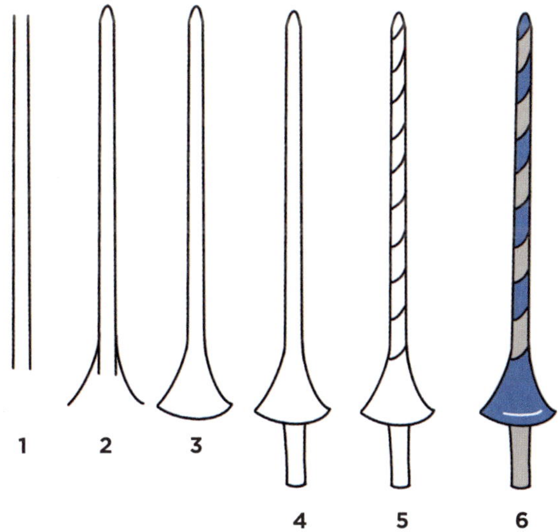

LONGBOW

The longbow, with its range of 450 to 1,000 feet, allowed a knight to hit their enemies while they were still a considerable distance away. Start your longbow doodle by drawing a vertical line that curves to form two equal-sized bumps. This will resemble a very rounded sideways "m." Draw a second line that mirrors the first but connects to it at the top and bottom ends. Now, make a straight vertical line connecting the top and bottom points of this shape to create the bow's string. Divide the back of the bow into three sections so that there is a grip in the center. Finally, color your bow.

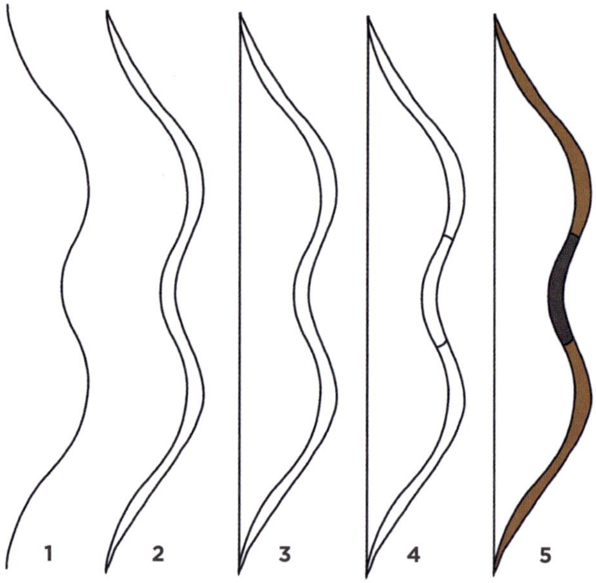

ARROW

To sketch an arrow, start with a pair of parallel vertical lines to form the shaft. Next, draw a "v"-shaped tip at the top that connects to the shaft with short diagonal lines. To create the fletching, sketch curved lines on either side of the shaft near the bottom, and connect them to the shaft. Add color to finish your doodle.

practice here

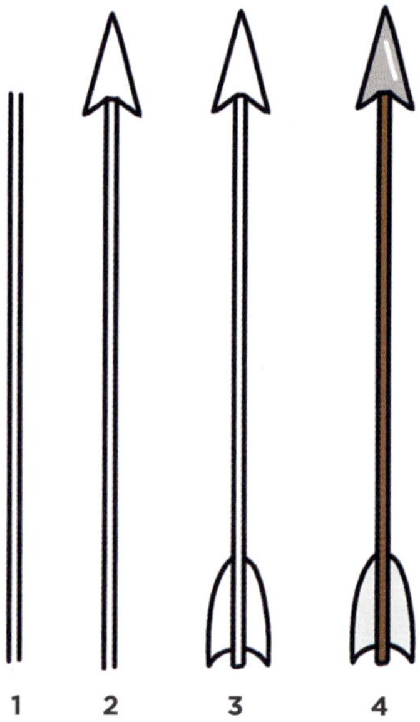

QUIVER

Knights kept their arrows in quivers, usually made from leather. To draw one, start by sketching a vertical line and a diagonal line, and connecting them with a slight curve at the bottom. At the top, draw a slanted oval to show the opening for the arrows. Sketch a line to divide the top third of the quiver from the rest, and then add a wavy strap to show that it's made of flexible leather. Finally, color your doodle.

To add arrows to your quiver, just draw the bottom section of your arrow doodle, which includes part of the shaft and the fletching. I drew four, but you can sketch as many arrows as you like, overlapping them slightly to show depth. Erase any areas where the arrows overlap each other and the mouth of the quiver. Then, add color to finish your drawing.

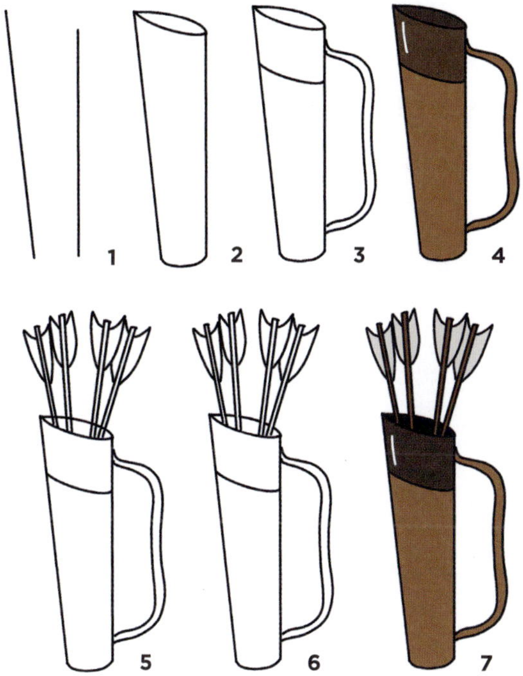

BATTLE AXE

The first step in drawing an axe is to sketch a “c” shape for the edge of the blade. Next, sketch two curving horizontal lines that connect to it and get closer together at the other end. Draw a line to finish the outline of the blade, and then add a vertical rectangle where you want the handle to be. Sketch parallel lines above and below the rectangle to form the handle. Finish your doodle by adding a triangle on the top of the handle, and then filling it in with color.

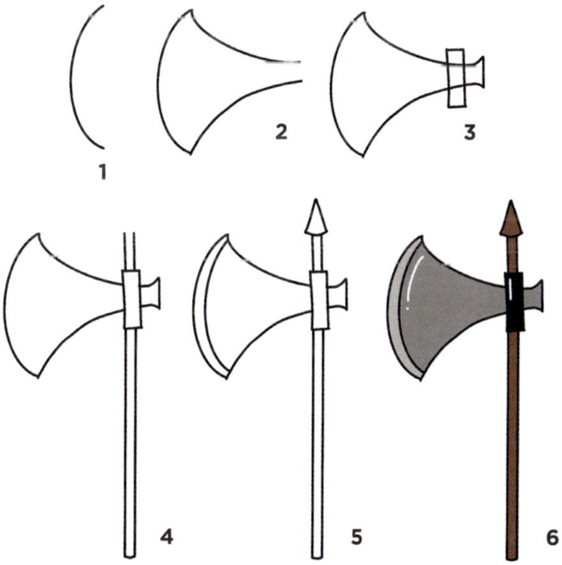

DOUBLE-HEADED BATTLE AXE

To doodle a double-headed axe, start with a long, thin rectangle for the handle, and then draw a decorative diamond shape on top. Sketch a line to divide the top section of the handle from the rest. Draw four curving lines coming out from this top section to form the sides of the blades. Connect the curving lines to create the blade edges. Add curving lines near the blade edges, as well as two small rectangles to indicate the top and bottom of the handle grip. Finally, color your drawing.

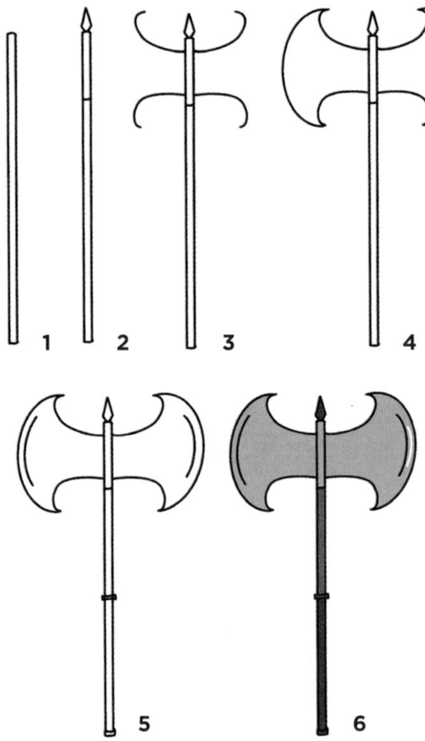

MORNING STAR

A morning star is a medieval weapon that consists of a spiked ball mounted on a shaft. To draw it, start with a circle, and then add thin "v" shapes extending out from inside it. Erase the areas where the spikes overlap the circle. Next, sketch a pair of parallel lines coming out from the ball for the shaft. Draw a rectangle at the base of the lines for the grip, and connect it to the rest of the handle with short, curving lines. Finally, add color to your doodle. I chose dark gray for the ball since most of these weapons were made from iron.

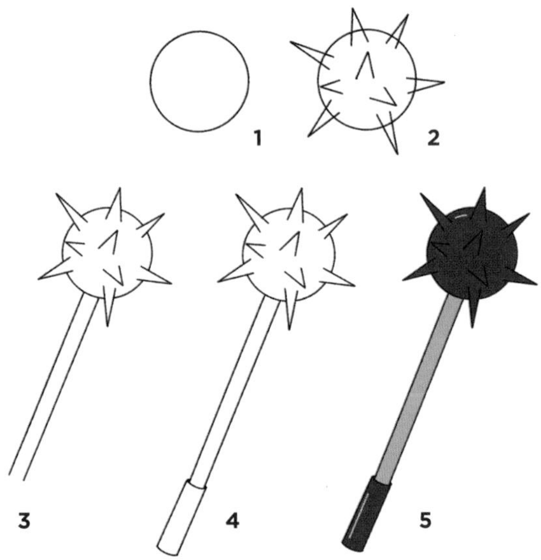

FLAIL

Like the morning star, a flail has a spiky metal ball, but it's attached to a flexible chain or rope rather than directly to a shaft. Start this doodle by drawing a circle and adding thin "v" shapes extending out from inside of it. Erase the areas where these points overlap the circle. Sketch a thin, rounded rectangle for the first chain link, and then draw a pair of rounded rectangles intersecting it to form the second link. Continue this pattern to draw a short chain, erasing the spots where the links overlap.

At the top of the last link, sketch a double circle that's attached to a long "u" shape. Connect the base of the shape, then extend a pair of lines down from it to form the grip. Connect the lines at the bottom, and then add detail lines in that grip section to show a wooden texture. Complete your doodle by adding color.

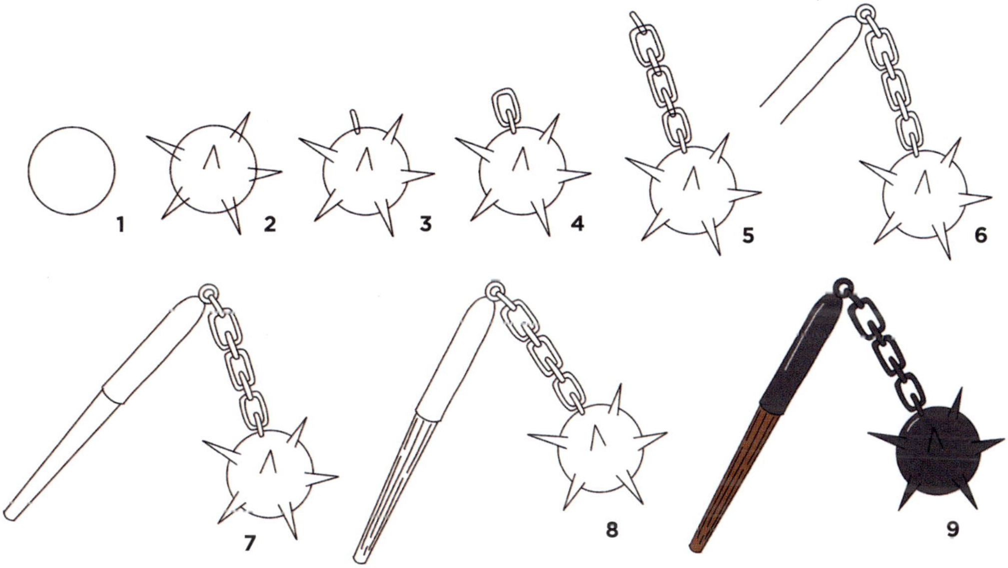

CATAPULT

To doodle this medieval weapon, start by sketching a "u" shape with a thin rectangle across the top. Next, draw a long, thin rectangle extending out to the right for the arm. Add two diagonal pieces of the frame, erasing the areas where the lines overlap. The left frame piece should look as though it's behind the arm, while the other piece is in the front. Draw two round wheels, and connect them with parallel lines. Sketch smaller circles inside each wheel, and add details like lines for wooden texture and a bolt. Finally, draw a bumpy rock loaded into the catapult, and color your doodle.

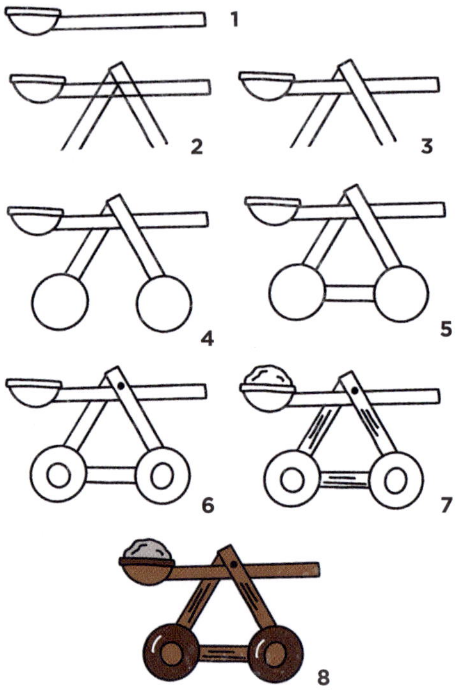

HORSE

Doodle your knight a noble steed to travel on adventures! Start with the head shape and add a pair of ears that point forward. Divide the outer parts of the ears from the inner parts. Draw a curving line for the chest, and a pair of front legs. Sketch the horse's back, belly and back legs. Add a tail, and then draw a mane on the back of the neck and the top of the head. Erase the areas where the mane overlaps the body.

Sketch detail lines inside the mane and tail for texture. Separate the hooves from the rest of the legs, and draw a face including eyes, nostrils and eyebrows. Once your doodle is finished, color it in any way you like to give your horse its own unique look.

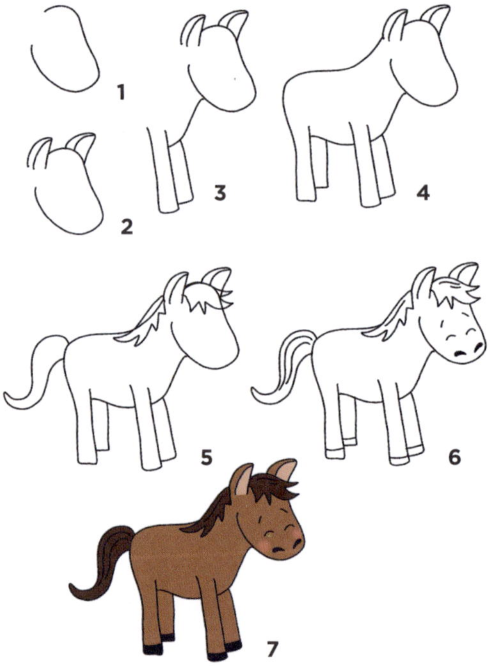

KNIGHT

Let's learn to draw the hero, our knight in shining armor! We'll start with the head, drawing a round helmet with the center part sectioned off for the visor, and a small rectangle on top. Add detail to the visor: a short vertical line in the top center, a crescent shape eye opening and a series of rounded rectangles in the mouth area. Draw a plume extending from the top of the helmet, as well as two short, curving lines for the neck area.

Add detail lines inside the neck, and a curving rectangle below. Draw a pair of semicircles with curving lines inside for the shoulder armor, and then sketch two vertical lines connected with a curve for the breastplate. Next, draw a curving rectangle for the tasset, with a few detail lines. Sketch the tops of the legs, and poleyns (knee coverings). Add a pair of boots.

Finally, draw a pair of arms extending out from below the shoulders, and sketch a glove on each hand. I positioned my knight this way so that I can add a shield and/or weapons in both hands. You can color your knight as is, or add one of the weapons to his hand, like the morning star. Also, feel free to add a heraldic symbol, like a cross or fleur-de-lis on the breastplate.

Have fun personalizing your knight doodle by adding different objects in his hands, using the weapons and shields we learned how to draw earlier in the chapter.

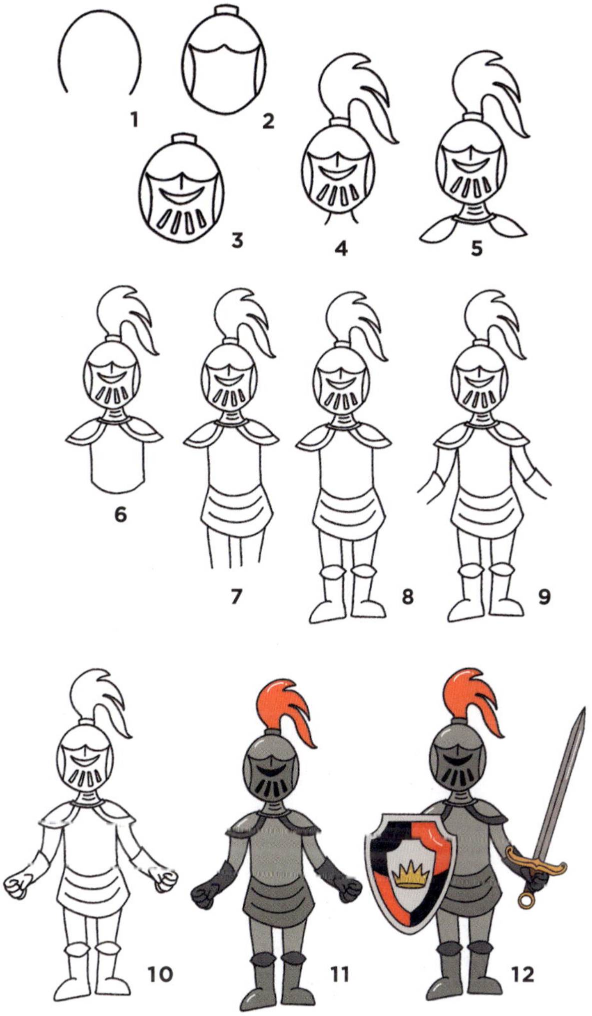

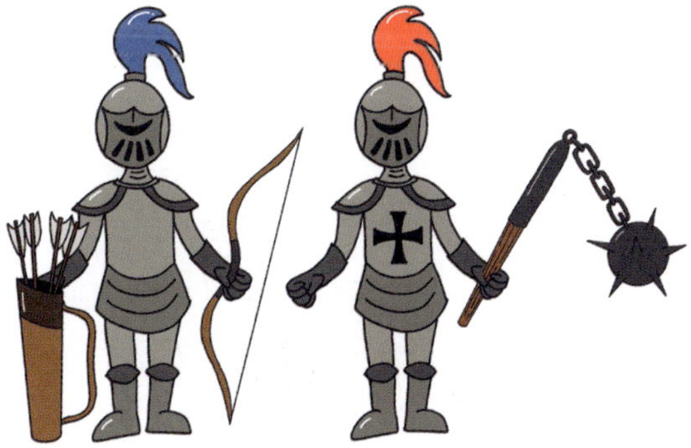

HORSE WITH ARMOR

In battle, knights would provide their horses with armor to protect them. To draw the horse's armor, start by following the steps for doodling a horse, except for the face. Then, use a curving line inside the head to separate out a center section covered by armor. Erase the top part of the mane, and add a circle where the horse's eye will go.

Sketch a rectangle shape on the horse's back, and then add a band around the neck with several squares attached. Draw wavy lines to add a blanket over the horse, and erase any areas where it overlaps. Finally, add the horse's eye inside the circle in the face armor. Complete your doodle by adding color.

Now, try drawing your knight next to his horse! Don't they make a great team?

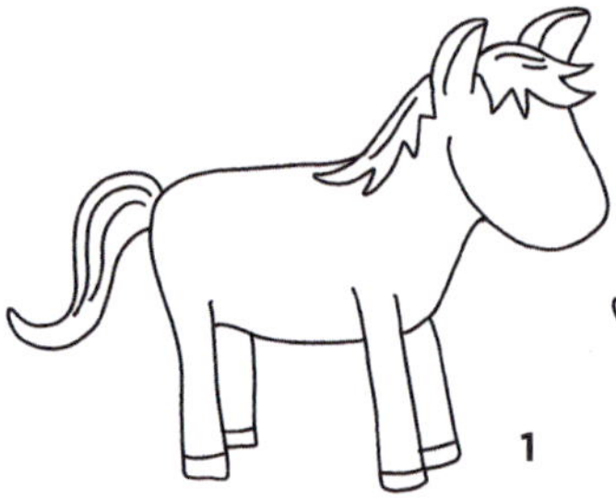
1

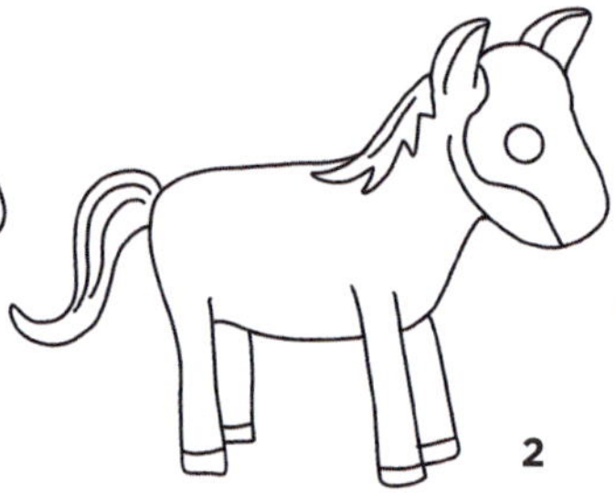
2

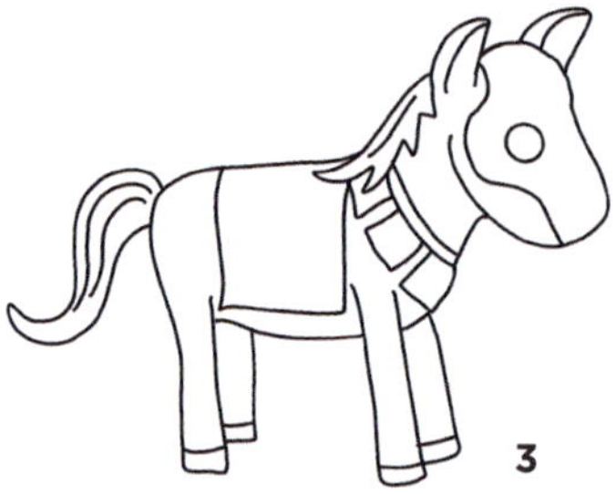
3

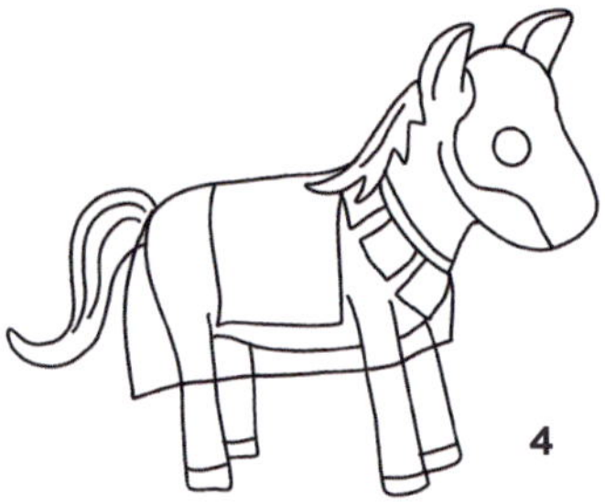
4

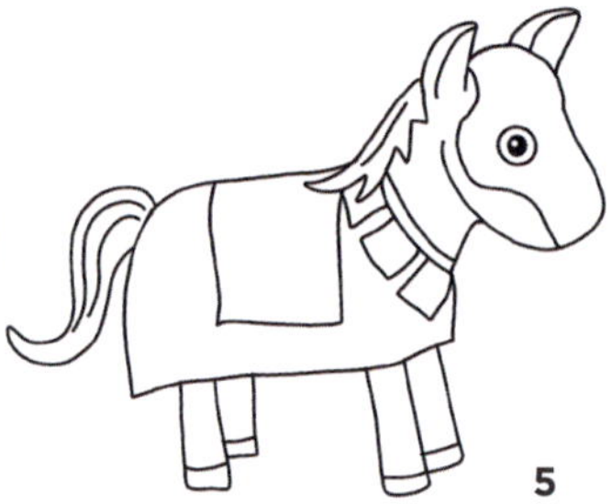
5

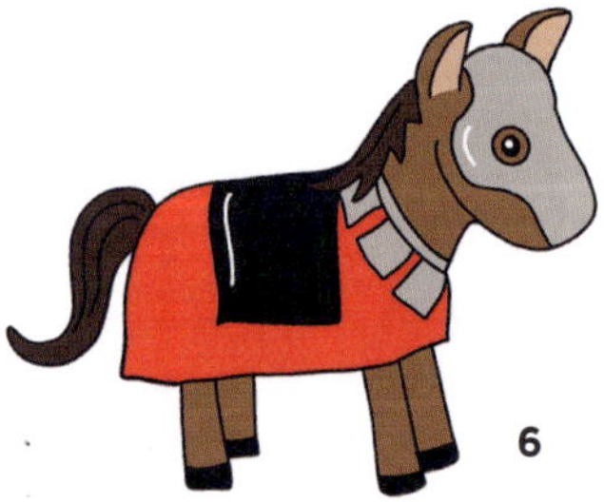
6

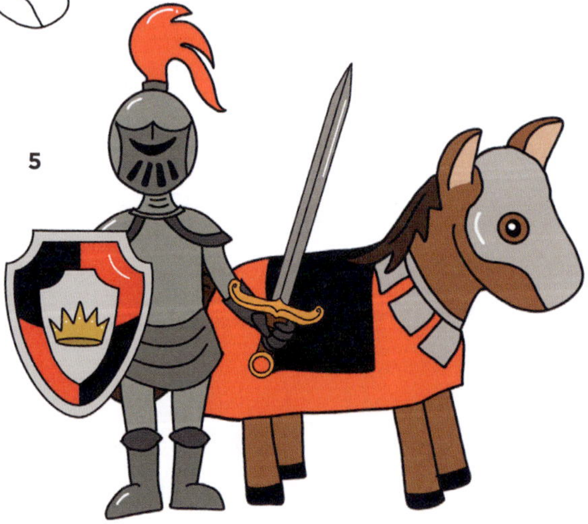

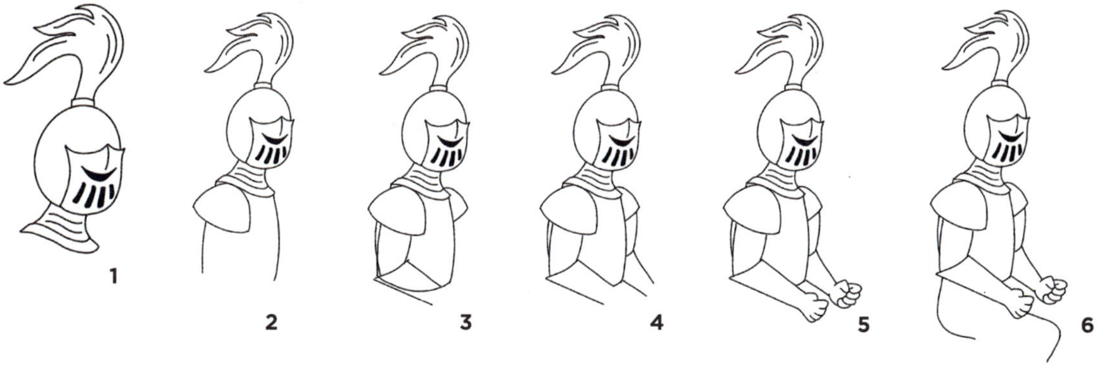

MOUNTED KNIGHT

Let's finish our knights and dragons chapter by drawing our knight mounted on his horse, riding to victory. Start your doodle by drawing the helmet we learned earlier in the chapter (page 39). Then, add a semicircle for the shoulder covering and two lines for the front and back of the body. Add a second shoulder on the other side of the body, and sketch arms extending down from the shoulders, erasing any overlapping areas. Draw a pair of gauntlets (gloves) with the fingers curled inward so that the knight can hold something in his hands.

Add a curving line for the upper leg and knee, and another curve below the back. Connect the lines to form the front leg and boot. Draw a curving line for the upper part of the back leg. Sketch curves to create the knee coverings. This completes the seated knight.

Now, draw the horse (I chose the armored version on page 50) below the knight, and erase any spots where the two overlap. Place the weapon of your choice in the knight's hand, and color your drawing.

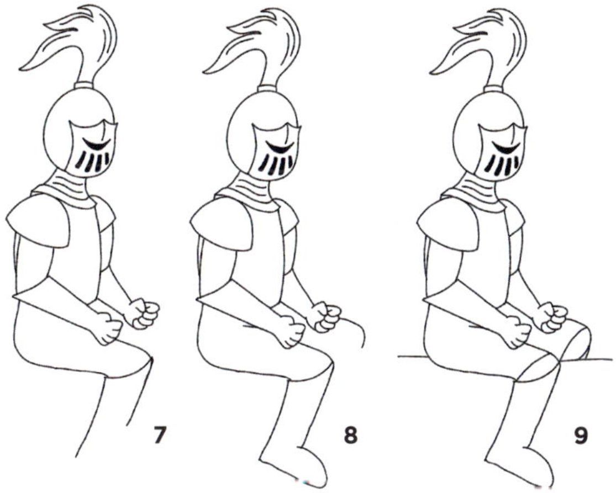

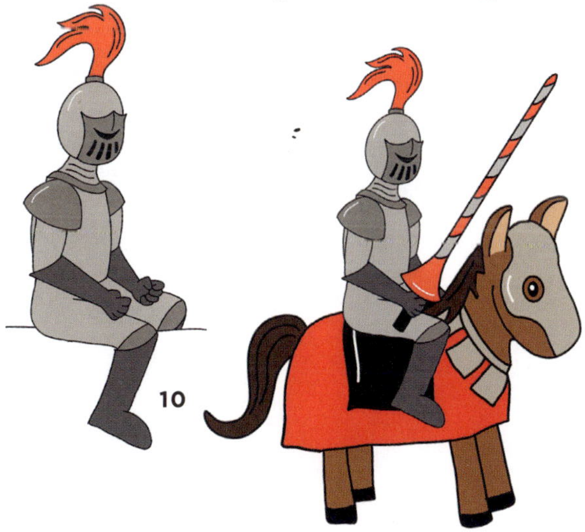

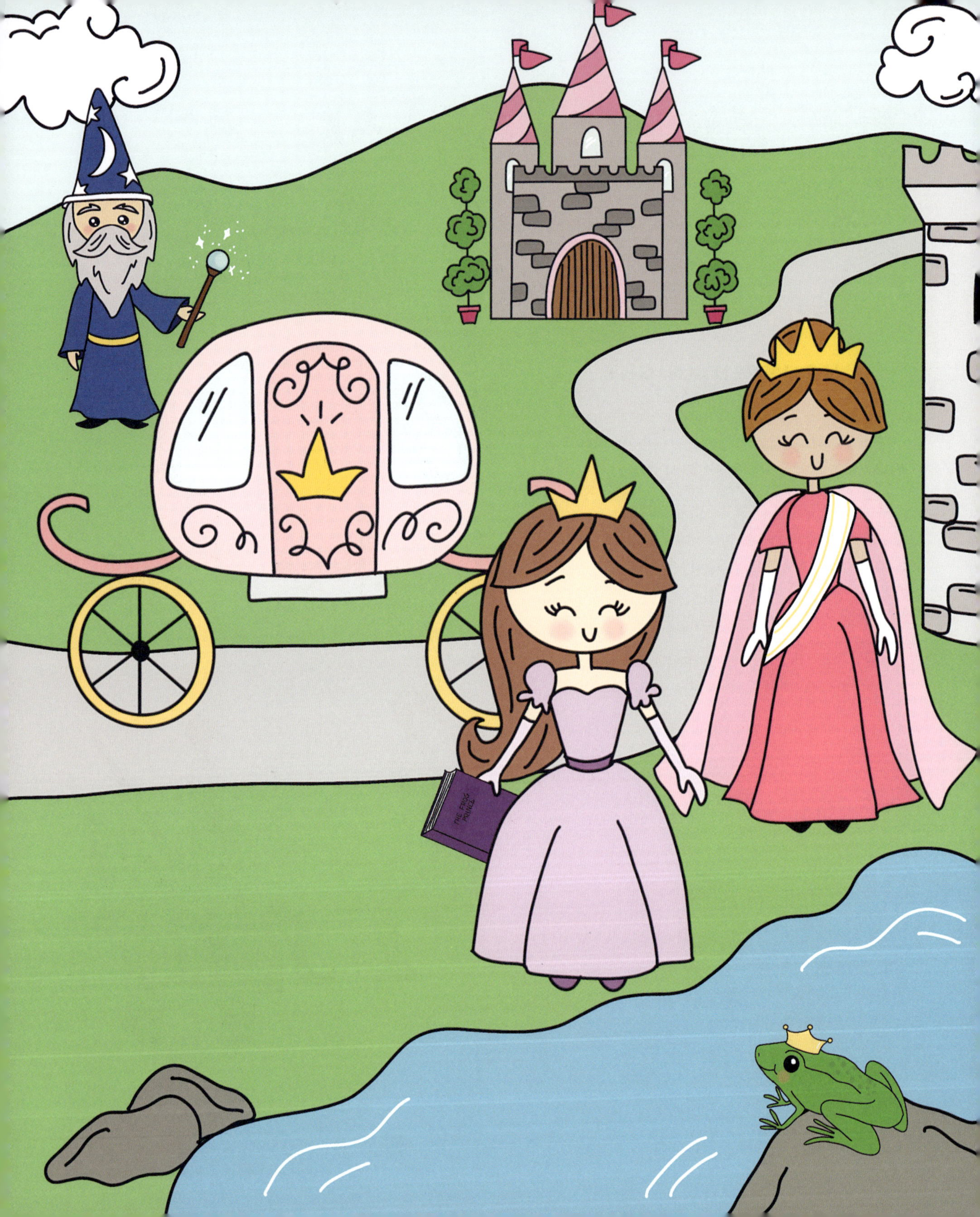
THE FROG
PRINCE

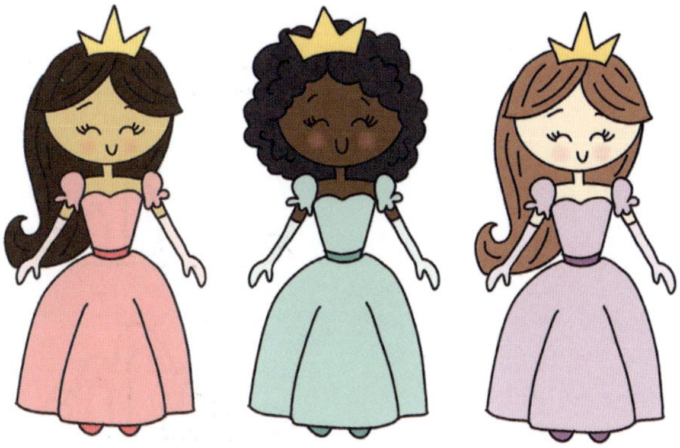

FAIRY-TALE Kingdom

Let's take a journey to a fairy-tale kingdom, where the beautiful princess and her Prince Charming live happily ever after together. Learn to draw the king and queen, their castle and carriage, as well as many other things you might find in this magical realm. Many of these doodles also make a perfect combination with those in the Land of Knights and Dragons chapter! Grab a pencil, and we'll get started with drawing everything you'll need to create your own royal family.

TIARA

To sketch a tiara, start with a thin oval. Then, draw a set of five scallops, making the center one the largest. Erase the area where the scallops overlap the oval, as well as a bit more to create the ends of the headpiece. Draw a second line below the front of the oval. Add upside-down "u" shapes inside the scallops. Erase the spots on the oval that are in between the "u" shapes. Finally, color your drawing. As a bonus variation, try adding some colorful gems!

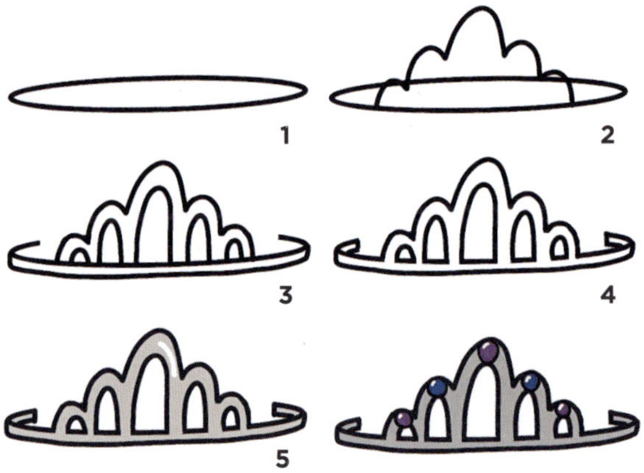

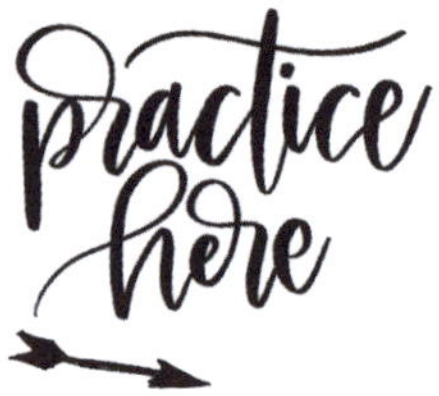

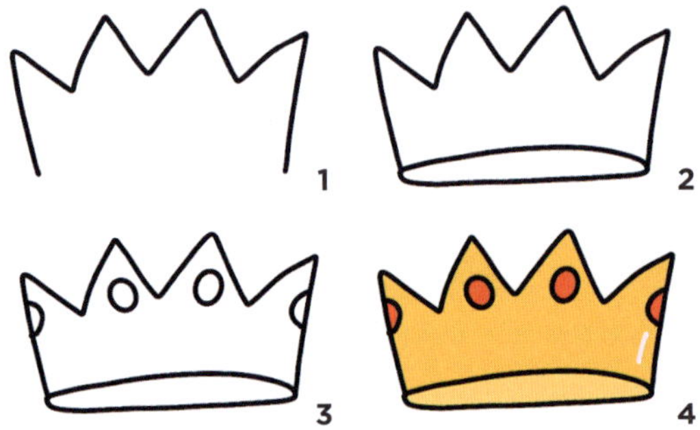

CROWNS

There are many ways to draw a crown. The easiest one is to sketch a pair of vertical lines, and then connect them at the top with a series of "v" shapes. You can do this so that all of the crown's points are the same size, or you can make the center point taller than the ones on the sides. Then, draw an oval at the bottom. Decorate your crown using circles or other shapes to represent gemstones, and then color it. Here are two variations to try: one with three points and one with four.

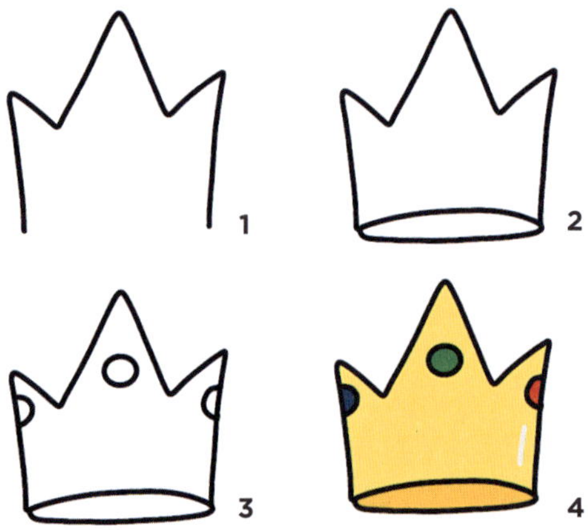

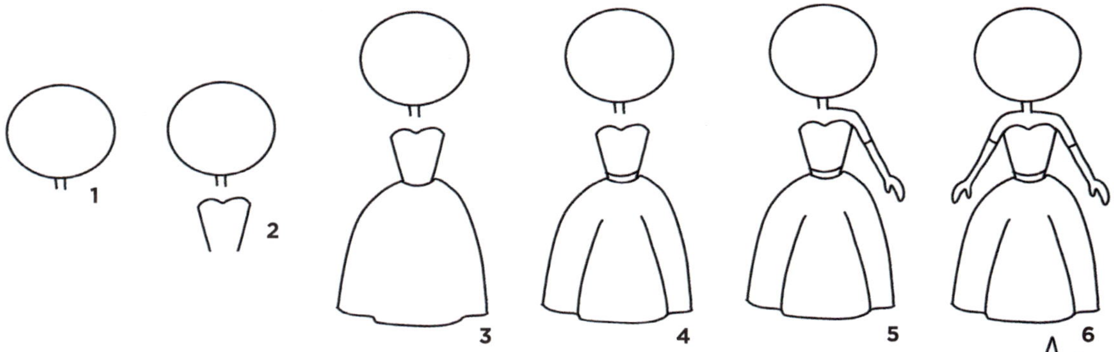

PRINCESS

Let's doodle a princess together! Start with an oval head and two small lines for the neck. Leave a bit of space, and then draw a rounded "m" shape with a diagonal line on each side for the bodice of her dress. Add a full skirt, and draw a few detail lines to show the flowing fabric. Draw a sash where the bodice and the skirt meet.

Give your princess shoulders, arms and simple hands wearing long gloves. Add a pair of puffy sleeves, and erase the areas where they overlap her arms. Sketch two soft raindrop shapes on top of her head for hair, and erase overlapping spots. Draw the rest of her hair, and add a crown on her head. Sketch detail lines inside the hair for texture, and add two small semicircle shoes. Finally, give your princess eyes, eyebrows and a smile, and add color to your drawing.

Personalize your princess in any way you like, using all kinds of skin and hair colors and hairstyles. Maybe your princess wears her hair in a bun, or perhaps she has curly hair!

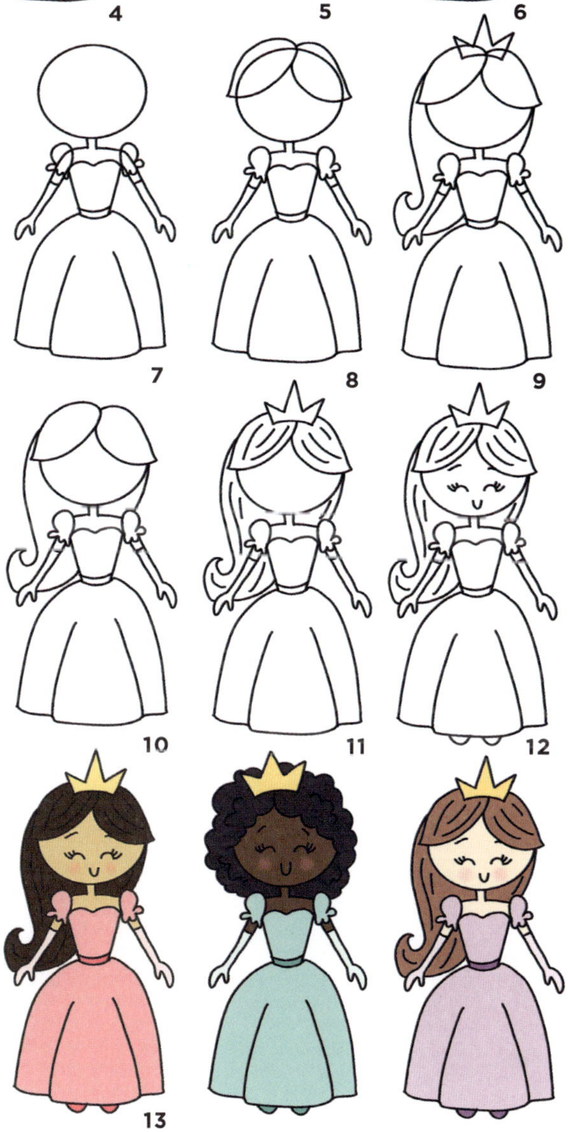

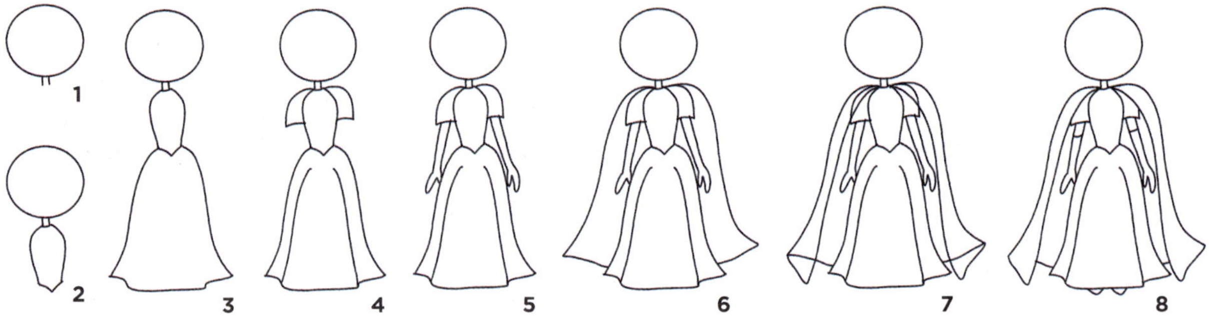

QUEEN

To draw a regal queen, start with an oval head and two short lines for her neck. Next, draw the upper body, with a point at the waist of her dress. Add a skirt with flowing lines, and a pair of rounded sleeves. Draw a pair of arms and simple hands. Sketch a line coming down from each shoulder and across the bottom to form a cape. Draw another pair of lines from the front of each shoulder, connecting them to the back of the cape. Erase the areas where the cape overlaps the queen's body and shoulders.

Add a line on each arm to indicate long gloves, and draw a pair of shoes peeking out from the skirt. Sketch two paisley shapes on the head for hair, as well as a rounded bun on top. Erase overlapping areas, and add detail lines to the hair. Draw a crown on top of her head, and give her a simple face of eyes, eyebrows and a smile. Sketch a sash that crosses the front of the body on a diagonal. Erase any extra lines, and then color your queen.

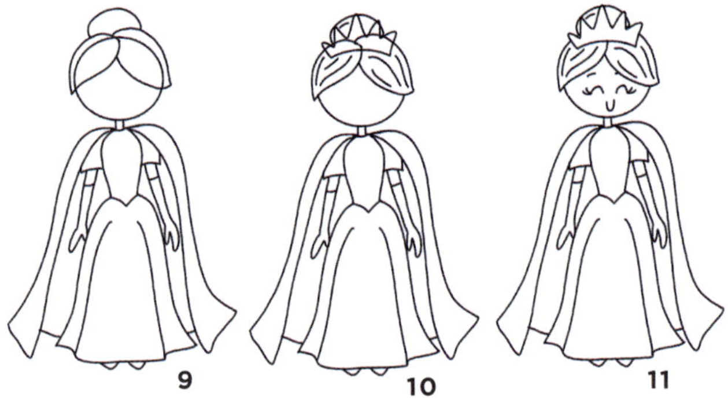

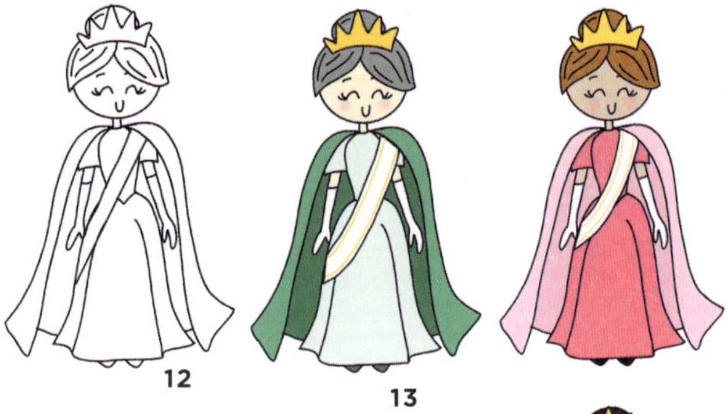

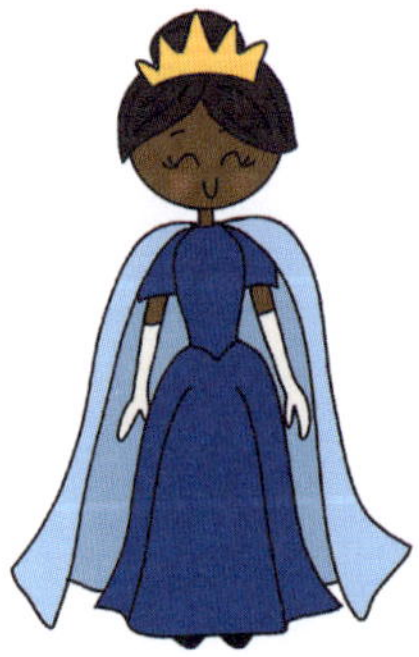

practice here

PRINCE

It's time to doodle a charming prince! First, sketch a circular head with two short lines for the neck. Then, draw two rounded shoulders and a torso with a belt at the bottom. Add two rounded triangles below the belt for the bottom of the tunic. Next, sketch a pair of legs with boots. Give your prince arms and hands, and then sketch his hair. Erase the lines where the hair overlaps his head, and then add a few lines for texture. Draw a crown, erasing any overlapping lines, and give him a smiling face. Add any additional details, like buttons on his tunic, and then color your prince.

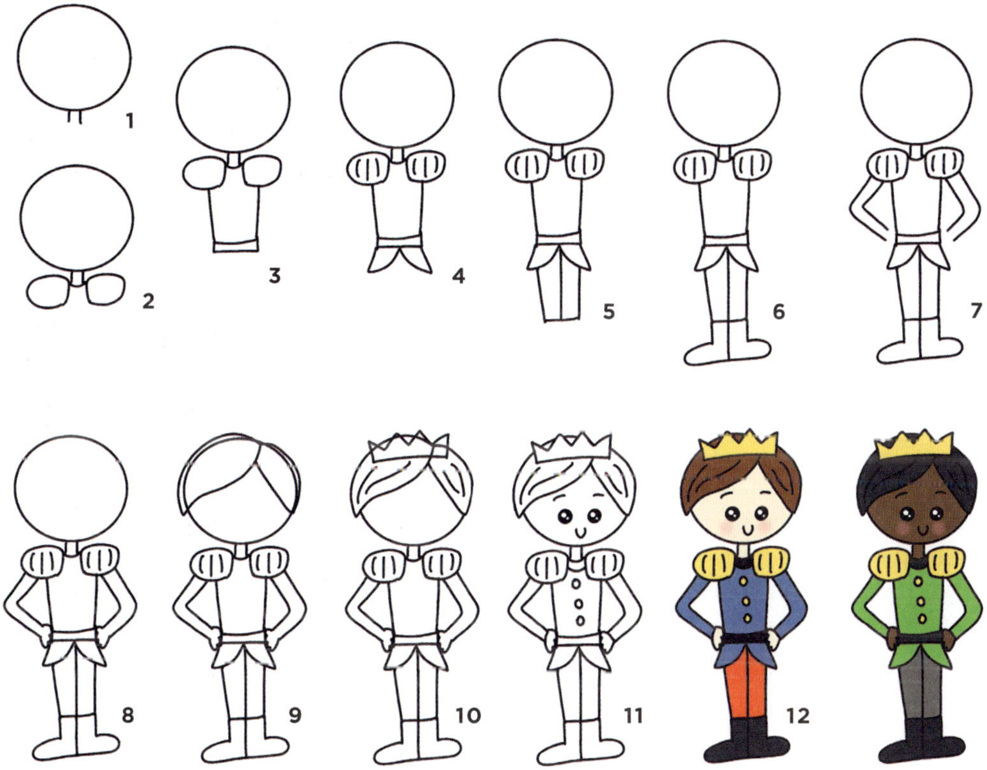

KING'S CROWN

Let's create a large, ornate crown fit for the king! First, sketch the basic crown shape, and add a circle to the top of each point. Next, draw a pair of curving lines above it, and another pair of curving lines inside the first two. Add embellishments on top, like a set of crescent shapes and a cross. Finally, draw a smaller crown shape inside the base. Color your crown using any combination of colors you like.

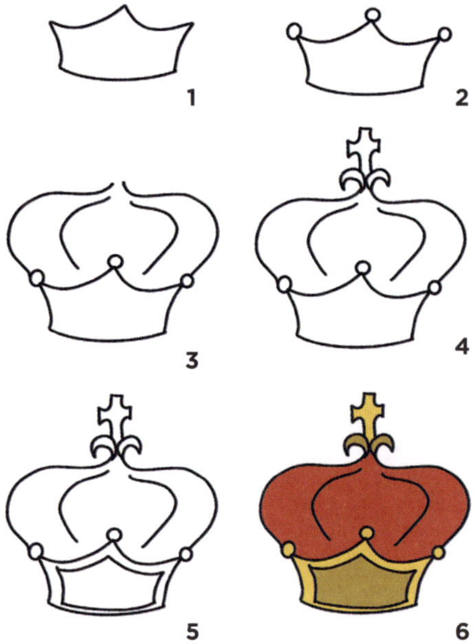

SCEPTER

Every king needs a scepter, so let's learn to draw one! Start with a pair of long, vertical lines, and connect them at the bottom. Draw a short rectangle at the top, then sketch a heart shape above it. Add a second heart shape inside, plus one more line to divide the upper section. Finally, draw a small circle on top. Color your scepter, and it's ready for your king to hold.

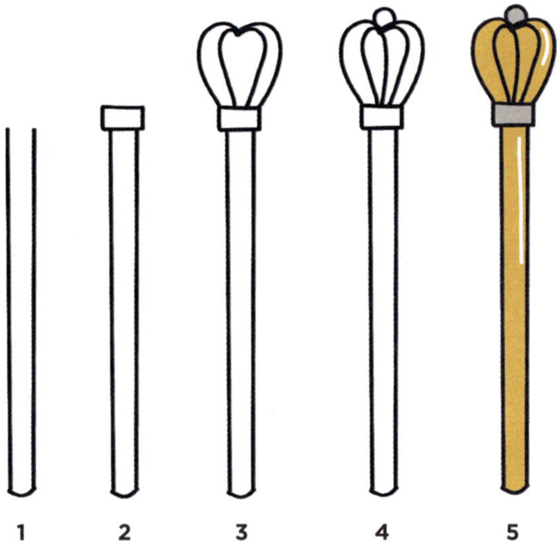

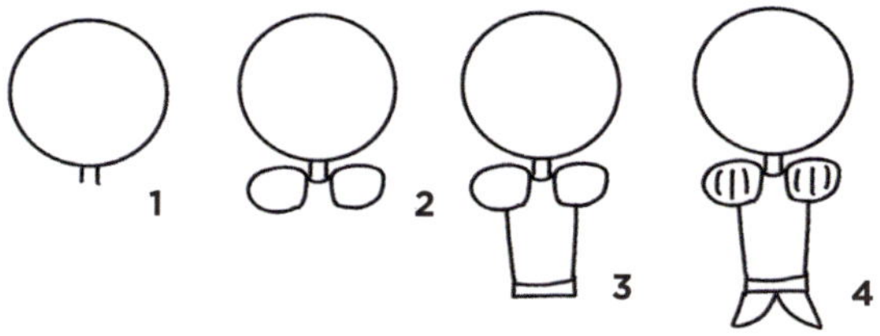

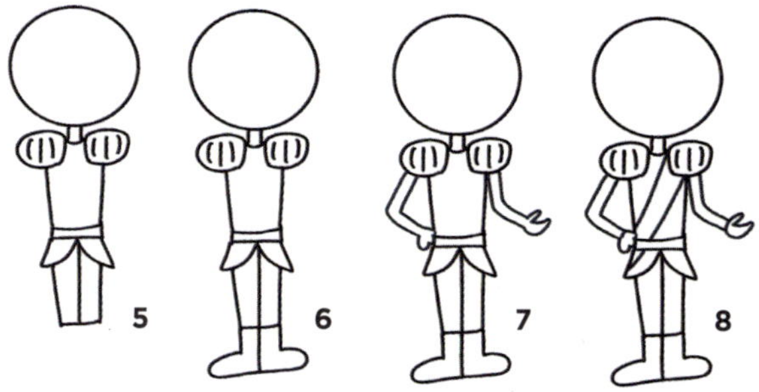

KING

Drawing a king is very similar to drawing a prince. Start in the same way, with a circular head, a neck, rounded shoulders and a torso with a belt. Add the bottom of the tunic, a pair of legs and boots, just like the prince. Then, give your king arms and hands. I like to draw one arm bending outward so that the king can hold his scepter (or the hand of a lovely lady). Sketch a sash diagonally across the torso, and then draw a cape that extends down from the king's shoulders. Add hair and a crown on his head, erasing any overlapping lines. I chose to use the special king's crown doodle from page 58, but you can use whatever type of crown you want him to wear. Add texture to the hair with a few detail lines, and give your king a face. Finally, add color to finish your doodle.

To make him look even more official, try adding the royal scepter in his hand.

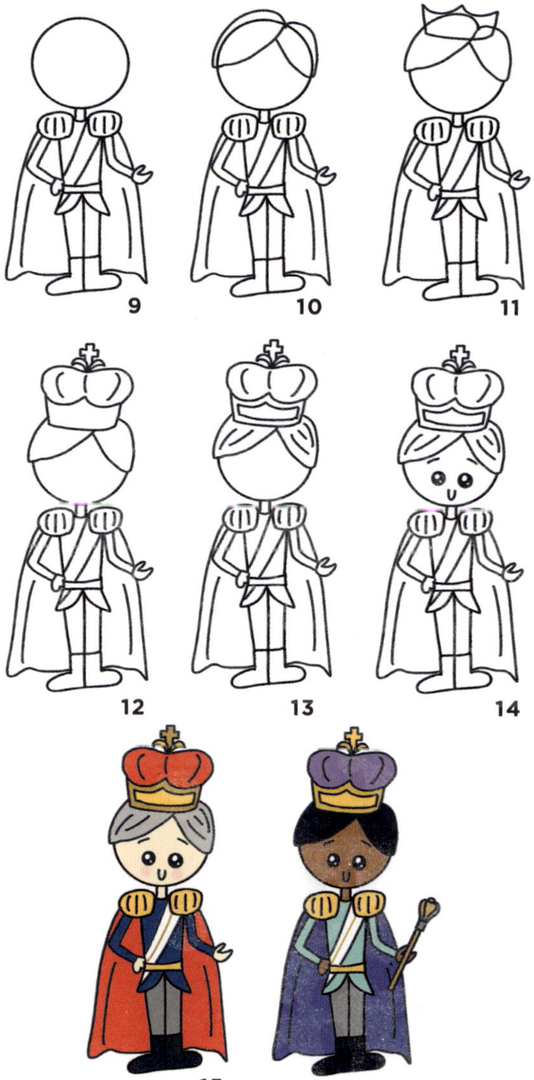

practice here

BONUS

Now that you've learned to draw a princess, a queen, a prince and a king, let's draw the whole royal family, all together for a family portrait!

Or, try drawing any two together, like the king and the princess.

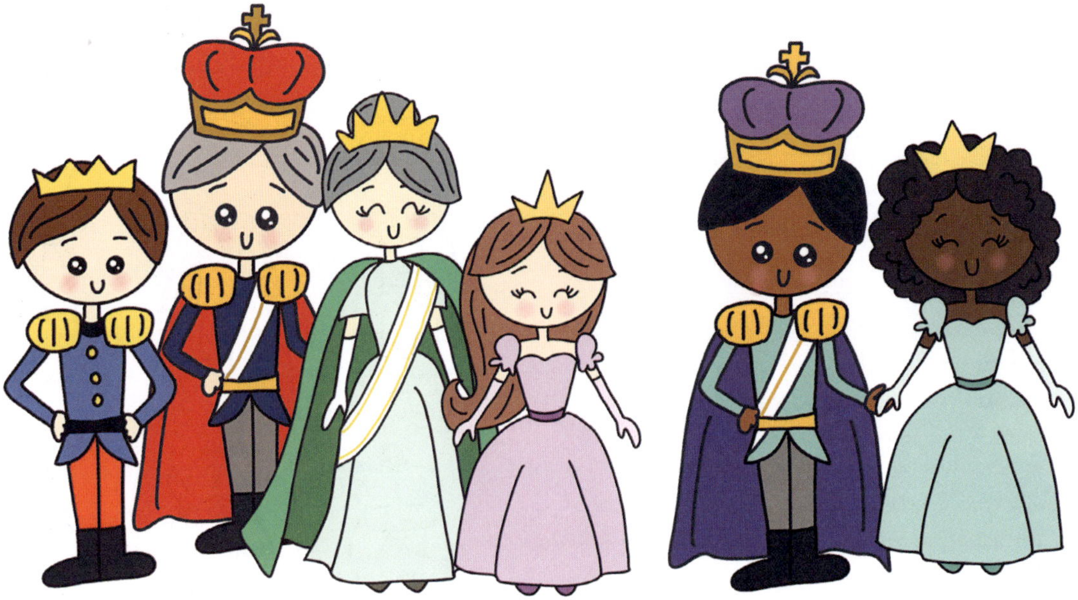

practice here

LADIES' HAT/HENNIN

This fancy, pointed hat with a long veil, which was popular during the Middle Ages, is perfect for the ladies in the king's court or even the princess herself. Start by sketching a cone shape, and then draw a long, wavy line coming from the top. Draw a second wavy line extending below the base. Connect the two lines, and then add detail lines inside to show the flowing texture of the fabric. Finish your doodle by adding color.

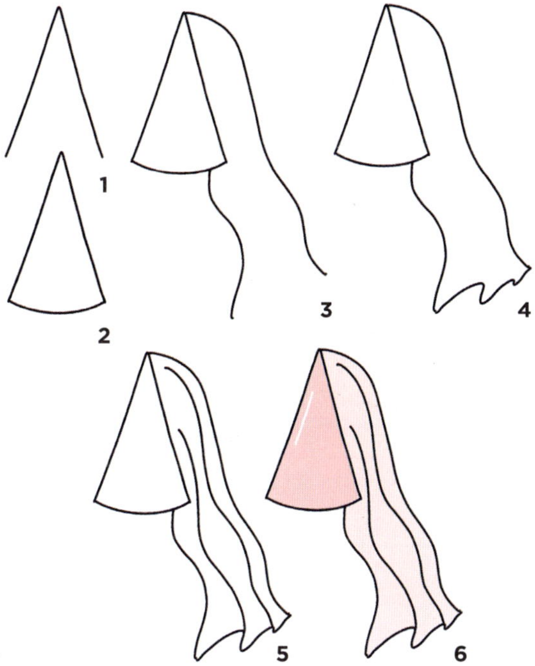

JESTER'S HAT

The first step in drawing a jester's hat is to sketch a curved rectangle for the band. Draw a wave shape extending out to the left, and then draw a second wave shape that curves to the right. Make a third wave shape behind the center one that also extends to the right. Sketch a large circle on each point, and erase any overlapping lines. Add details to the circles to make them resemble bells. Finally, color your doodle. Traditionally, jester's hats are often green, purple, and/or yellow, but feel free to choose any combination of bright colors.

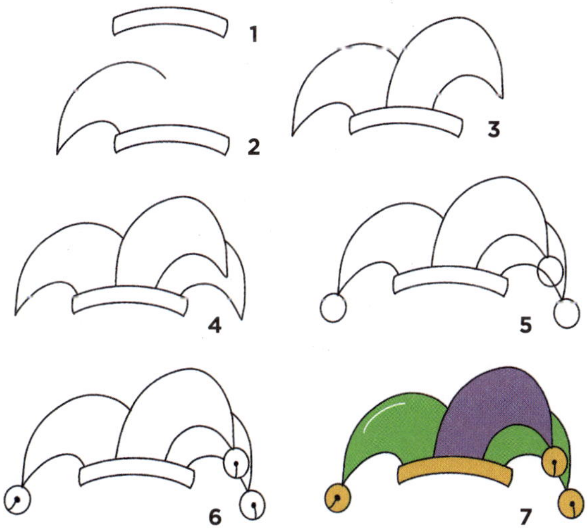

FROG PRINCE

Sometimes you have to kiss a few frogs before you find your prince! Let's draw a frog prince, starting with a curved line for the head and back of the body. Next, sketch a bent back leg, and a foot with three long toes. Add a short front leg and another three-toed foot, and connect it to the back leg with a short line for the belly. Draw a second front foot, and then sketch a bumpy line inside the body. Add a large round eye, a nostril and a smile. Finally, give your frog a crown, erasing the areas where the crown overlaps the body. Color your frog, adding some darker spots on his back for a more realistic look.

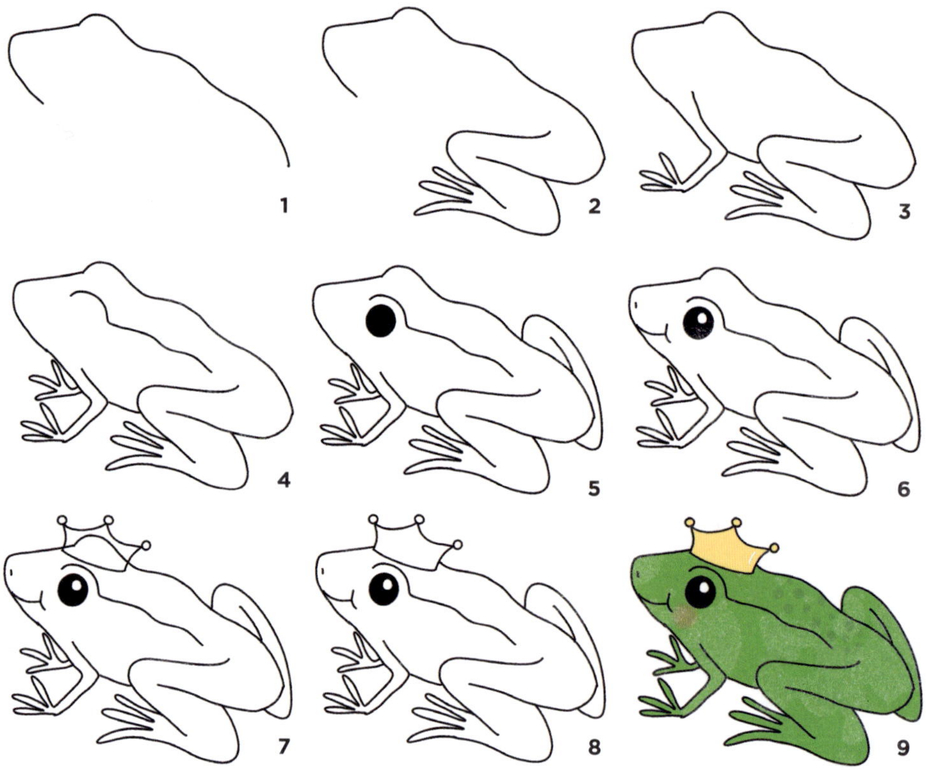

WIZARD'S HAT

Start this doodle by drawing a tall, upside-down "v." Connect the bottom with a curving line. Then, draw a "c" shape around the base. Decorate the hat with drawings of a crescent moon and stars. Erase any extra lines, like the ones inside the stars. Then, color your hat. Typically, wizard hats are blue and white, or blue and yellow, but feel free to use any combination of colors you can imagine.

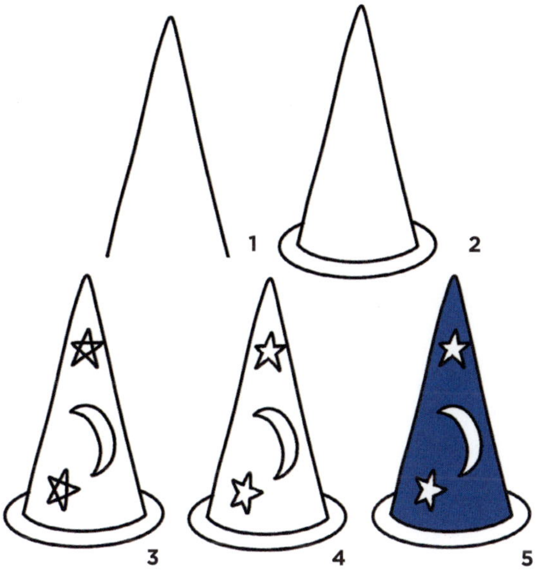

WIZARD'S WAND

In a magical kingdom, you might expect to find a wizard's wand, which happens to be very easy to doodle. Start with a long, thin rectangle, and then draw an upside-down trapezoid on top. Finally, doodle a circle for the ball at the top of the wand. Color your drawing in any way you like. I added a lighter circle and a white highlight line inside the ball to make it look reflective and a little bit magical.

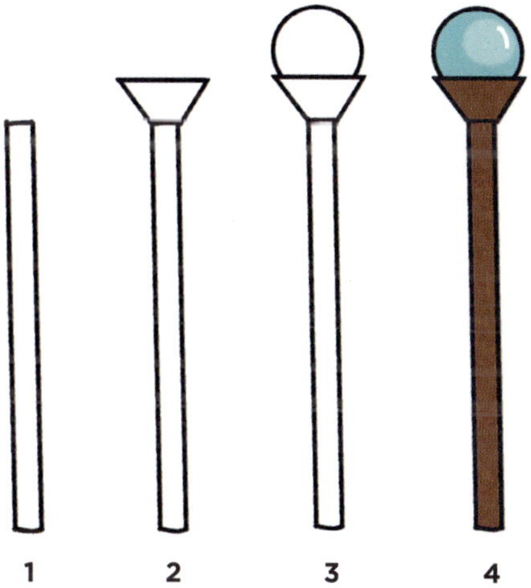

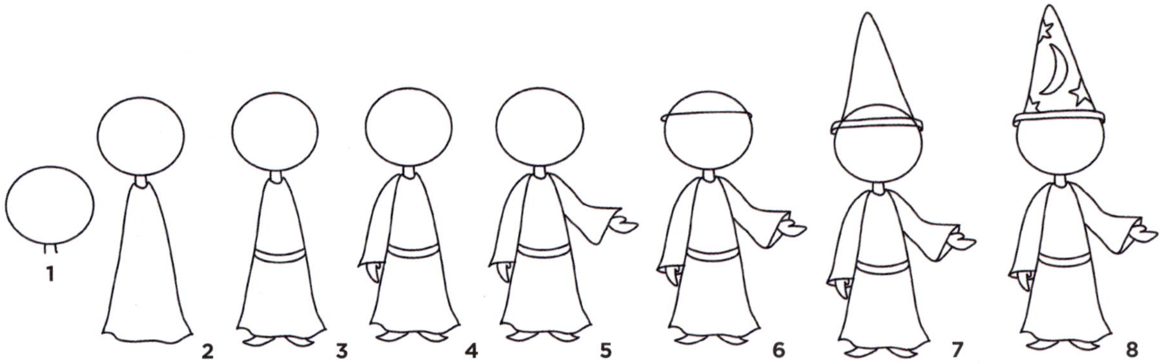

WIZARD

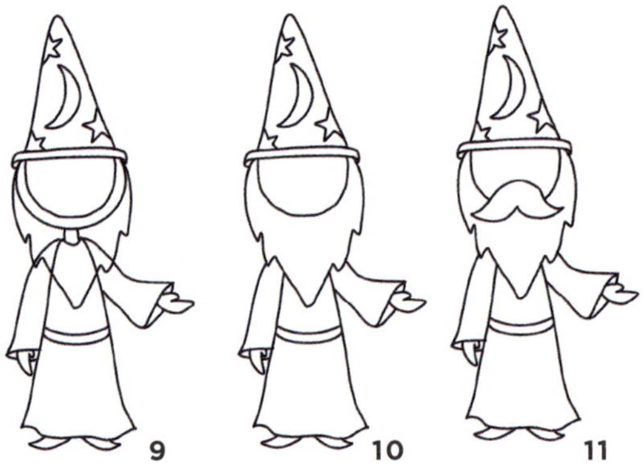

Now, it's time to draw the wise wizard himself. Begin by sketching an oval head with two lines for the neck. Add a long, flowing robe with a belt across the waist. Draw a pair of shoes coming out from the bottom of the robe. Sketch a pair of arms in long sleeves and simple hands. I like to draw one arm outstretched so that he can hold a wand. Next, draw a band across the center of the head, and the tall, "v"-shaped base of the wizard hat. Sketch the moon and stars inside the hat. Draw a long, zigzag beard, erasing the areas where it overlaps the head. Add a mustache, eyes and thick eyebrows. Finally, sketch a wizard's wand in his outstretched hand, erasing any extra lines. Color your masterpiece to complete the doodle.

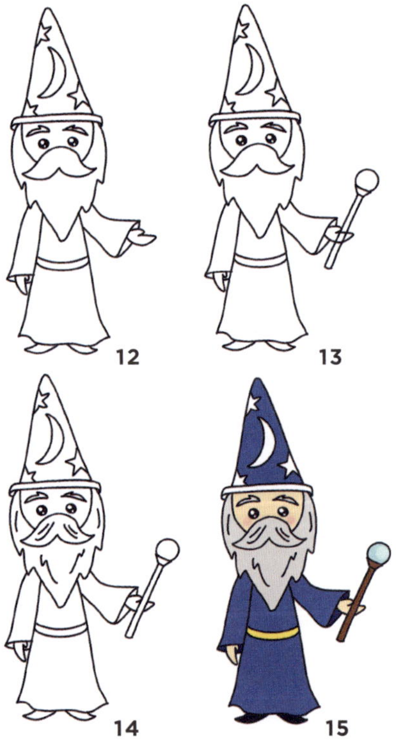

practice here

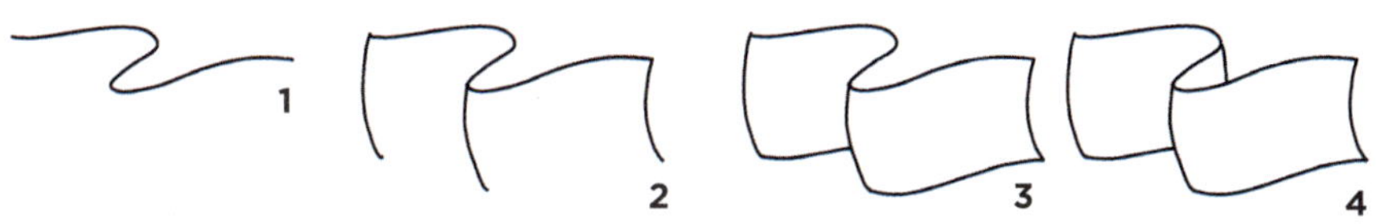

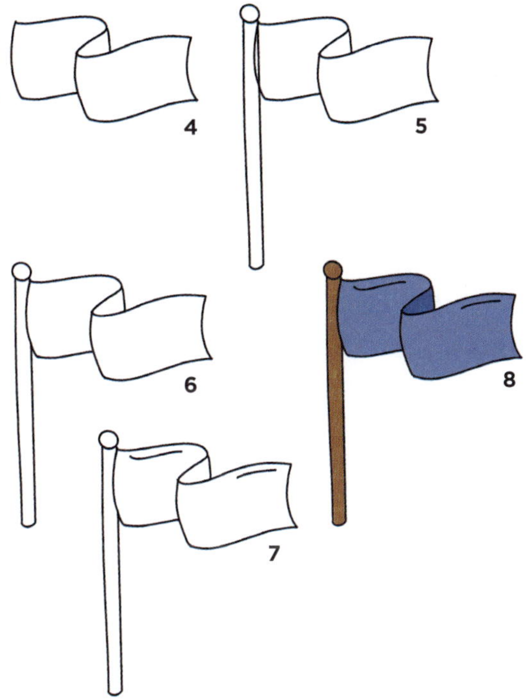

FLAG

Flags can be found throughout the kingdom, including at the tops of towers on the castle. Start this doodle by drawing a wavy, "z"-shaped line. Next, draw three short, vertical lines coming down from the left, right and center of the "z." Connect the lines on the bottom. Add another short, vertical line connecting the top curve to the front part of the banner. This creates dimension and makes the flag look like it's waving. Draw a flag pole with a circle on top, and erase any areas where it overlaps the flag. Finish your doodle with detail lines and color.

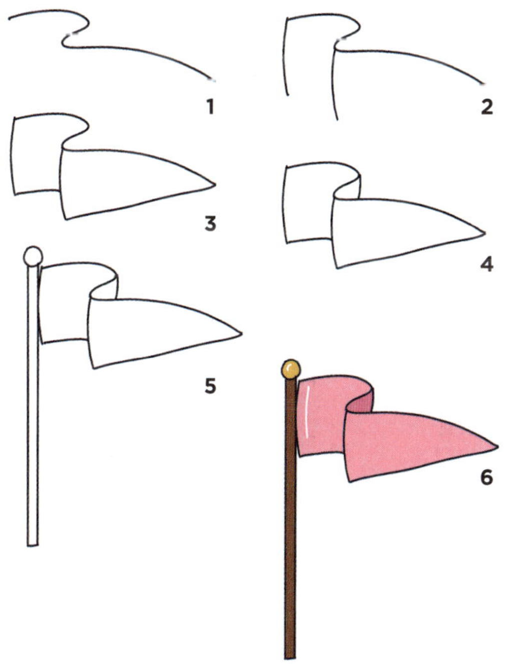

FLAG VARIATION

If you prefer to have a pointed pennant, here's how to create it using the same basic steps as the basic flag. Start with another wavy "z," but let the tail curve down at the end. Draw short, vertical lines on the left side and in the center, and then connect the center line to the end of the "z," forming a triangle point. Add one more short line to form the fold in the fabric, and then draw a flag pole. Draw detail lines, and finish by coloring your flag.

BANNER

Royal banners can decorate the outside and inside of a castle. To draw one, start with a pair of vertical lines that are connected with an upside-down "v" shape at the bottom. Draw a line across the top to finish the basic shape. Then, draw a smaller version of the same shape inside. Add a rectangle across the top for a hanger. Decorate the banner with a small doodle inside, like a crown, a flower, a letter or anything else you'd like to use to represent your royal family, and then add color.

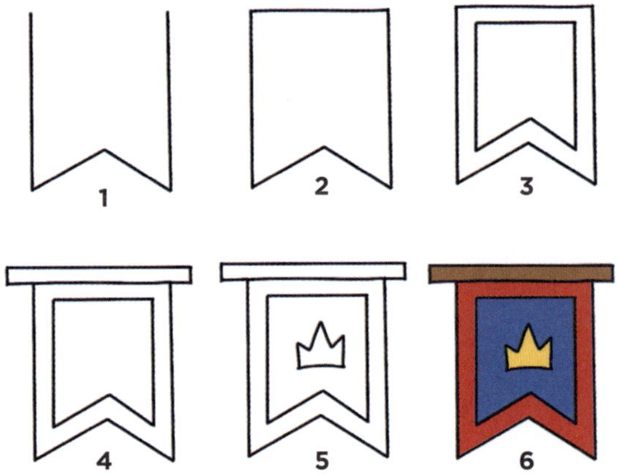

BANNER VARIATION

Here's a slight variation on the banner doodle. Start with a pair of vertical lines, but this time, connect them with a "v" at the bottom. Draw a line across the top to close the shape, and then sketch a smaller banner shape inside. Add a rectangle hanger, and then sketch your favorite doodle inside the banner. Color your drawing, and then it's ready to decorate the palace.

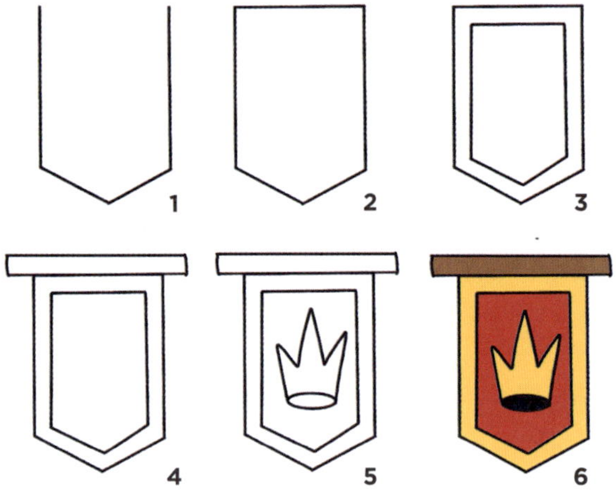

practice here

TOWER

Towers can be part of a castle, or they can stand alone as a remote hideaway for prisoners or princesses. To draw one, start with a pair of vertical lines. Then, add short diagonal and vertical lines to form the top part of the tower. Connect the top with a pattern of "u" shapes, and divide it from the rest of the tower with two horizontal lines. Draw an arch-shaped window, and then add texture by sketching rounded rectangle stones in random spots throughout the base of the tower. Add detail lines to the bricks, and color your tower gray.

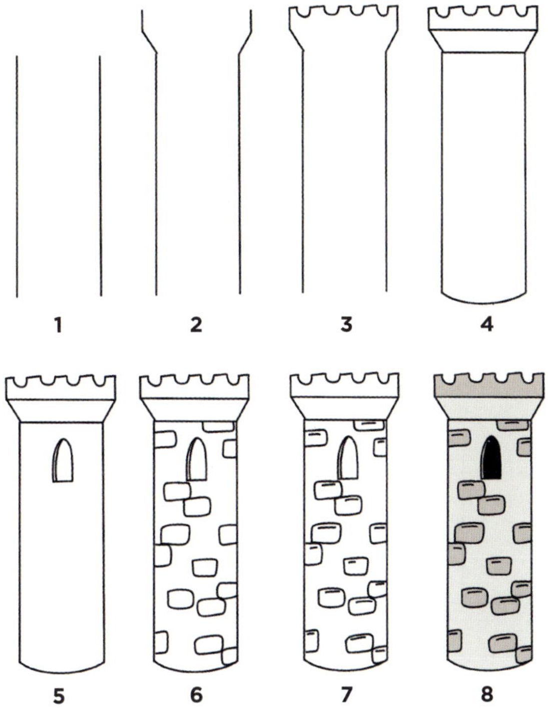

SCROLL

Hear ye, hear ye! To draw a scroll, start by sketching a backward "c" shape with a little spiral on each end. Next, extend a horizontal line out from the top and the bottom of your shape. Connect the lines to create the main part of your scroll. Draw horizontal lines from the top and bottom of each spiral that connect to the main scroll. This will give it a 3-D effect, as though the paper has been rolled. Add detail lines and color your doodle. To finish it off, you can add tiny words or squiggles to show that something is written on your scroll.

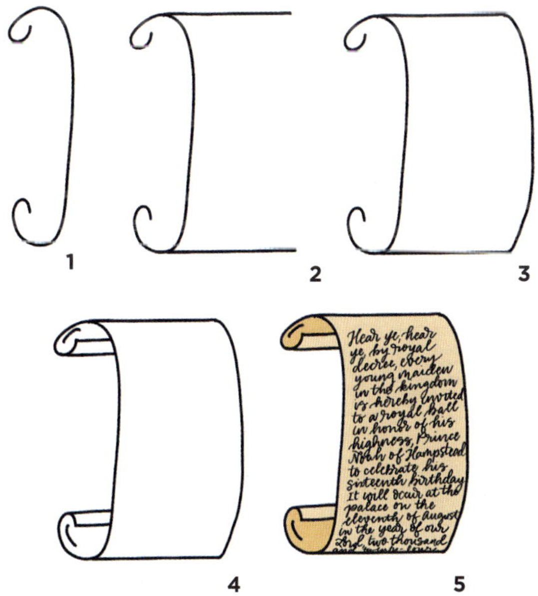

CASTLE

Your royal friends will need a castle to live in; here's how to doodle one! Start by forming the main section, which is two vertical lines connected with a series of lines and "u" shapes across the top. Add a bottom with an arch-shaped doorway. Draw a tower extending up from behind the main shape, as well as a tower on each side. Sketch an arch-shaped window near the top of each tower, and then cover the surface with rounded rectangles for texture. Add texture to the door with a series of vertical lines, and then draw a flag at the top of each tower. Finish your castle by adding color.

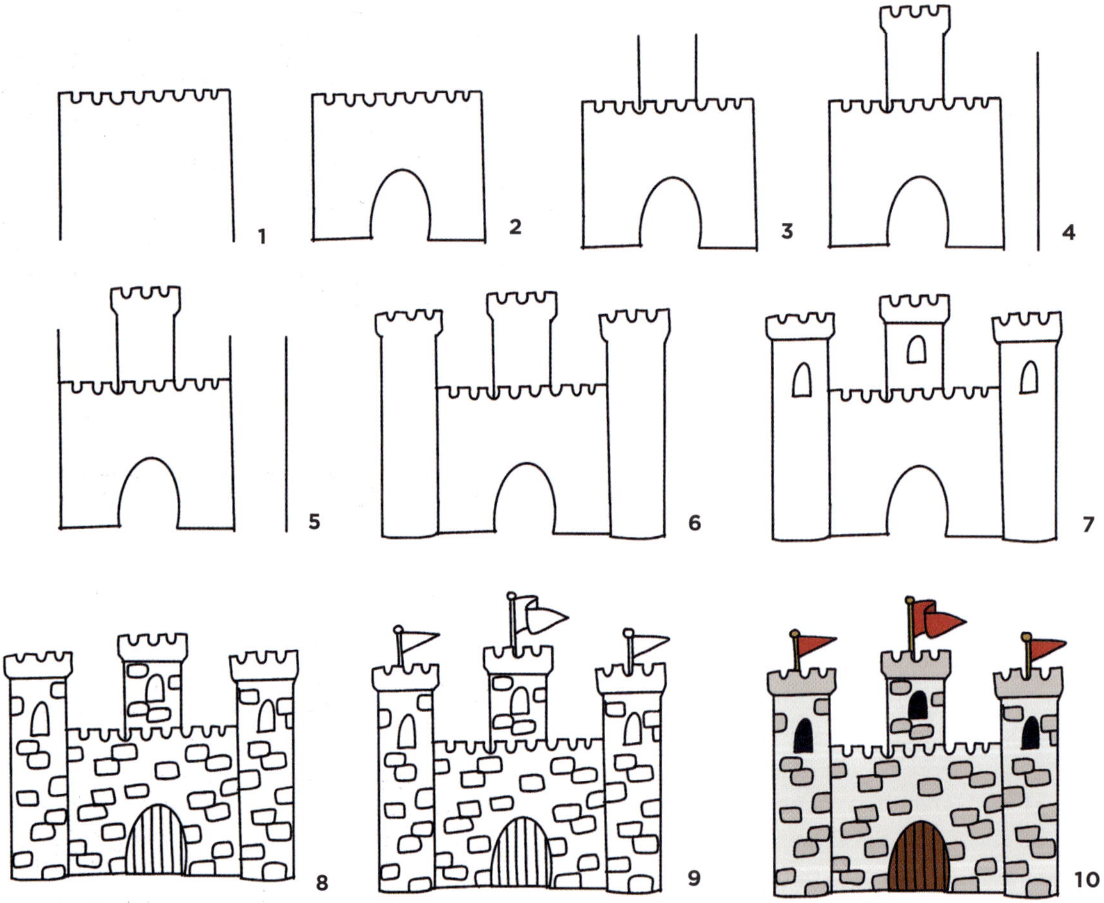

PRINCESS CASTLE

Here's another variation on a castle doodle that your princess is sure to love. First, draw two vertical lines, and connect them at the top to form a tower. Add a triangle and decorate it with diagonal stripes. Repeat the same steps to draw two slightly smaller towers, one on each side. Next, draw a rectangle in front, overlapping the center tower and parts of the side towers. Erase the overlapping lines, and then draw a pattern of "u" shapes across the top.

Erase the extra lines, and sketch a large, arched doorway with vertical lines running through it for texture. Draw a small, arched window near the top of each tower. Add rounded rectangle shapes scattered throughout the front of the castle to represent stones. Sketch a flag on the top of each tower, and then add topiaries on each side of the castle. Finish by coloring your doodle.

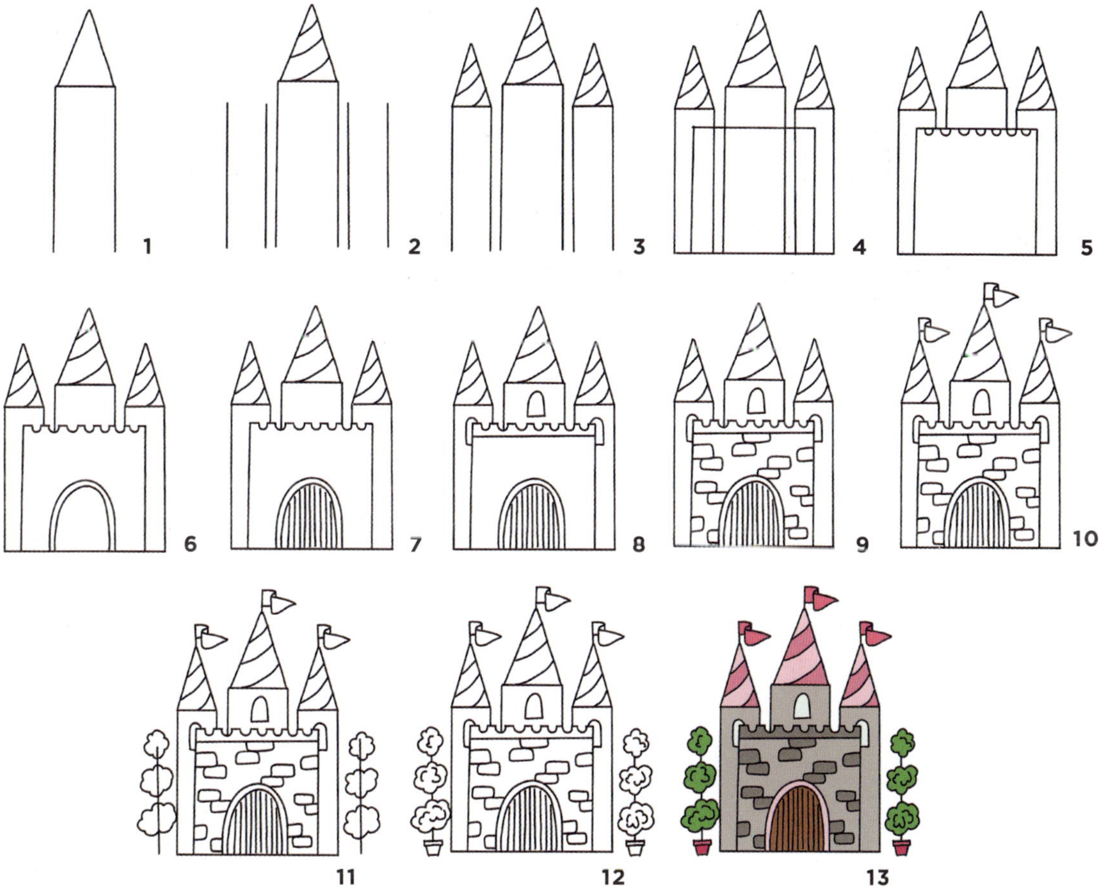

CARRIAGE

Let's give our royalty a stylish way to travel—a fancy carriage! Start this doodle with a rounded shape, and then add an arched door and a rectangular step. Add two rounded triangles for windows, and then decorate the side of the carriage with a crown and any other swirling, looping embellishments you like. Add a curving "J" shape on each side of the carriage, and then draw a pair of wheels made of smaller circles inside larger ones. Divide the center of each wheel with three intersecting lines, and draw a circle where they meet. Draw several diagonal detail lines in the windows, and then finish your doodle by coloring your carriage.

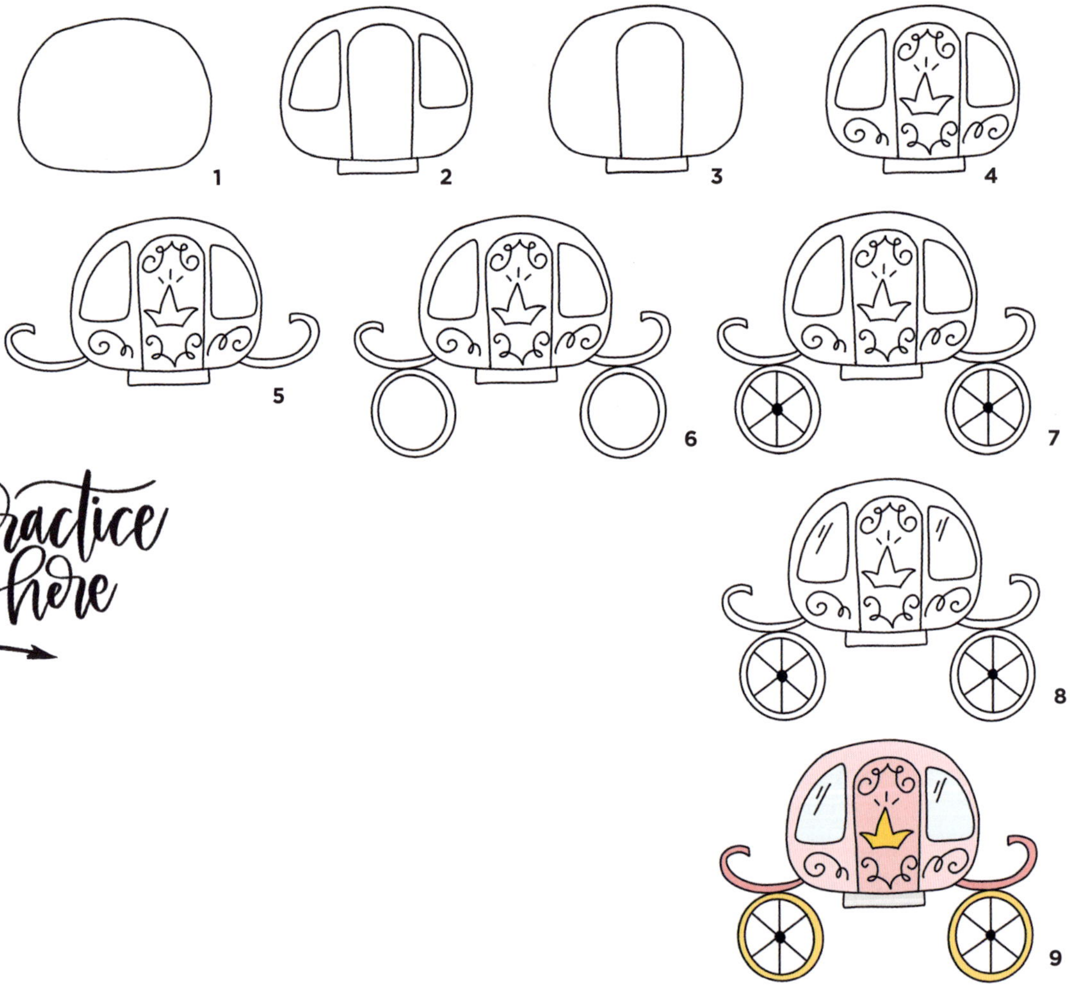

practice here

GOBLET

To sketch a goblet, start with a "u" shape, and then draw an oval on top. Add a long, thin stem, and then draw a rounded triangle base around it. Decorate the cup with whatever kind of pattern you like, to make it ready for royal use. Finish your doodle by adding color.

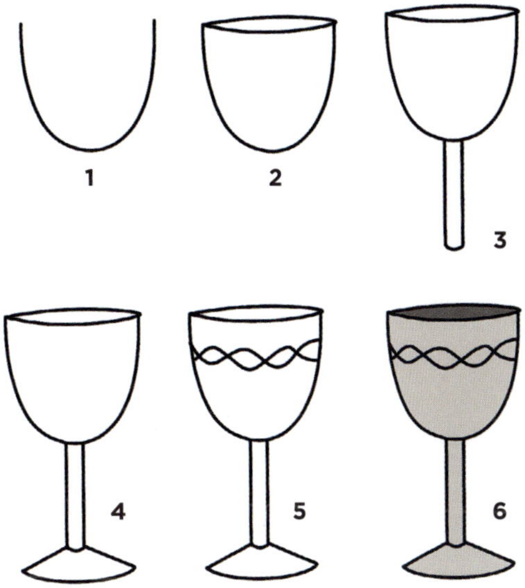

KEY

Learn to draw a key that unlocks special secrets in the castle. First, sketch a pair of spirals that curl toward each other. Add a second spiraling line and connect it to the first one. Draw a circle on top, with a smaller circle inside. Sketch two small rectangles below the spirals, and then make a long, thin vertical rectangle for the shaft. Draw the key's bit on one side of the shaft at the bottom. You can give it any type of pattern you like. Finish your doodle by drawing detail lines and adding color.

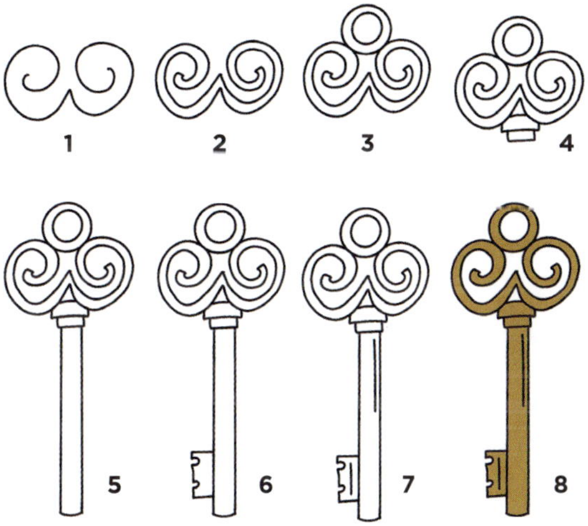

HANDHELD MIRROR

To give your princess a mirror to hold, start by drawing an oval. Draw a second, larger oval around the first one, and then add a handle. Erase the line where the shapes overlap, and draw a small circle in the bottom part of the handle. Embellish the mirror by drawing swirls or any other fancy pattern you can create. Draw a few diagonal detail lines on the mirror's surface to give it a 3-D effect. Finally, color your doodle, using any color you like for the outside, and a very light gray or blue for the reflective mirror.

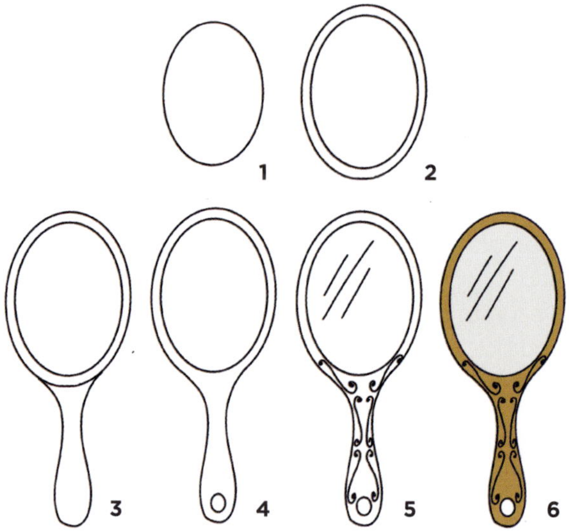

WALL MIRROR

Now, let's draw a mirror that can hang on the castle wall. Start by making a large oval, and then draw a bracket on the top, bottom, left and right. Connect the brackets by drawing sets of three scallops in between, with the largest scallop in the center. This will form an elaborate frame for the mirror. Add detail lines inside the frame, as well as a few diagonal lines on the surface of the mirror itself. Finish your doodle by adding color.

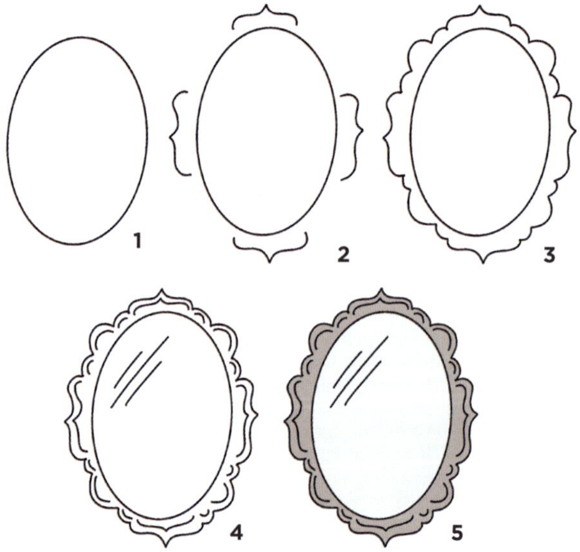

CLOSED STORYBOOK

Let's draw the storybook that contains our fairy tales! First, sketch the book's spine by drawing a pair of vertical lines that connect at the top and bottom with short diagonal lines. Draw a rectangle extending from the right side for the front cover. Then, draw a horizontal line for the back cover, and connect it to the front with a small curve. Add more horizontal lines to represent the book's pages. Finally, color your book. Feel free to add the title of your favorite story on the front.

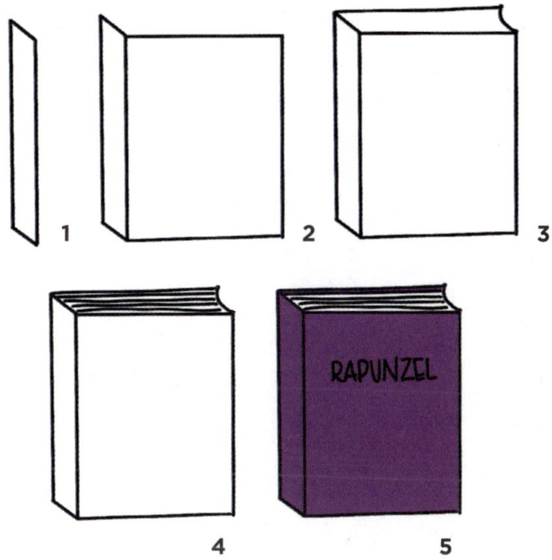

OPEN STORYBOOK

Now, it's time to draw an open storybook. Start with a vertical line for the center, and then draw a curving line extending out from the top to the left and the right. Draw the same kind of curving lines at the bottom. Connect your lines to form two pages. Add two more lines to the side and bottom of each page to give the illusion of more pages below. Sketch a line across the bottom to form the cover, with a "u" shape in the center for the spine. The last step is to add squiggles or tiny words to the pages of the book, and then color the cover.

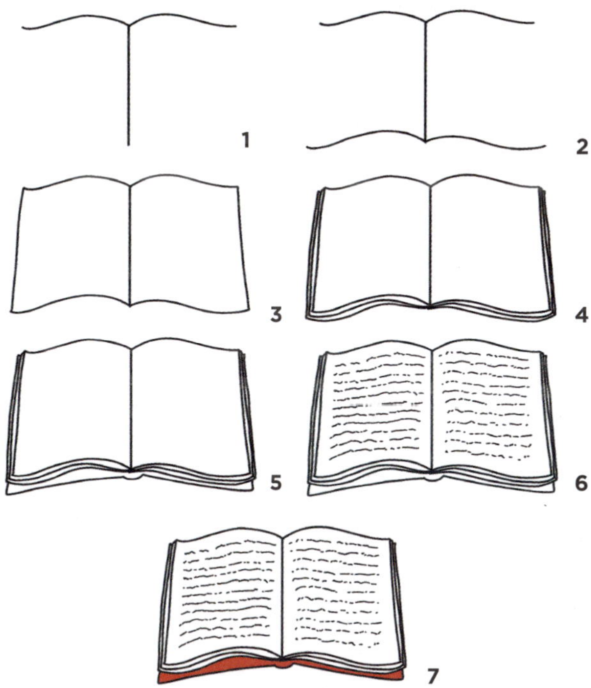

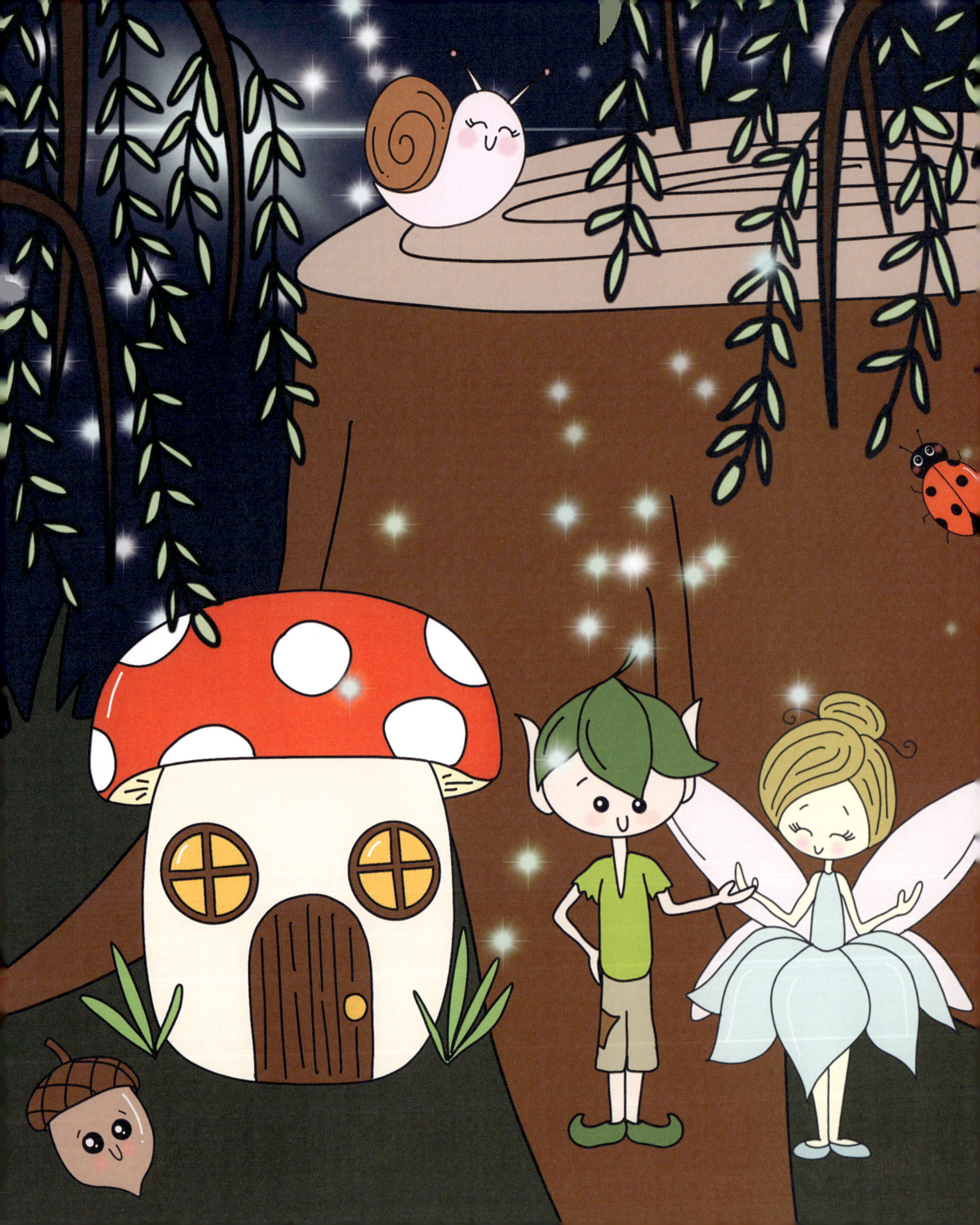

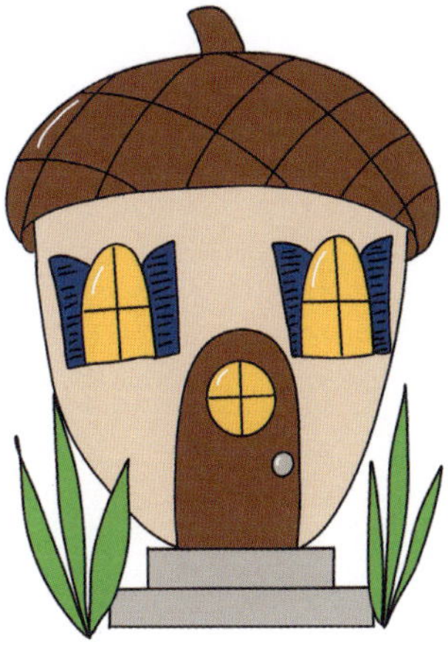

Enchanted Forest

Let's take a trip to the Enchanted Forest, where you'll find all kinds of magical creatures! Fairies flit from one tree to another, elves play among the tree stumps and homes are made of toadstools and acorns. You can easily get lost in these woods and discover another world, where trees can talk and centaurs roam. Grab your pencil and let's get started!

TOADSTOOL

Fill your forest floor with bright, cheerful toadstools. To doodle this form of mushroom, start with a wide, upside-down "u" shape. Draw an oval at the bottom of the shape, and then sketch a slightly curving stalk extending down from the oval. Erase the spot where the stalk overlaps the cap. Draw a line across the top of the stalk, and then draw two vertical lines connected with a zigzag to cover the top third of the stalk. Erase the overlapping lines. Sketch a series of lines running from the outer edges of the oval to the center. Then, add circles to the top of the cap. Draw a few detail lines, and add color to complete your doodle.

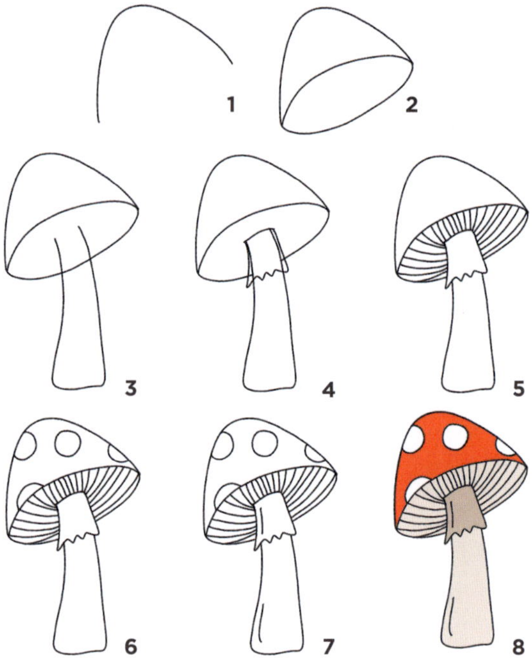

MUSHROOM VARIATION

In addition to toadstools, there are many other kinds of mushrooms that can grow in the forest. Here is a variation you can draw, starting with a wide "u" shape. Next, draw a wavy oval on top. Add a thick, rounded rectangle for the stem, and then sketch detail lines around the top of the mushroom. Add a detail line to the stem as well, and then color your drawing.

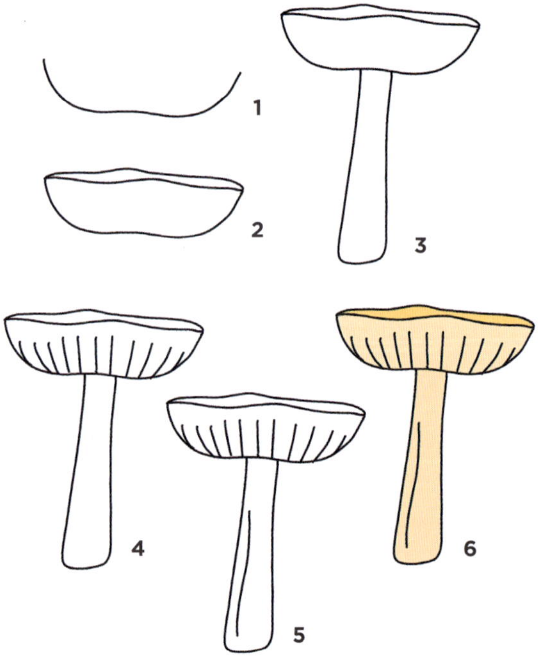

TOADSTOOL HOUSE

Not only are enchanted forests full of regular toadstools, these fungi can also be turned into wonderful homes for small forest creatures. To draw a toadstool house, sketch a slightly squared "u" shape for the base, and add a cap on top. Connect the edges of the cap to the sides of the house, and fill the cap with round spots.

Next, draw an arched doorway with a round handle and some vertical lines for texture. Add two circular windows with smaller circles inside. Then, divide the windows into four sections. Draw a few detail lines on the bottom of the cap, and add a sprig of grass on each side of the house. All that's left to do is color your toadstool house, and then it will be ready for magical creatures to inhabit.

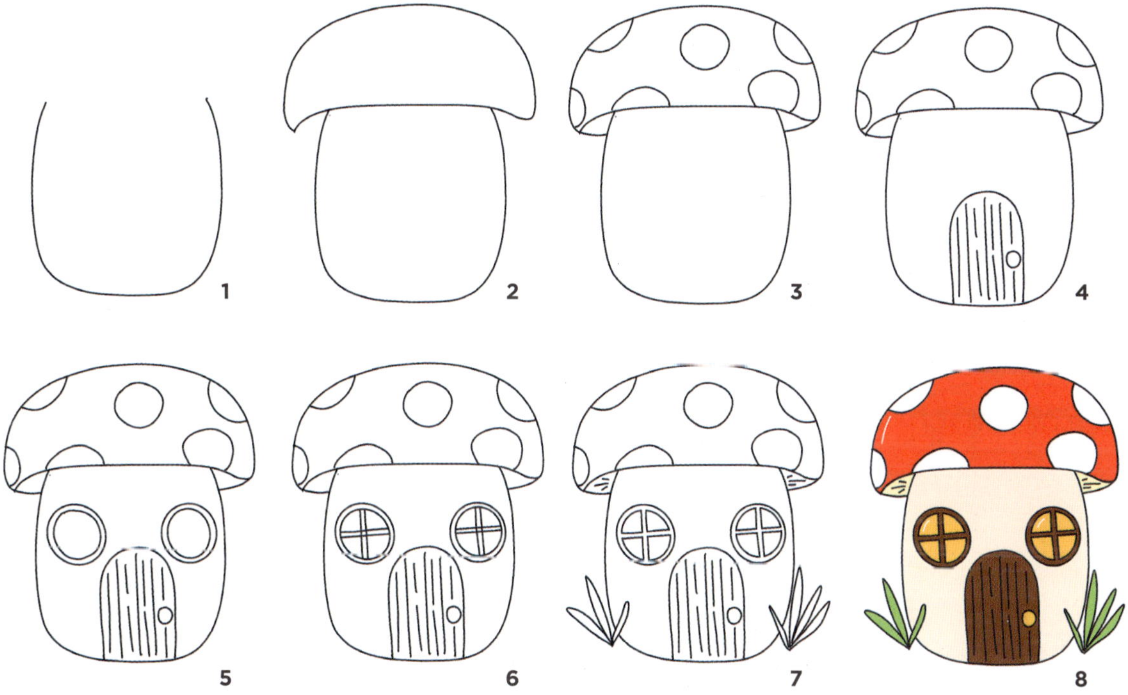

ACORN HOUSE

Like toadstools, acorns can also make excellent homes for tiny forest friends. Create your own, starting with a large, wide "u" shape. Draw a "c" shape across the top and form the cap, and then add a stem and diagonal texture lines. Add an arched door with a round handle and a round window divided into four sections.

Next, draw two arched windows, also divided into sections, and a pair of shutters on each window. Sketch two rectangles below the acorn to create steps, and erase the spot where the top step overlaps the house. Finally, draw a few blades of grass on each side of the house, and then color your doodle. Feel free to experiment by changing the shapes of the door and windows to create your own unique acorn house variation.

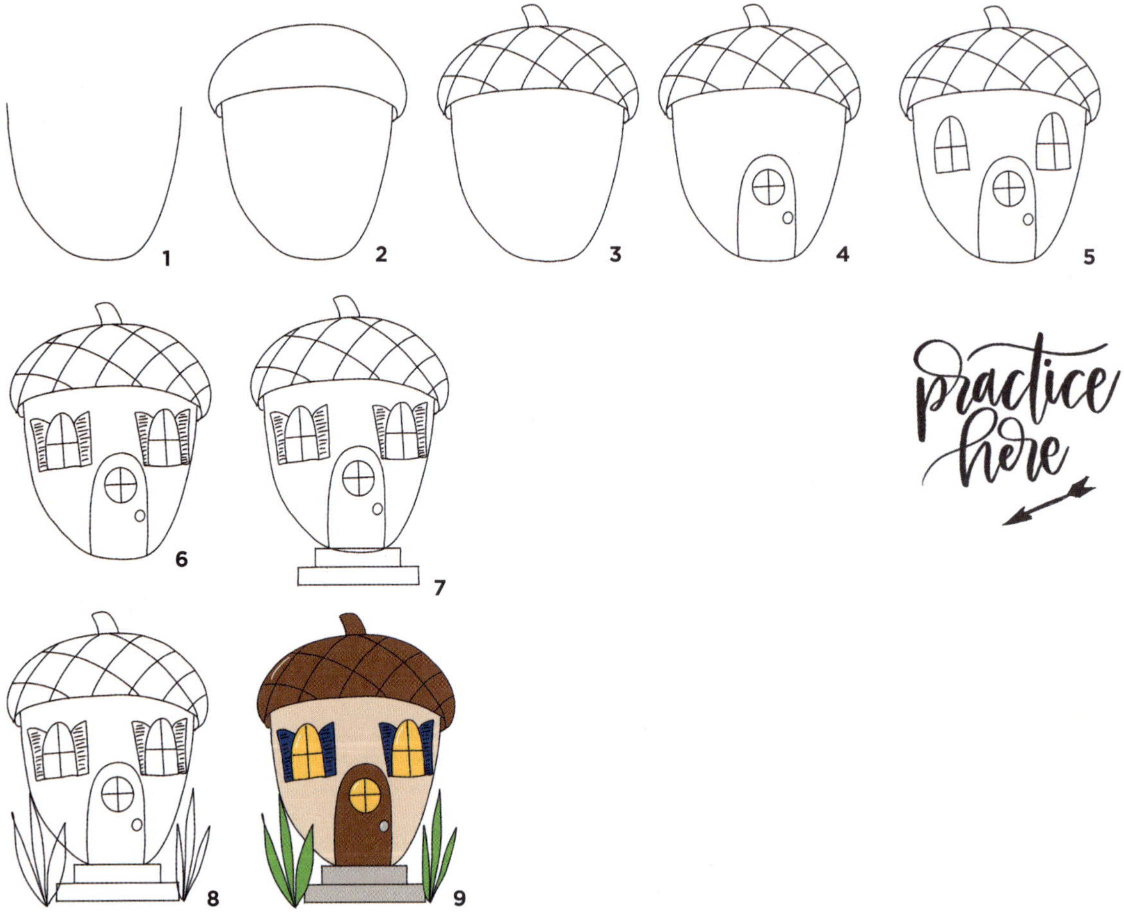

ACORN

Enchanted or not, every forest has plenty of acorns. Start this drawing with a "u" shape that has a point at the bottom. Close off the top, and then add a "c" shape to create the cap. Draw a short, thin stem. Add texture to the cap by sketching intersecting diagonal lines. You can finish your doodle here and add color, or you can take it to the next level by adding a cheerful face!

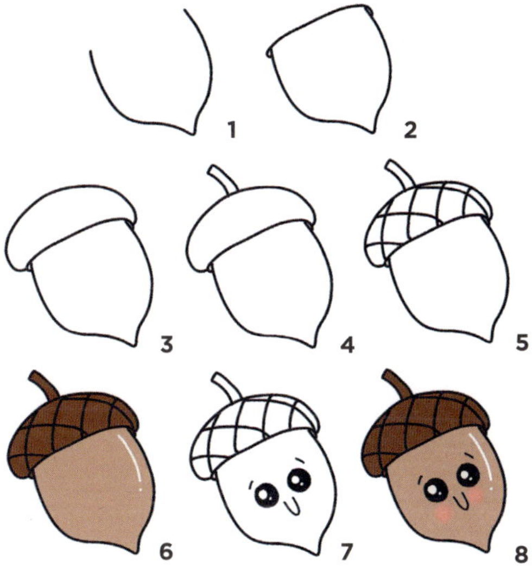

WAND

The Enchanted Forest is a great place to find magical creatures like fairies (which we'll learn to draw next). To get ready for encountering them, we're going to start by drawing a magic wand. First, sketch a five-pointed star, and then erase the lines on the inside so that just the outline remains. Draw a long, thin rectangle for the handle, and add texture by dividing it into sections. Doodle two wavy lines, one on each side of the handle. Then, add a few more curving lines to create streamers. Draw a second, smaller star inside the first one. Finally, add some tiny dots, diamonds and "x" shapes around the wand to show how magical it is! Have fun coloring your wand using whatever color scheme you like best.

Once you learn how to draw the fairy on the next page, you can try adding the wand in her hand!

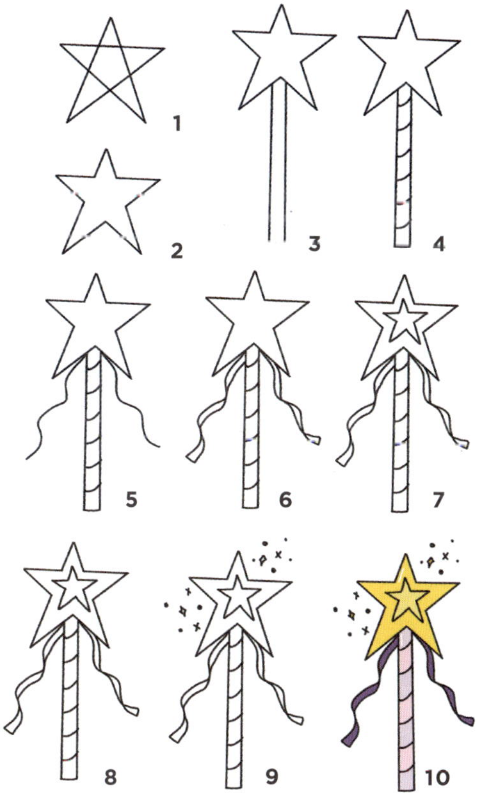

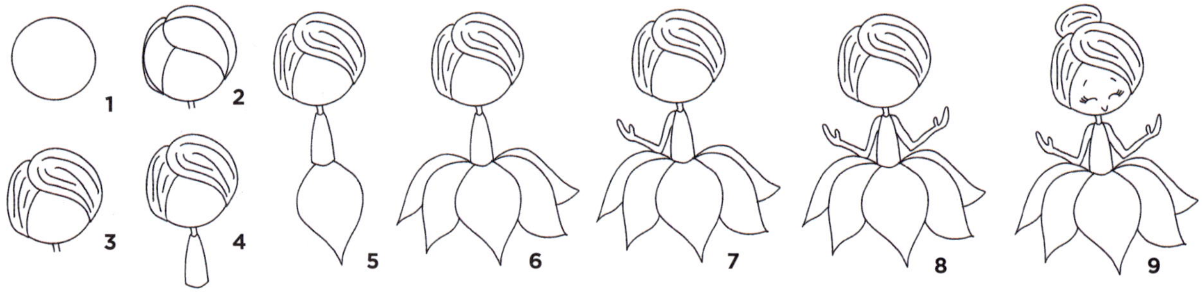

FAIRY

Don't be surprised to find fairies flitting among the trees and toadstools in your enchanted forest. Start this magical doodle with a circle for the head. Add two paisley shapes on top to form hair, erasing the areas where they overlap the head. Draw two lines for a thin neck, and add detail lines inside the hair.

Sketch the upper body, and then add a large, pointed petal below it. Continue adding more petal shapes, two on each side, to form the fairy's skirt. Doodle a pair of arms and hands. Add an oval-shaped bun with detail lines on top of her head, and draw a simple face with eyes, eyebrows and a smile.

Give your fairy a pair of wings, adding detail lines. Then, sketch three vertical lines to form her legs, and draw a pair of shoes. Add any final details, like little curls coming out from each side of the bun, and then color your fairy to bring her to life. Of course, don't forget you can add a wand in her hand so she's ready to do some magic!

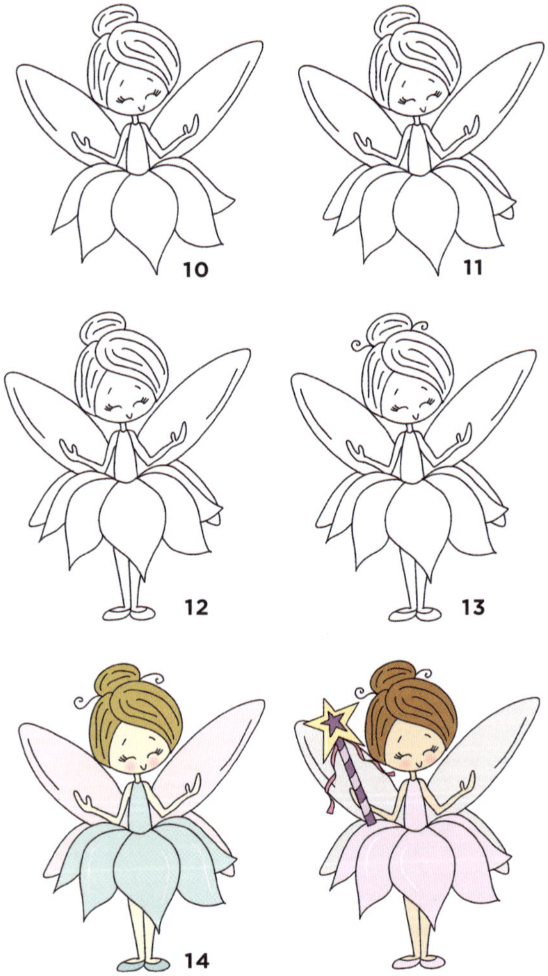

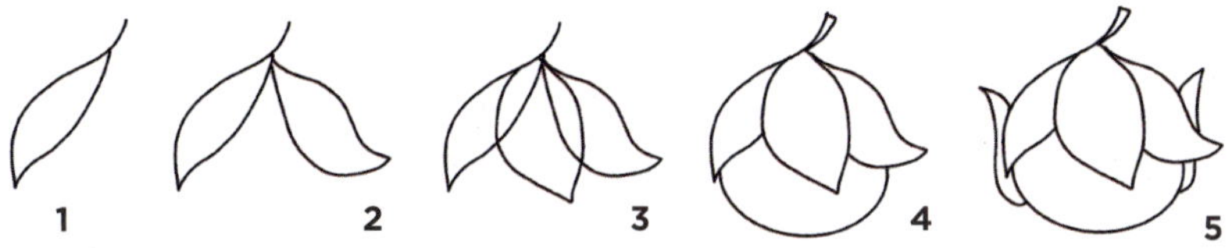

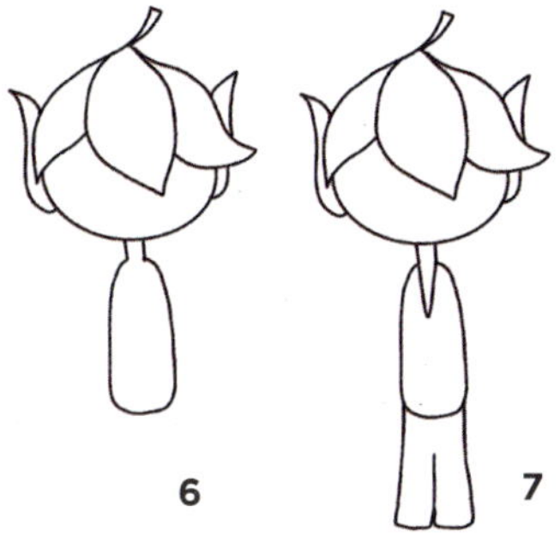

BOY WOOD ELF

Let's draw an adorable wood elf together! Start by sketching a leaf shape, and then add two more to form the hat. Erase the areas where the lines overlap, and draw a thin stem on top. Sketch a semicircle below the hat, and then give your elf a pair of pointed ears. Draw a thin neck and a rounded rectangle for the upper body.

Add a "v" neckline, and then sketch a pair of shorts below the body. Draw two arms with simple hands. You can position them however you like. Add sleeves to the shirt, and erase the extra/overlapping lines. Give the elf legs and a pair of shoes with curling toes. Finish your drawing by adding details, such as eyes and a smile, a patch on the clothing and detail lines. Then, color your doodle!

Try pairing your elf doodle with another of the drawings from this chapter, like the bird (page 88)!

practice here

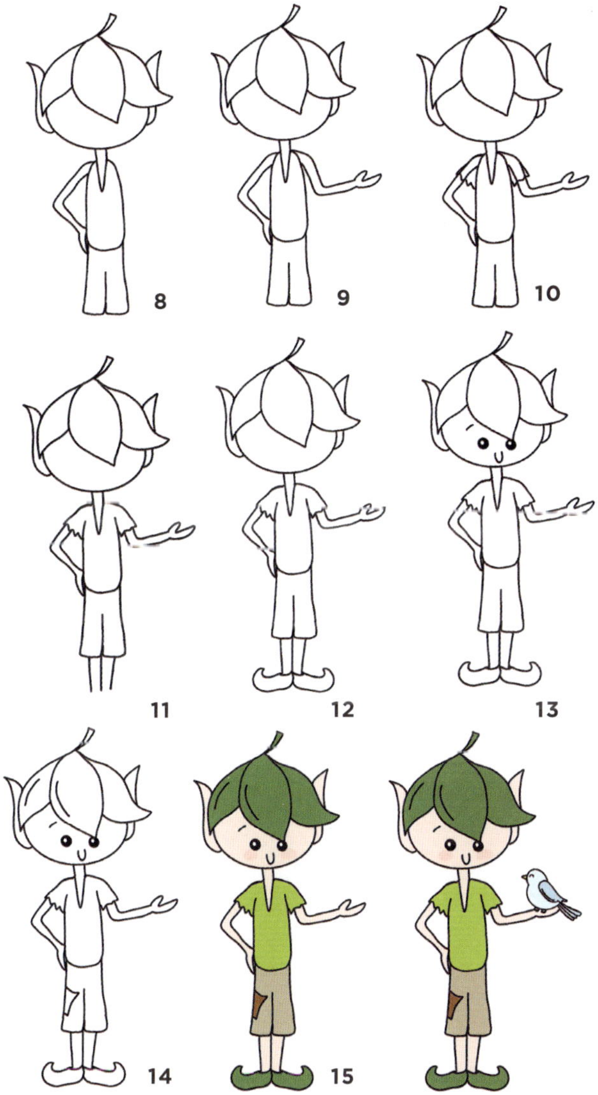

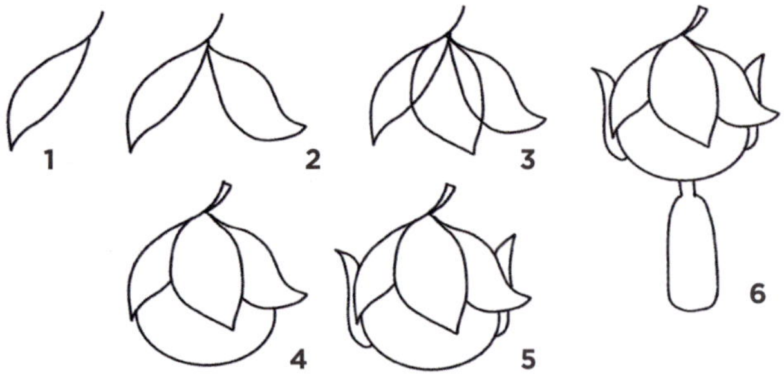

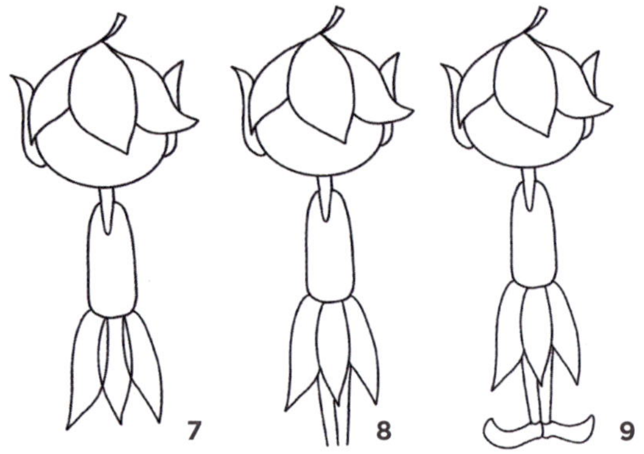

GIRL WOOD ELF

Want to create a female elf? First, follow the same initial steps as the boy elf, up through drawing the body. Then, instead of adding shorts, draw three overlapping petals, and erase the extra lines to create a skirt. Add a pair of thin legs and curling shoes. Sketch two arms with simple hands in any pose you prefer. Draw leaf/petal shapes for sleeves, and erase any overlapping lines. Give your elf a ponytail, and a face with eyes and a smile. Add detail lines, and then color your drawing. Try placing another doodle in your elf's hand, like the butterfly (page 89).

practice here

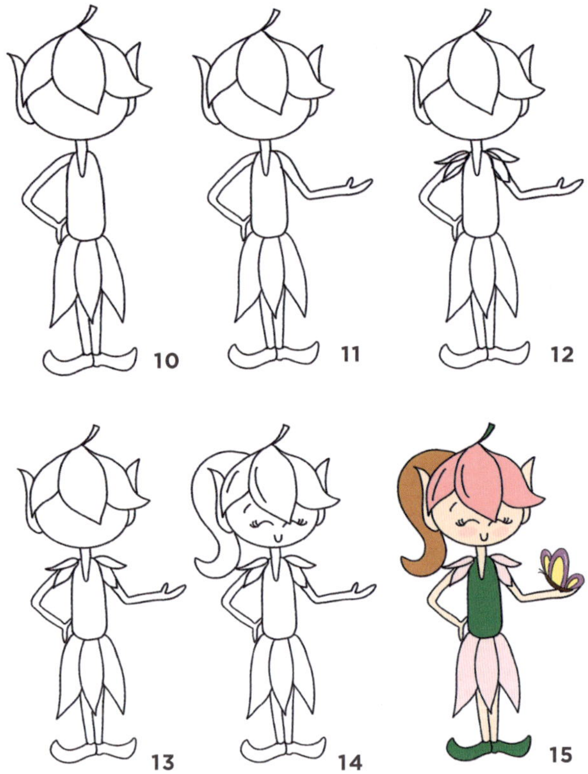

GNOME

What would an enchanted forest be without a gnome? Sketch this fine fellow starting with an upside-down "v" for the hat. Draw a curving line at the base, and then add a large oval nose just below it. Sketch a zigzag line on each side of the hat, curving toward the center. Join the lines to form the beard shape, and then draw detail lines inside for texture. Give your gnome a pair of rounded shoes, as well as a pair of short arms with semicircle hands. Finally, add a pattern to the hat, like stripes, dots or a heart shape. Color your gnome to complete your doodle.

practice here

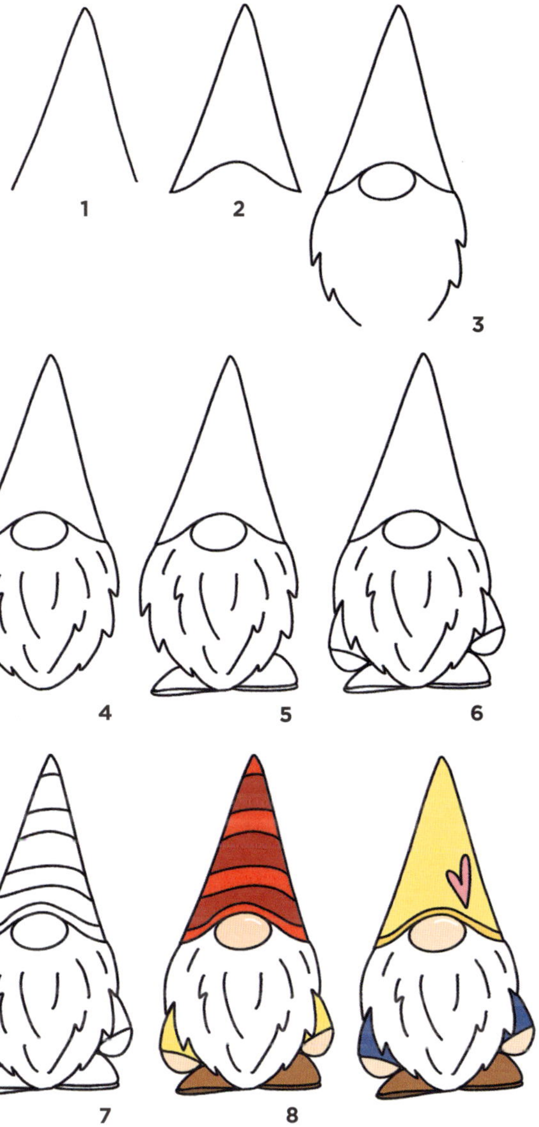

GIRL GNOME

To doodle a female version of the gnome, start in the same way, with a "v"-shaped hat, curved line for the brim and a large, oval nose. Then, draw a semicircle for the rest of the head, and add a smile. Draw a rounded rectangle on each side of the head, and then sketch a long, curling pigtail coming down from each one. Add a dress, with a rounded collar and a stripe across the bottom. Draw two "u"-shaped shoes, and then sketch a round hand on each side of the body. Decorate the hat with flowers or any other pattern you like, and then color your adorable gnome.

practice here

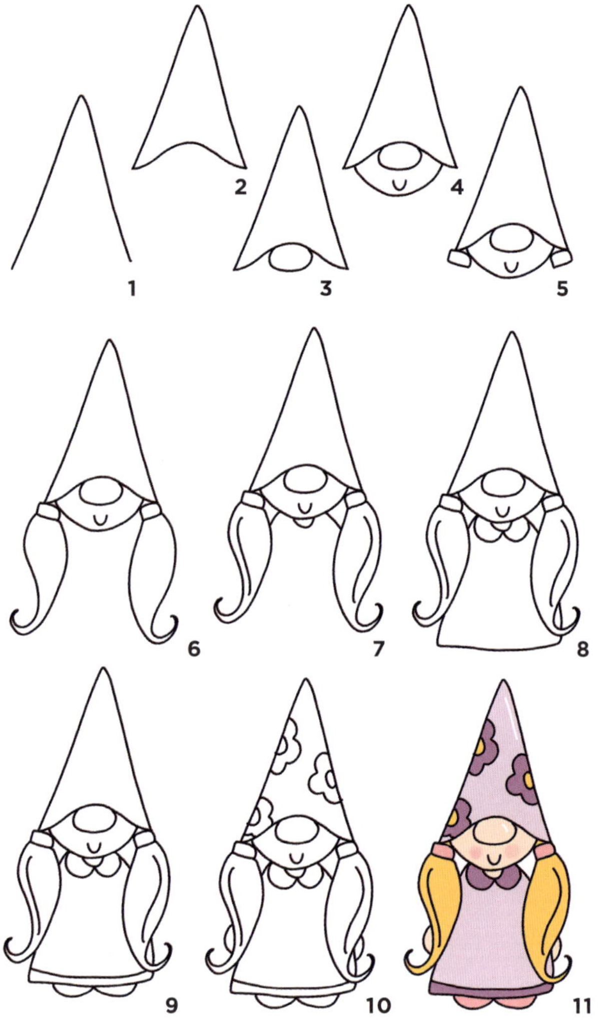

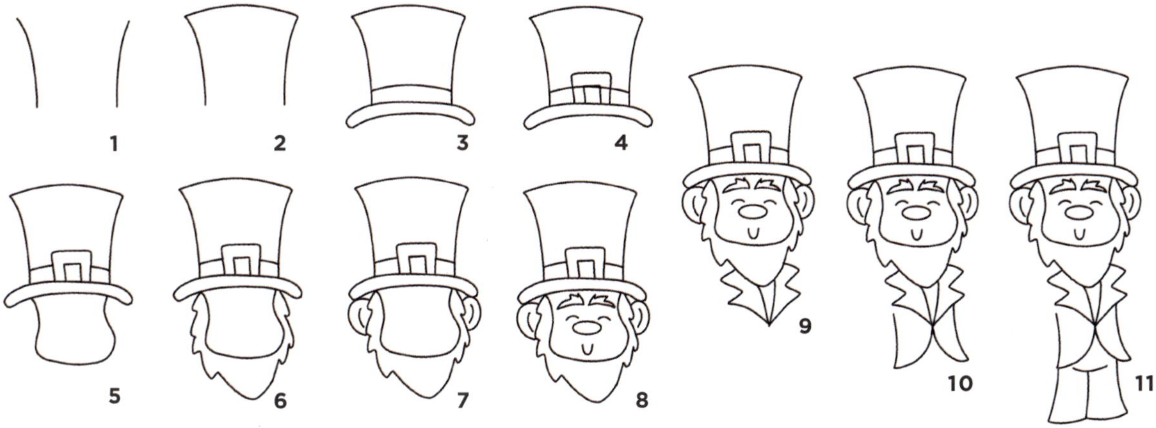

LEPRECHAUN

Let's sketch a mischievous leprechaun living in our woods. First, draw the sides and top of his hat, and then add a band and a curving brim. Draw a buckle in the center of the band, and erase the overlapping lines. Sketch a head shape below the hat, and add a beard around it. Give your leprechaun ears, bushy eyebrows and a face.

Next, draw the collar and body of his jacket. Sketch a pair of shorts below the jacket, and then draw a pair of arms and hands. In one hand, make a four-leaf clover out of four heart shapes. Add legs and pointed shoes, and then draw details, such as stripes on the socks, a button on the jacket and a detail line on the hat. Finally, complete your doodle by coloring your leprechaun.

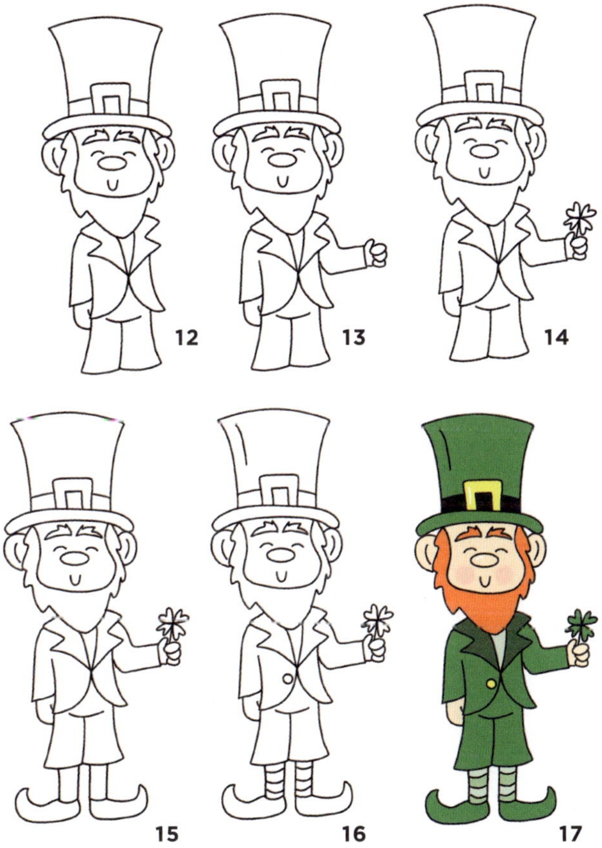

CENTAUR

One of the more unusual mythical creatures is a centaur, which is half human and half horse. Start your centaur sketch with a bean shape, and then add a back leg. Draw a second back leg next to the first one, and add a pair of front legs, too. Erase any areas where the legs overlap the body shape, and then divide the bottom part of the legs to form hooves. Next, draw a tail, as well as a round head and a neck. Erase the extra overlapping lines, and draw an ear on the side of the head.

Draw a line above the front legs to separate the human part of the body from the horse part. Sketch whatever type of hair you like, and erase the areas where it overlaps the head. Add detail lines to show texture in the hair and tail. Draw a pair of arms, erasing the extra lines, and then give your centaur a face. Finish your doodle by adding color.

To take your drawing to the next level, choose another doodle and add something to the centaur's hands. Here are examples of mine holding a bird and a bow. Remember, just as humans and horses come in many colors, your doodles can, too!

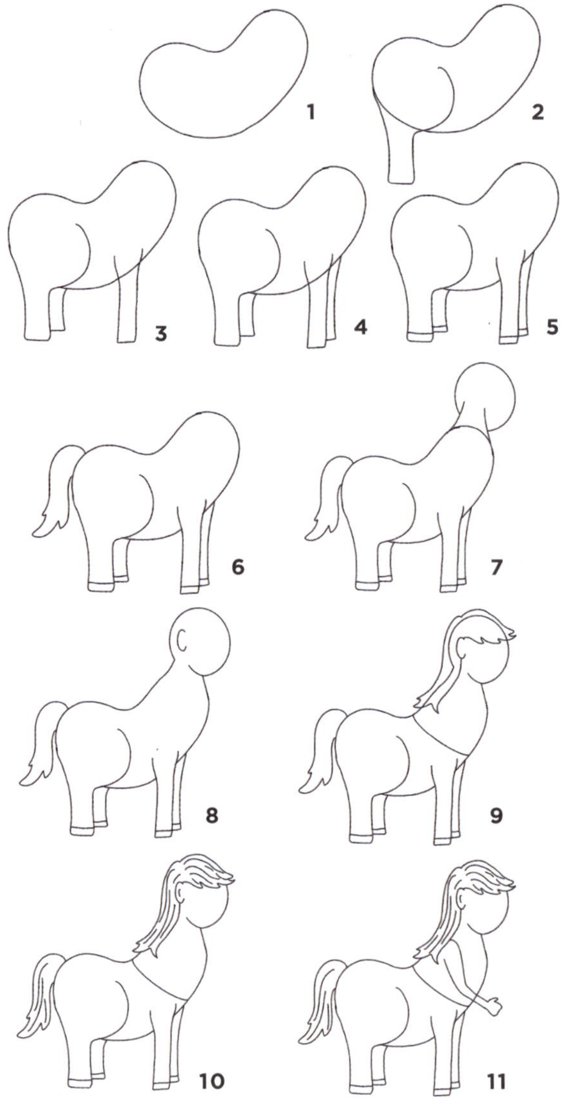

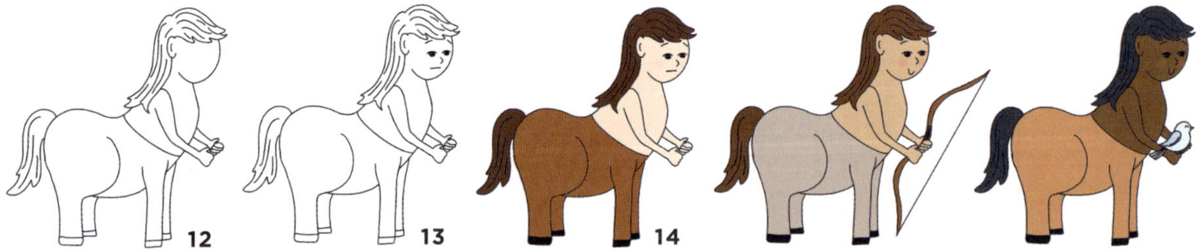

SNAIL

Let's doodle a cheerful snail to add to the forest. Start with a paisley shape for the body, and then add a large spiral on top to form the shell. Add two long, thin triangles with circles on top to make a pair of antennae. Draw a simple face with eyes and a smile, and add detail lines to the shell. Finish your doodle by coloring your happy snail.

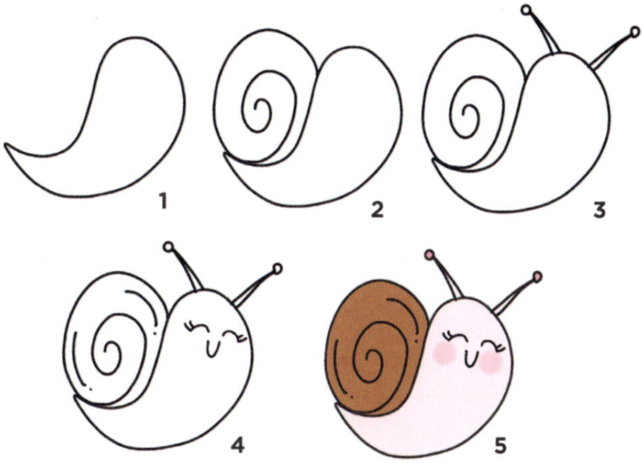

LADYBUG

To create a ladybug doodle, start with an oval body. Add an oval-shaped head on top, and then use an upside-down "Y" shape to divide the body into a pair of wings. Draw a pair of antennae, and fill the wing areas with round spots. Add six "L"-shaped legs, three on each side of the body. Give your ladybug a pair of eyes, and then color her to finish the drawing. The body and head are typically black, while the wings are red with black spots.

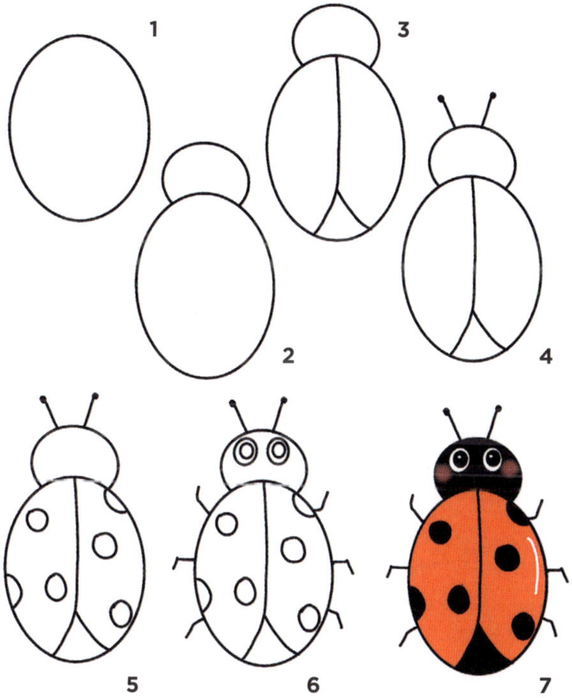

BIRD

Let's fill the trees with some feathered friends! To draw a basic bird doodle, start with a curving head, and then sketch a plump body. Sketch a paisley-shaped wing with a few scallops at the bottom, and erase the areas where it overlaps the body. Next, add a long tail with three scallops, and draw lines dividing the tail into three sections. Give your bird a small triangle beak and an eye, and add a detail line to the wing. Finally, add a pair of feet. Color your bird in any combination of colors you like.

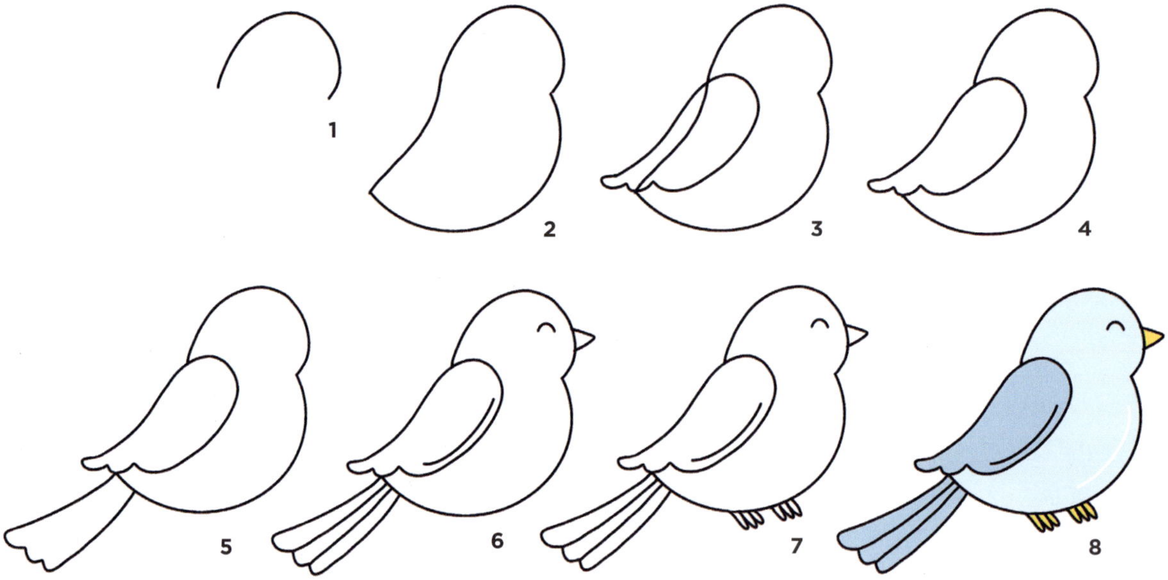

practice here

BUTTERFLY

To doodle a butterfly in flight, start with a curving line, and then turn it into a long, thin body shape. Draw two "u" shapes, one large and one small, for the front wings. Then, add a third wing shape. Add detail to the wings by drawing smaller shapes inside each one. Finally, color your butterfly. In nature, butterflies come in all colors, so feel free to be as creative as you like!

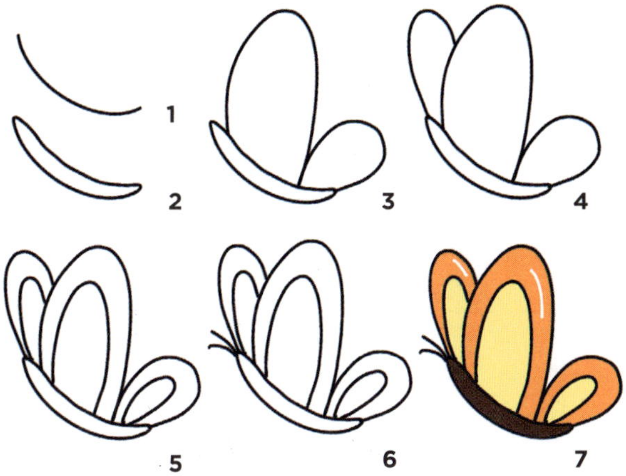

OWL

Sketching an owl starts with a slightly curved line for the top of the head, with a little "v" shape on each side. Next, draw curving lines to form the head and basic body shape. Add a curving "m" shape near the top of the head, and then draw a wing on each side of the body. Erase the areas where the wings and body overlap. Add two scalloped lines to the belly to show a feathery texture. Give your owl two large, round eyes and a triangle beak. Finally, draw a small pair of feet, and add detail lines to the wings. All that's left to do is color your feathered friend.

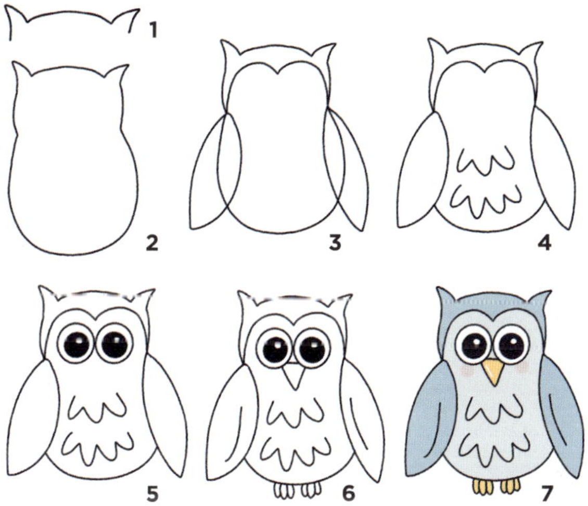

practice here

LEAVES

One thing you're sure to find in every forest is leaves. To draw a basic leaf, start with a simple teardrop shape. Then, add a line for the stem. If you like, you can stop here, color your leaf and call it finished. Or, you can choose to add details by drawing a series of "v"-shaped veins.

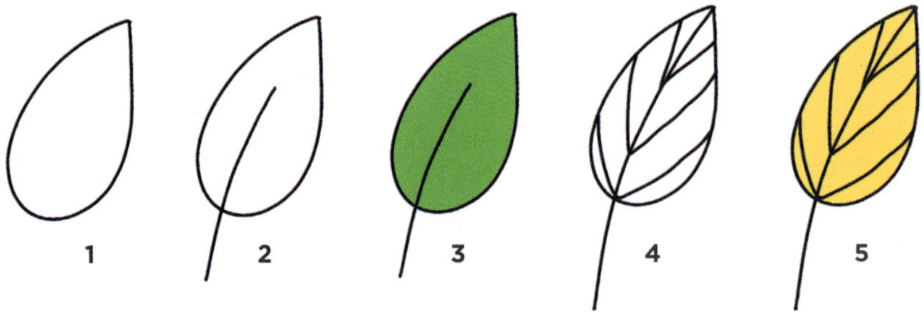

For a slight variation on your leaf drawing, try sketching the starting shape upside down! This will give you a rounded leaf instead of a pointed one, which looks like it came from a totally different kind of tree. Add a stem, and if you like, you can add veins as well. Finish your drawing by coloring your leaf.

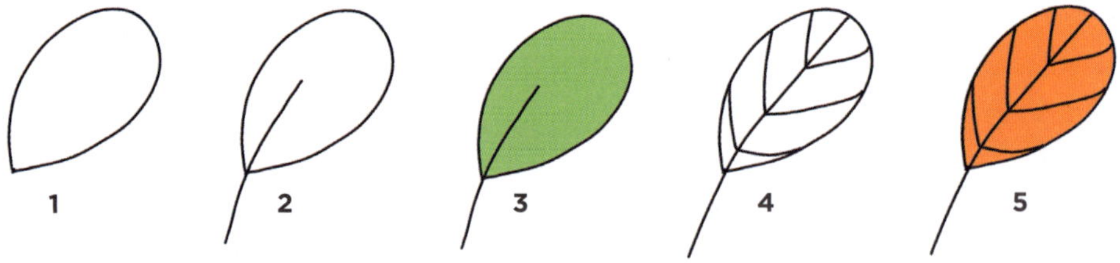

practice here

PINE TREE

To draw a pine tree variation, start your sketch with an upside-down "v" shape. Add small zigzags to each end. Then, create the next layer of the tree by drawing a diagonal line on each side with a zigzag at the bottom. Repeat that step to draw a third layer, and add a short zigzag in the center, as well. For the final layer, draw your diagonal lines, and then connect them with one long zigzag line. Sketch the tree's trunk on the bottom, and then add color to finish your doodle.

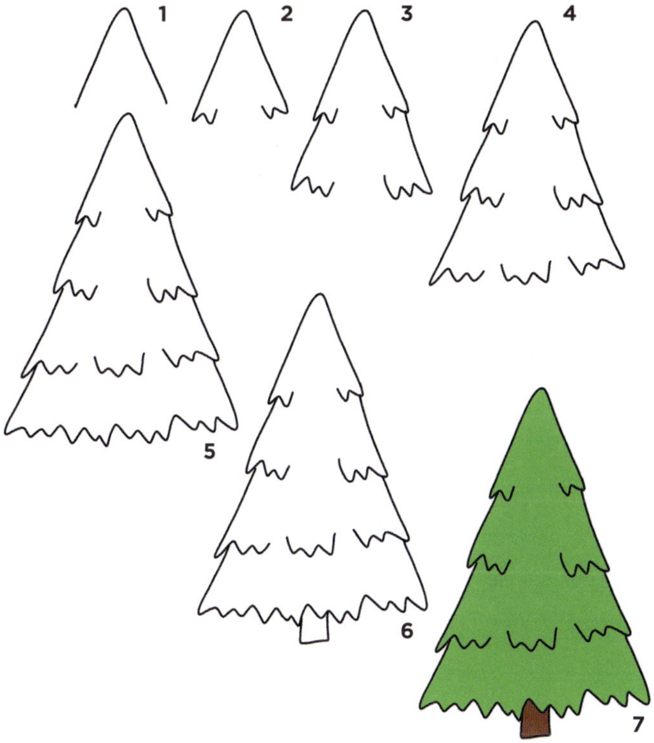

TREE STUMP

To doodle a tree stump, start with two short lines that curve away from each other at the bottoms. Next, sketch an oval on top, and draw a spiral inside of it. Draw a line to connect the bottom of the stump, including a triangular root. Add texture lines to show dimension. Color your stump, making the sides darker than the top, and feel free to add a face.

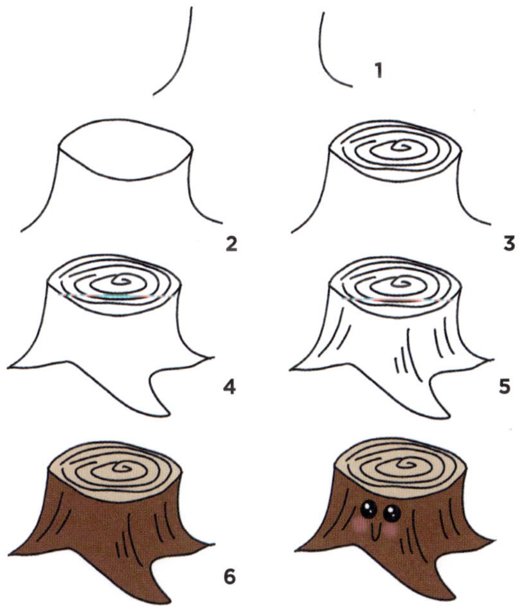

TREE

No forest would be complete without trees, and in our enchanted forest, the trees have whimsical personalities! To draw a simple tree, start by sketching two vertical lines that curve outward at the bottom for the trunk. For the leafy area, alternate between drawing scallops and swirls to create a round shape. Erase the areas where the trunk lines overlap the treetop. Add short, curving lines inside the top area to show a leafy texture. Finish your doodle by coloring it. Since this is an enchanted forest, you can bring your drawing to life by adding a happy face to the tree trunk.

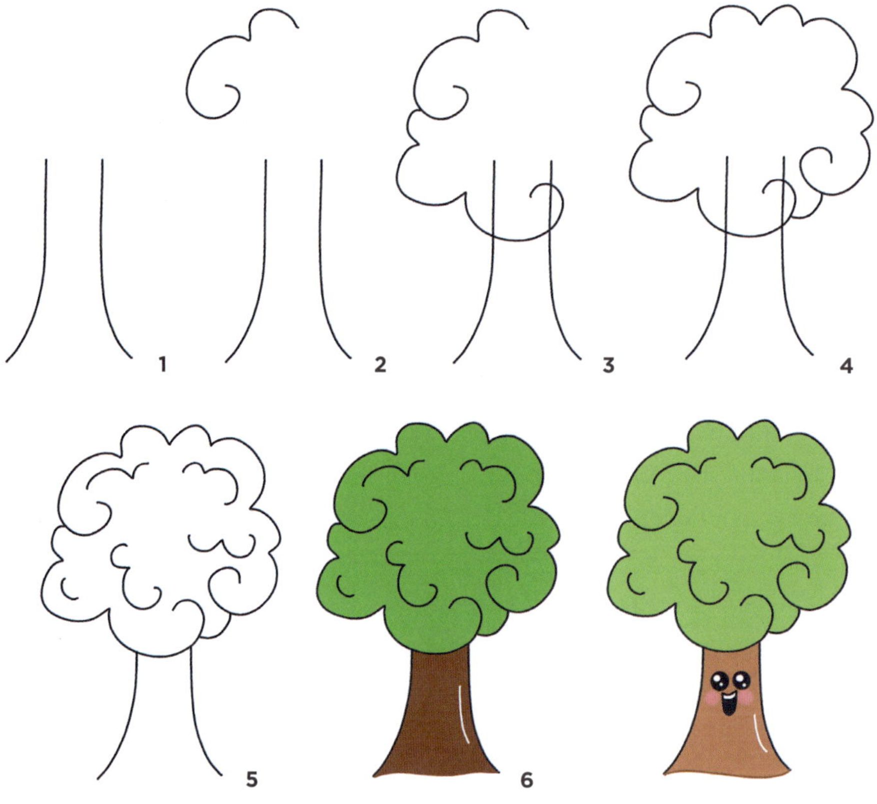

WILLOW TREE

Let's draw a graceful willow tree! Start with a large, upside-down "u" shape that's slightly higher on the left side. Then, draw a smaller "u" on the right side. Add a pair of curving lines to create two drooping branches. Draw another set of branches by adding two more "u" shapes and making a big curving "m" shape to connect them. Continue adding more branches anywhere you like, erasing the areas where they overlap one another. To add leaves, draw a series of lines descending from each branch, with small leaves going up and down each side. Finally, color your tree. Feel free to add a face as you place it in the enchanted forest.

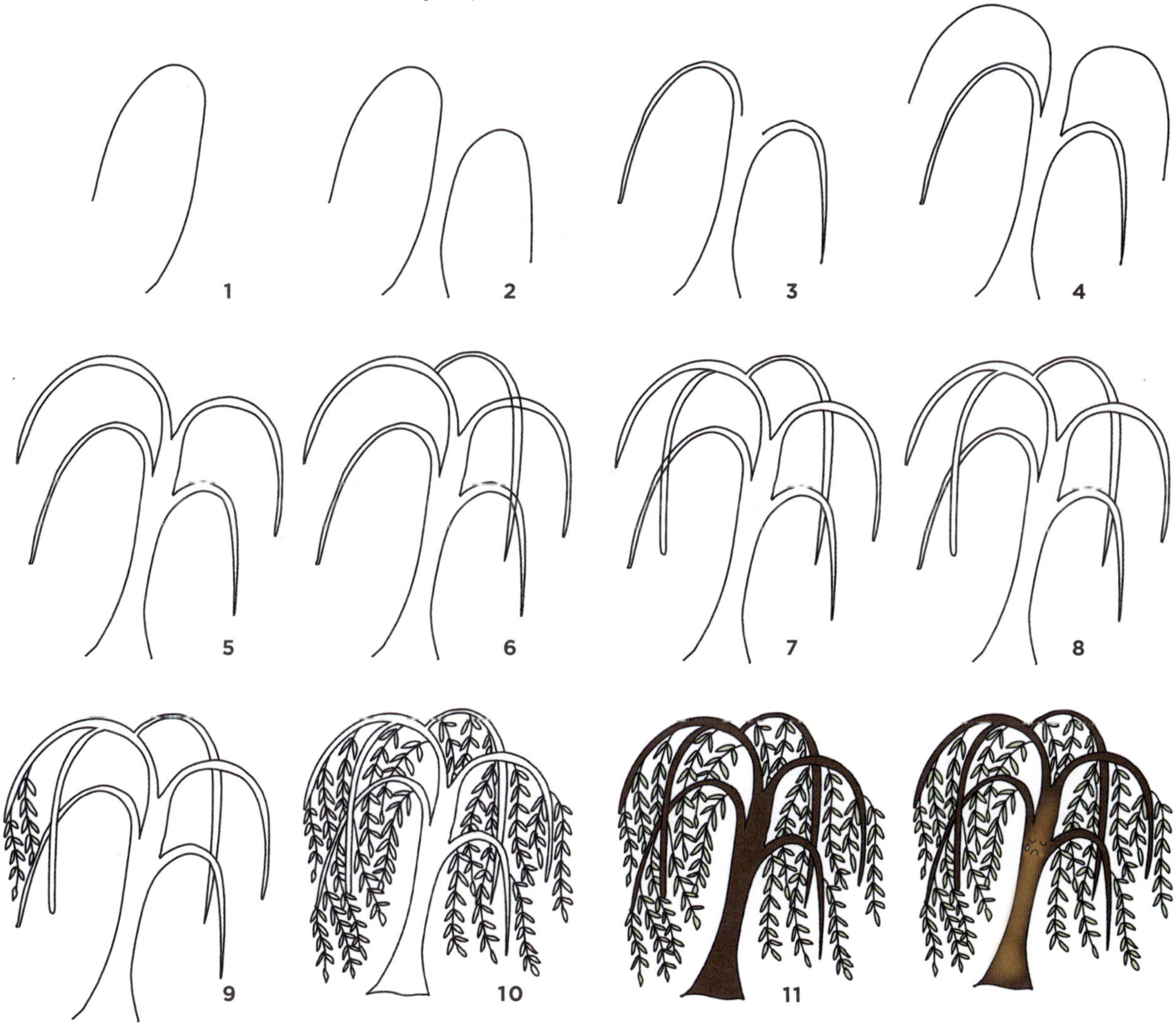

STRAWBERRY

Fairies and elves love to enjoy the berries that grow wild in our enchanted forest! Drawing a strawberry starts with a basic shape, a rounded triangle. Then, sketch a leafy patch on top, and erase the overlapping line. Add a thin stem, and draw a short, curved line at the base. Fill the strawberry with tiny dots to create the seeds. If you like, you can also give your berry eyes and a smile, or you can leave it as is. Finish your doodle by coloring it red and green.

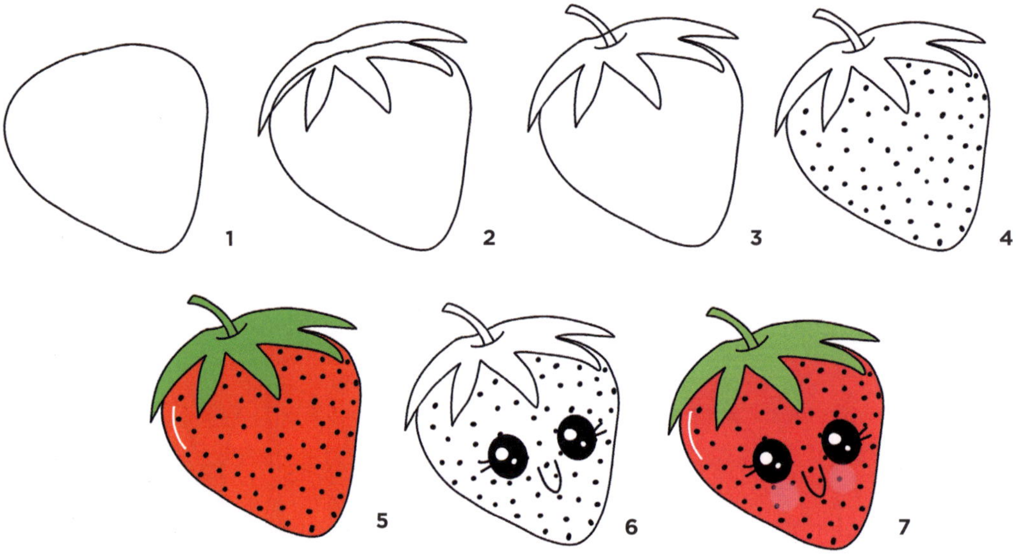

practice here

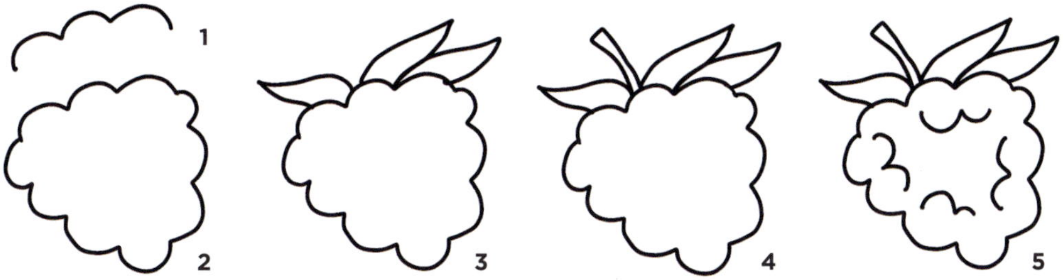

RASPBERRY

Start doodling a raspberry by drawing three scallops for the top of the berry. Continue sketching scallops to create sides and a rounded bottom. Add three leaves to the top, as well as a long, thin stem. Draw several more scallops inside the berry to give it texture. All that's left to do is color your doodle, and add a face if you like.

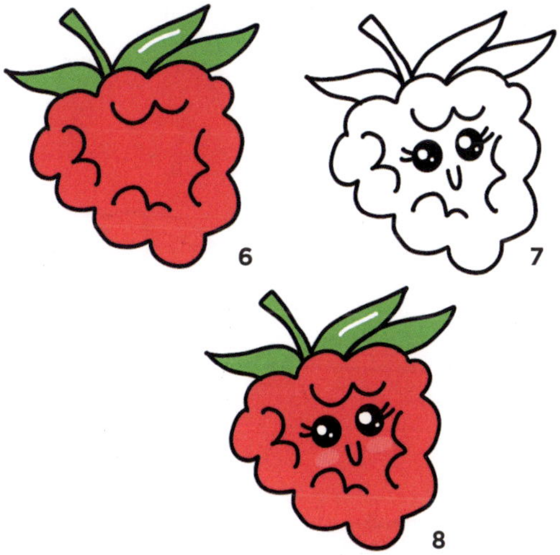

BLACKBERRY VARIATION

By coloring the raspberry doodle a deep purple, you can turn it into a blackberry!

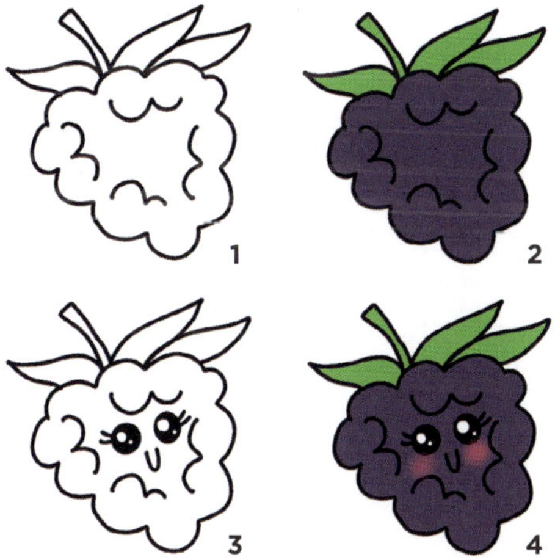

POCKET WATCH

To recreate a favorite story in the woods, let's draw a pocket watch. First, draw a circle with a slightly smaller circle inside. Add a rounded rectangle and a pair of short, vertical lines on top. Sketch a bow shape with two diagonal lines and a curve above it. Draw two ovals extending from the bow shape, and add texture lines to the crown. Next, sketch a small circle in the center of the watch, and write Roman numerals or numbers in the twelve, three, six and nine positions. In the remaining positions, make short lines. Add a pair of hands to the watch, indicating the time. Finally, color your doodle.

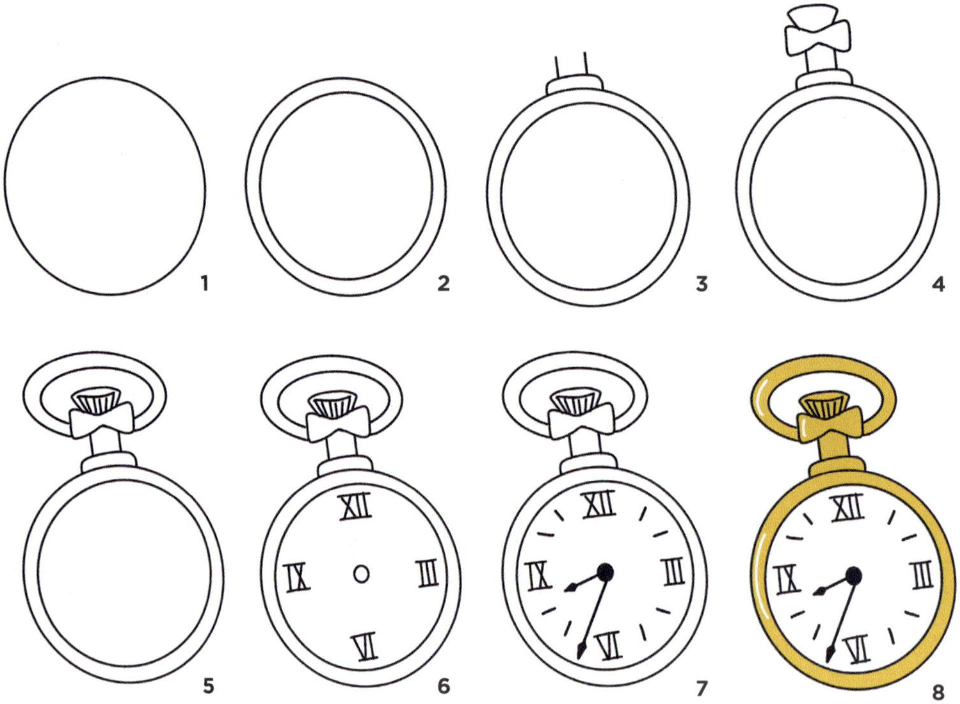

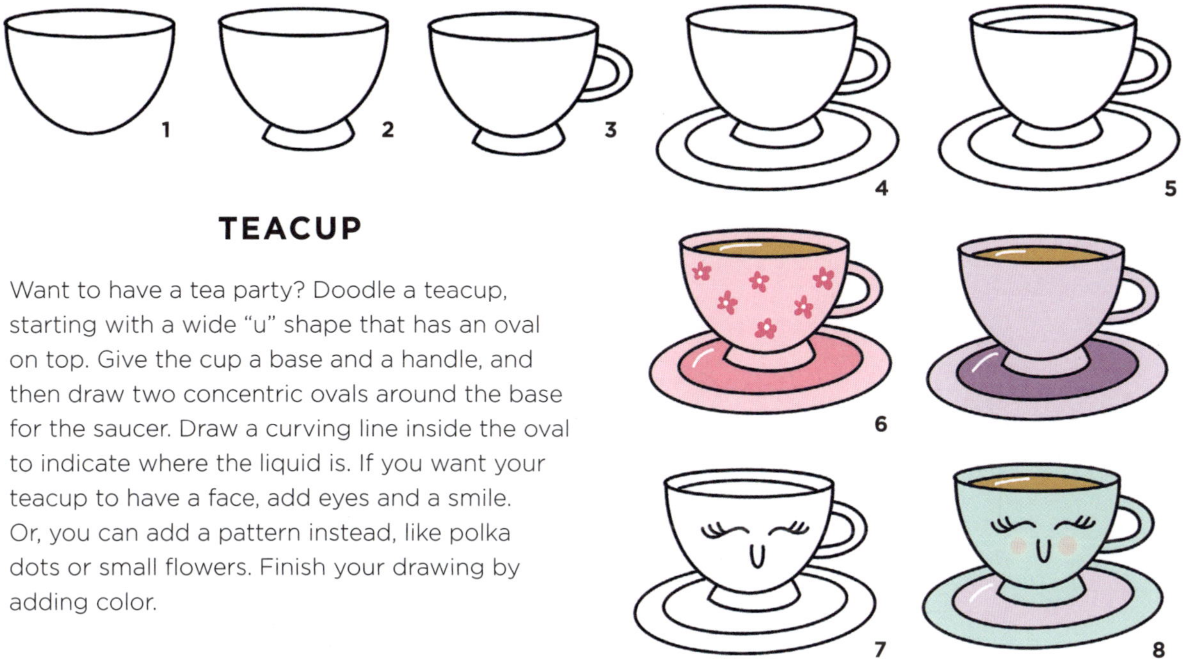

TEACUP

Want to have a tea party? Doodle a teacup, starting with a wide "u" shape that has an oval on top. Give the cup a base and a handle, and then draw two concentric ovals around the base for the saucer. Draw a curving line inside the oval to indicate where the liquid is. If you want your teacup to have a face, add eyes and a smile. Or, you can add a pattern instead, like polka dots or small flowers. Finish your drawing by adding color.

TEAPOT

It's hard to have tea in your cup if you don't also have a teapot! Start your teapot sketch by drawing an arch, and then closing it off with a slightly curved bottom. Divide off a small area at the top for the lid, and then add a round handle on top. Draw curving lines to form a spout on one side of the teapot, and a handle made of two "c" shapes on the other. Finish your doodle by adding color. If you like, you can add a pattern, like flowers, polka dots or stripes to give your teapot some extra pizazz.

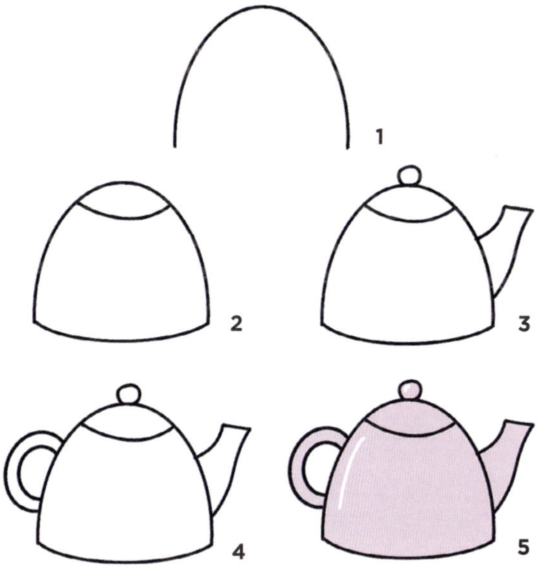

TOP HAT

Begin your top hat drawing with a pair of vertical lines that get closer together at the bottom. Connect them at the top with a curving line, and then sketch a large, rounded brim around the base. Divide off a section for a band, and add a few texture lines inside. You can stop here and color your doodle, or you can add a curving rectangle tucked beneath the band on one side first. Use your imagination, and choose any color combination to finish your drawing.

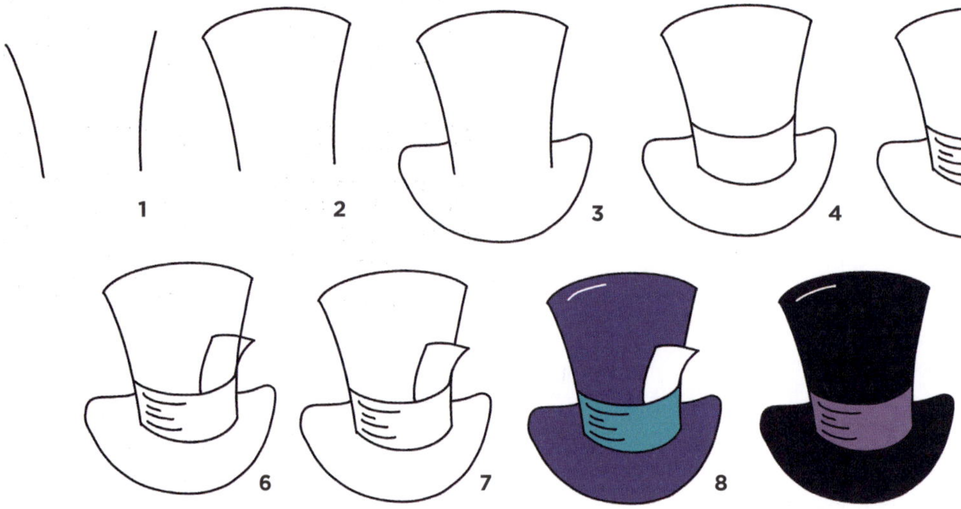

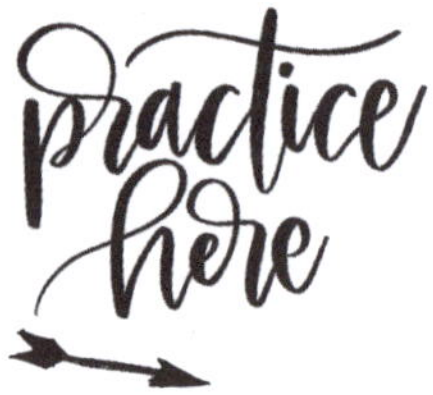

BRIDGE

To help you create a full scene, here's how to draw a special bridge that will carry you over the river and into the enchanted forest. Start with a wide arch, and then draw a curving line that meets it a little past the center. Draw another arch below this line. Add a curving line to show the underside of the bridge, and then sketch horizontal lines to show the wooden texture.

Next, draw five rectangle posts. Sketch two curving lines that connect the front four posts across the tops. Make a wavy line to indicate the land on the far side of the bridge, and add a few rocks. Draw three more posts for the back railing, and connect the four back posts with a pair of curving lines. Erase all the extra lines so that you're left with just the outlines of both railings. Sketch a rock and a patch of ground on the near side of the bridge. Add color to finish your doodle.

Try combining this bridge doodle with several of the tree drawings you've already learned to create the backdrop for a magical scene.

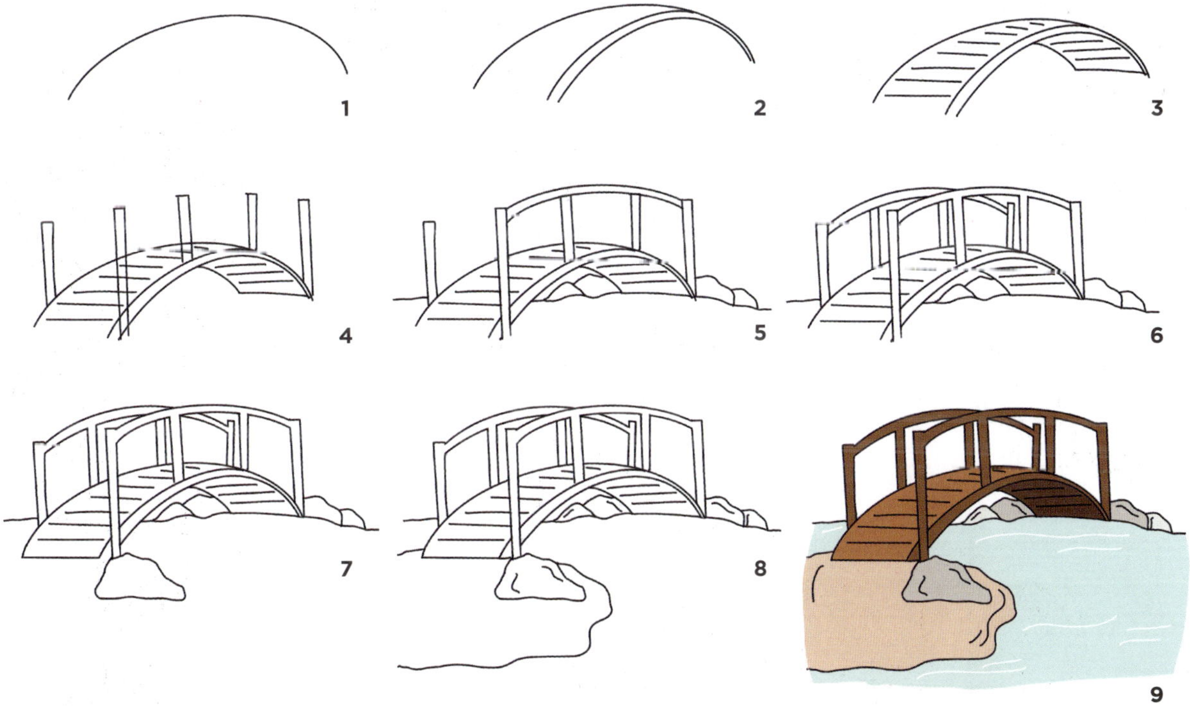

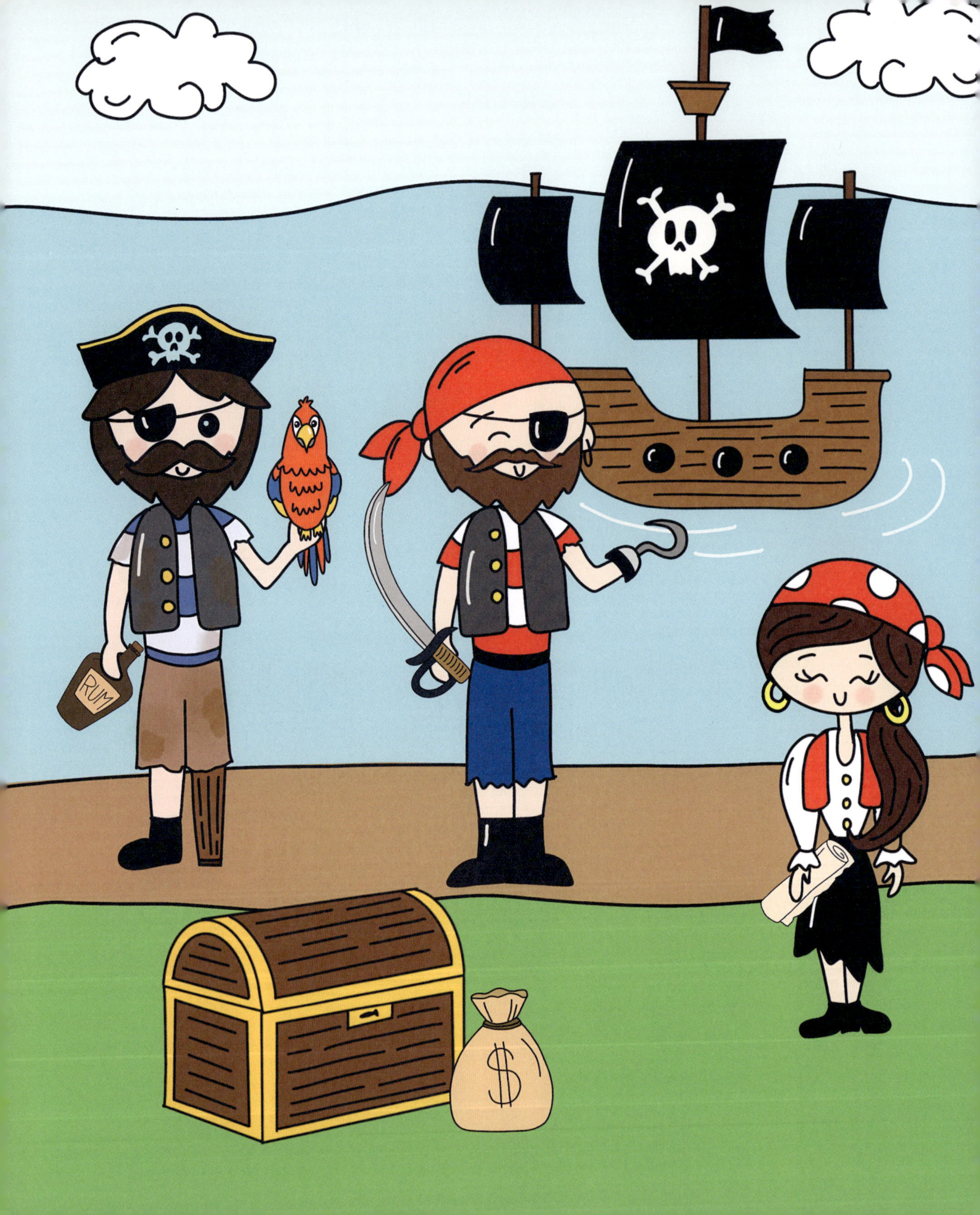
RUM
$

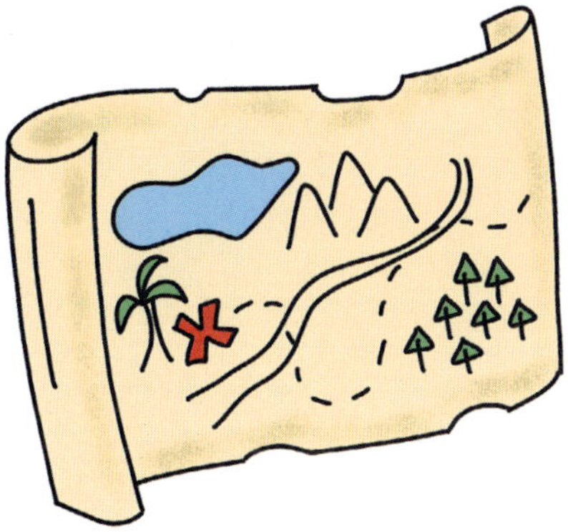

TREASURE *Island*

Ahoy, matey! Adventures await on the seven seas when you sail with a crew of pirates. You may find buried treasure, like gold coins or precious gems! Or, you might just discover a mystical mermaid swimming alongside your ship. Hoist your sails and grab your spyglass, the adventure is about to begin, as we learn to doodle these fun characters and treasures.

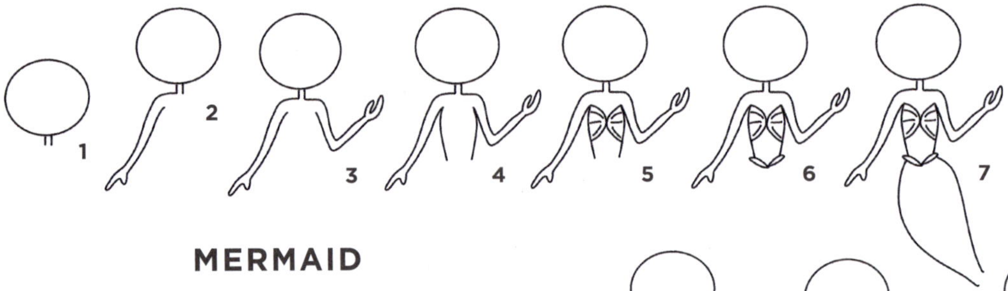

MERMAID

Draw your very own magical mermaid, starting with an oval-shaped head and a thin neck. Add a pair of arms, positioned in any way you like. Next, draw a pair of curving lines for the upper body, and add two semicircles with lines for her seashell top. Sketch two teardrop shapes that meet to form a "v" at the waist, and then draw the mermaid's tail. Add tiny "u" shapes and lines to the tail to show the scaly texture.

Next, sketch some flowing hair, and give your mermaid a cheerful face. Finish your doodle by adding color. Feel free to change the texture and style of your mermaid's hair, and use any skin and hair colors you like to make her unique.

practice here

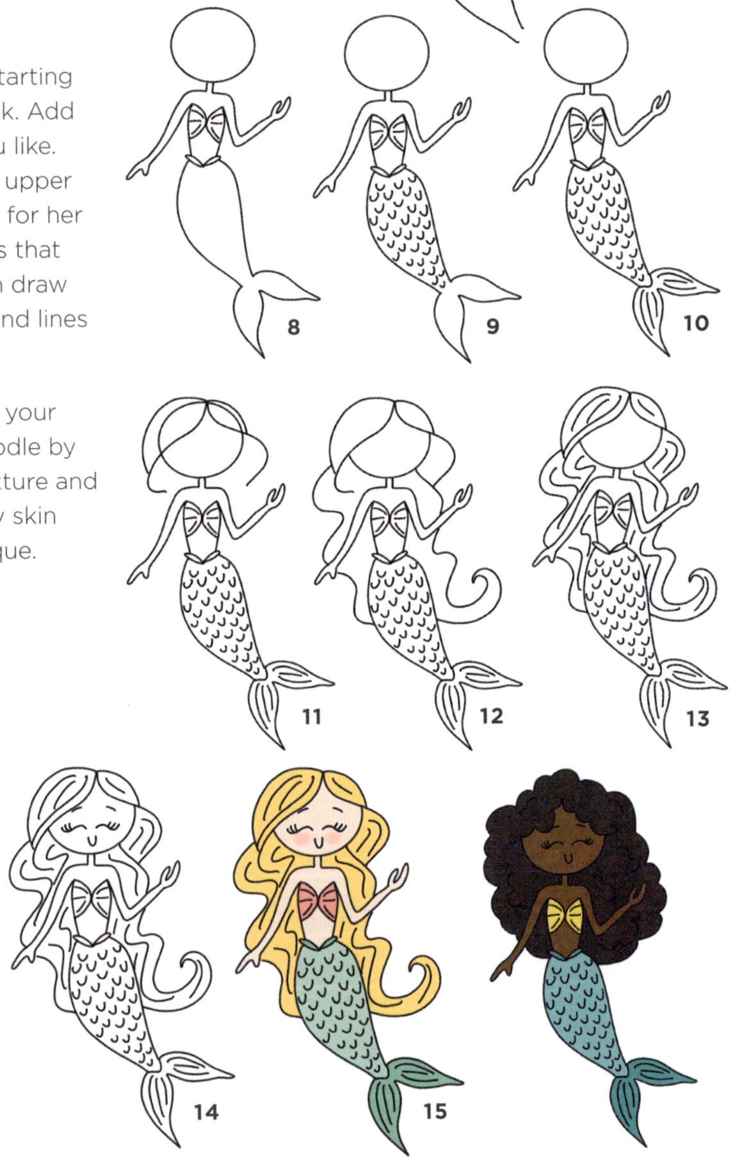

CORAL

The mermaids love to swim among colorful coral and look for beautiful shells! Coral is easier than you'd think to draw. Start by sketching a series of bumps that are different heights and widths. Each main "branch" of the coral can have several smaller sections. Add small detail lines at the top of each rounded area, and close off the doodle at the bottom. Color your coral in any bright shade of pink, orange, yellow or purple.

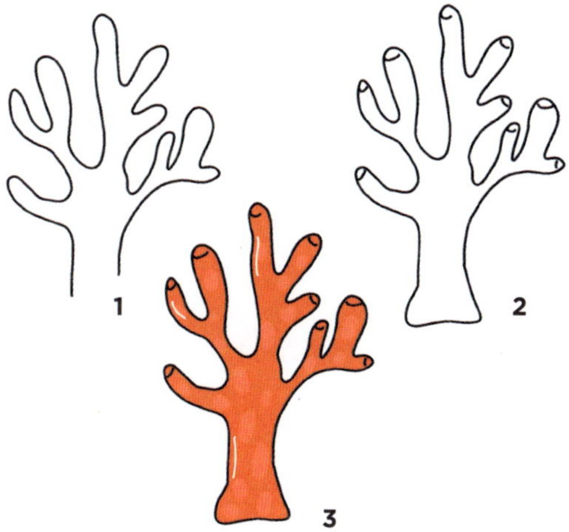

SHARK'S EYE SHELL

The ocean is full of shells, so let's learn to doodle a few of them to set the scene. To doodle a spiral shark's eye shell, start with a simple spiral, and then connect the outside end to the line right below it. That's all there is to it! Add a detail line or two, and then color your shell. I used two shades of light brown for mine, but feel free to use whatever colors you like best.

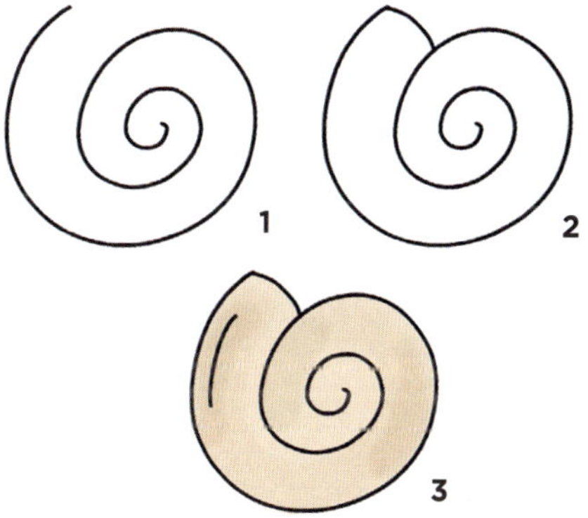

TULIP SHELL

To draw a tulip shell, start with a paisley shape for the inside. Then, add a curving line to the left to form the shell's outer base. Draw three rounded rectangles on top, each one decreasing slightly in size. Finally, add a small, rounded triangular tip. Finish your tulip shell doodle by adding color.

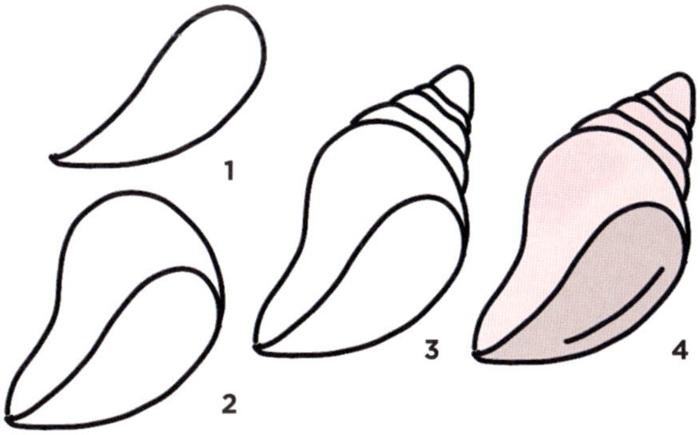

SCALLOP SHELL

Draw a scallop shell by making a scalloped curve with sides that extend down toward each other. Connect the lines at the bottom to form a triangular base. Then, draw ridges that go from the bottom of each scallop to the base of the shell. Finally, color in your drawing. Most shells are shades of white, gray, brown or pink, so using a combination of those colors will give you a doodle that looks more realistic.

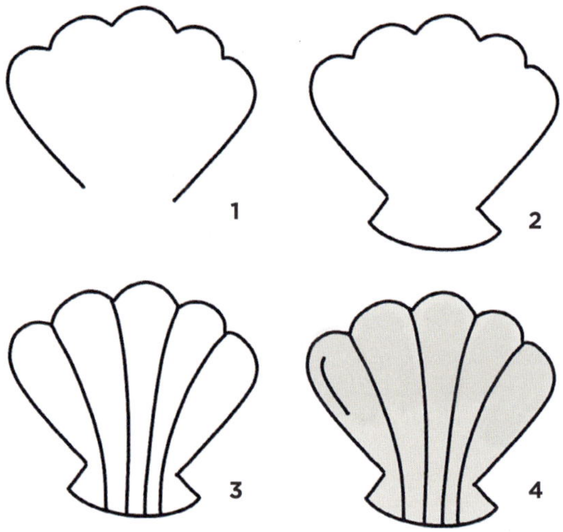

STARFISH

Let's sketch a cheerful starfish to accompany our mermaids. Start with a rounded, five-pointed star shape. Don't worry about perfection; all starfish are unique! Add a cheerful face with eyes, a smile and eyebrows in the center of the shape. Then, draw a series of oval-shaped spots on each arm. Finish your doodle by coloring it yellow, tan, brown or any other color you like.

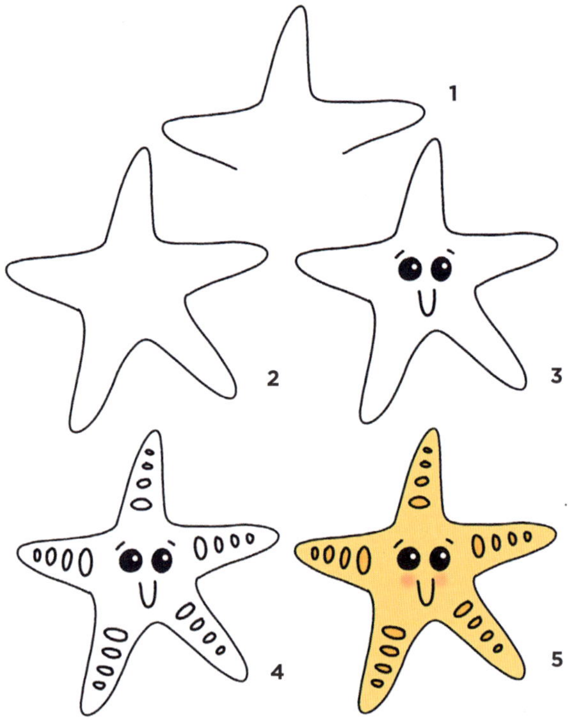

practice here

SKULL AND CROSSBONES

The traditional symbol for pirates is the infamous skull and crossbones. To doodle this symbol, start with an oval that's open on the bottom. Then, draw two lines extending down from the opening, and connect them with a wavy line to form the bottom of the skull. Add two oval eye sockets, and a triangular shape in the nose area. Next, sketch four bone shapes that form an "x" behind the skull. Color the eye and nose areas black, and leave the rest of the drawing white. This doodle can stand alone, or you can use it on the pirate's hat, flag and more.

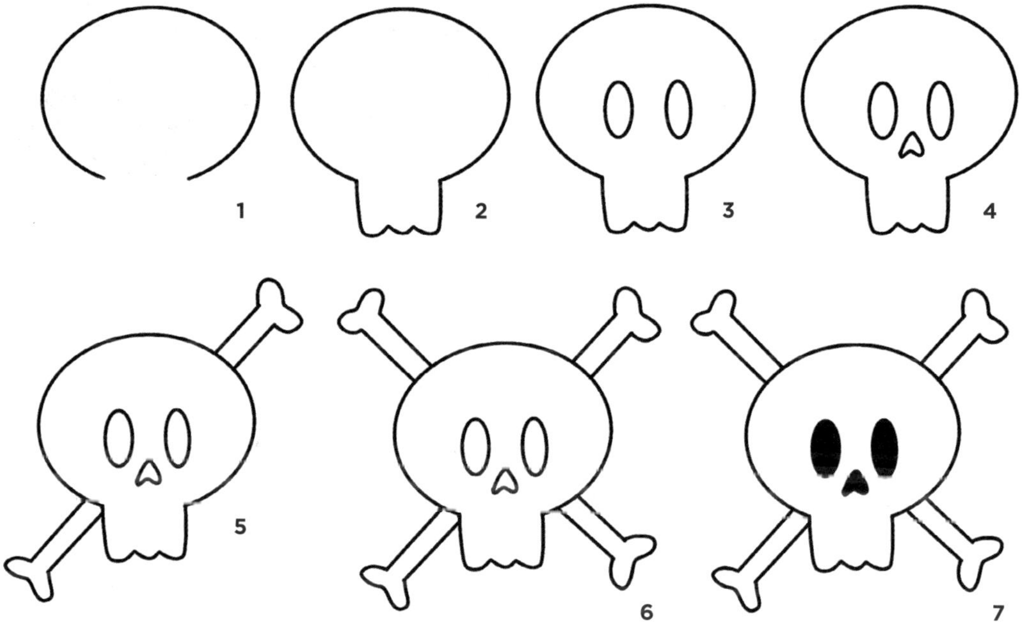

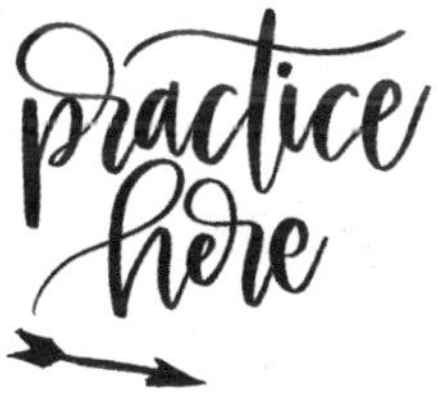

PIRATE HAT

To give your pirate a hat, start with two short, diagonal lines extending in opposite directions. Connect them at the bottom, and draw a curving line across the top that raises up in the center. Draw a second curving line above the first one, and then erase any of the diagonal lines that extend higher than the top of the hat. Draw the skull and crossbones symbol in the center, starting with the skull, and then adding the "x"-shaped bones behind it. Color your hat using black, white and gold/yellow. This doodle can stand alone, or you can draw it directly onto your pirate's head!

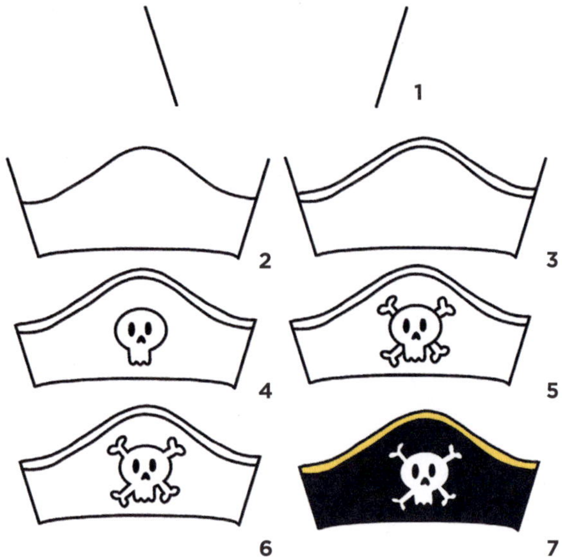

BANDANA

While some pirates wear hats, others cover their heads with a bandana. To draw this, sketch an upside-down "u" shape with a line across the bottom to form a semicircle. Add a round knot on one side, and then draw two short fabric tails extending from it. If you like, sketch a pattern or design on the bandana, like polka dots! You can also add a few detail lines to show folds in the fabric. Finish your drawing by coloring it.

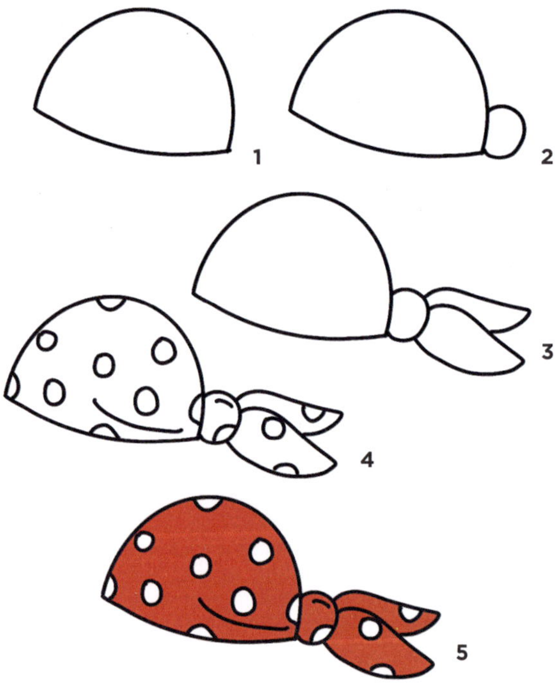

EYE PATCH

Arrrrr, it's a rough life when you lose an eye! Sketch an eye patch for your pirate, starting with a "u" shape that's connected across the top with a slightly curving line. Add a wavy oval shape that connects to each side of the patch for the strap. Draw a second line below the front and back parts of the oval to thicken the strap. Color your eye patch black. If you're drawing this doodle directly onto your pirate, you won't need to worry about the whole strap; just sketch the patch itself and part of a strap extending out to each side of the head.

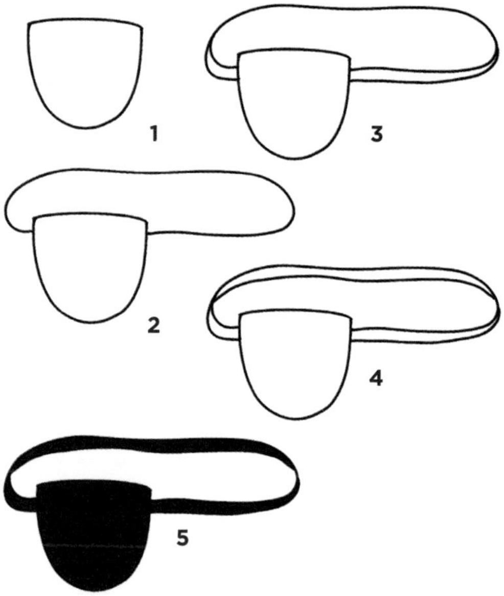

HOOK

Let's learn to draw a hook for any pirate who's unfortunate enough to lose a hand. First, draw an arch, and then connect the bottom with a curving line. Sketch a curving rectangle below it. Add a series of vertical lines inside the rectangle for texture. Draw a shape resembling a question mark, and then draw a second shape next to it that connects at the top point to form a sharp hook. Sketch a short, curving line at the base of the hook, and erase any overlapping lines. Finish your doodle by adding color and highlight lines.

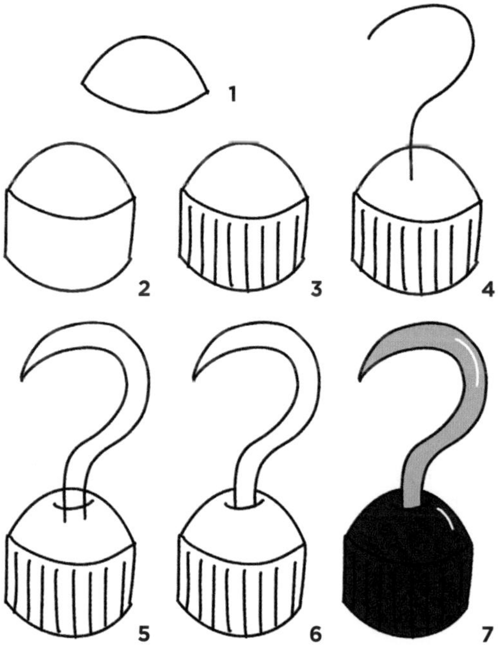

BOTTLE OF RUM

Yo ho ho, and a bottle of rum! Start this doodle by drawing the curving sides of the bottle. Connect them at the bottom, and then add a mouth at the top. Draw a rounded, rectangular cork above the mouth. Next, sketch a label and write "RUM" on it. Add a detail line on the bottle, and then color your drawing. I colored my bottle dark brown, but you can use any shade you like for your doodle.

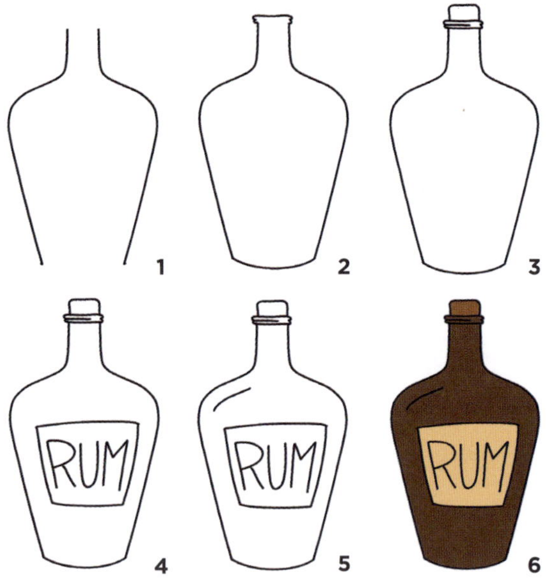

SWORD

Start your sword doodle by drawing a curved blade with a point at the end. Draw a detail line to divide the blade into two sections. Add a guard and a rounded, rectangular grip, and then sketch a series of lines on the grip for texture. Draw a "c"-shaped knuckle guard on one side of the handle, then finish your sword by adding color.

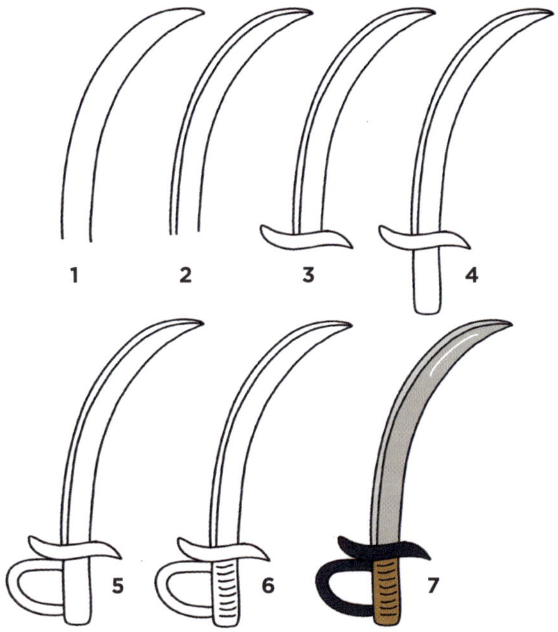

PARROT

Give your pirate a pet by sketching a talkative parrot. Start with an upside-down "u" shape, and connect it at the bottom with a scalloped line to show the head's feathery texture. Add an oval-shaped body and a pair of wings. Draw a long tail made of five thin "u" shapes. Sketch a beak and a pair of eyes, and then add scalloped detail lines on the wings and belly. To give your parrot a perch, draw two horizontal lines below the body for a branch. Add a pair of feet, erasing the areas where they overlap the branch. Draw leaves on the branch, and then use bright colors to bring your doodle to life.

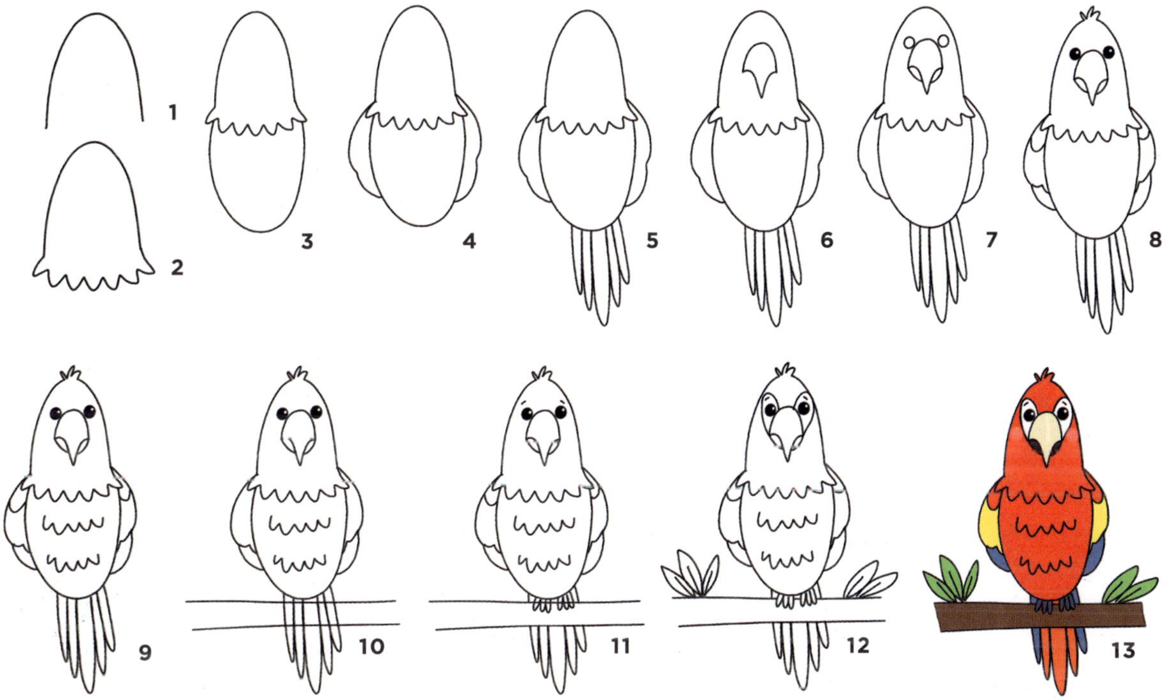

practice here

PIRATE WITH PEG LEG

It's time to put some of our doodles together to draw a pirate. First, sketch an oval-shaped head and a thin neck. Then, add an upper body, and draw a vest overlapping each side. Erase the areas where the lines overlap, and then add triangular short sleeves. Feel free to use a jagged line to show that one or both of the sleeves is ripped. Draw the arms, and then give your pirate shorts, making the bottom slightly wavy to show they're worn out.

Sketch a simple leg and boot on one side, and then draw a peg leg on the other. Detail lines on the peg leg will help show a wooden texture. Use curving lines to divide the shirt into stripes, and draw a few round buttons on one side of the vest. Give your pirate a hat, and draw the skull and crossbones symbol in the center.

Sketch zigzag lines for a ragged beard, hair and a mustache, erasing the areas where there are overlapping lines. Give your pirate a face, including an eye, a smile and an eye patch. Finally, color your doodle.

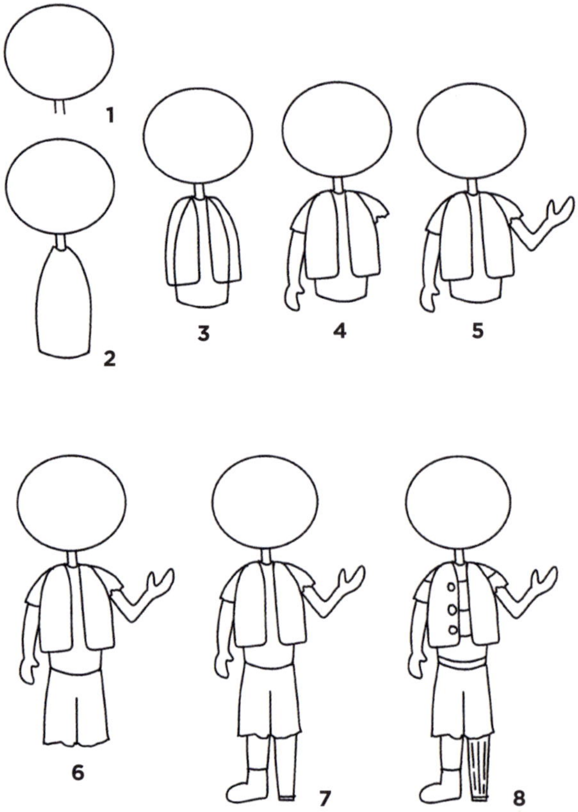

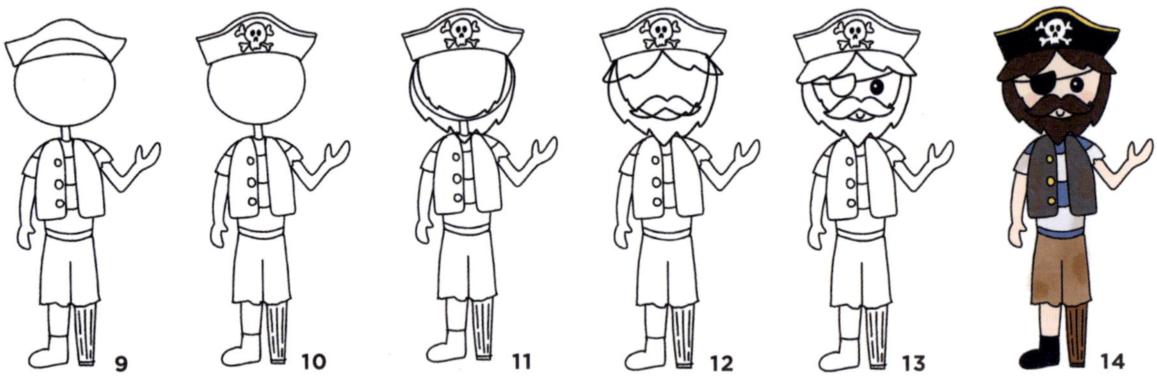

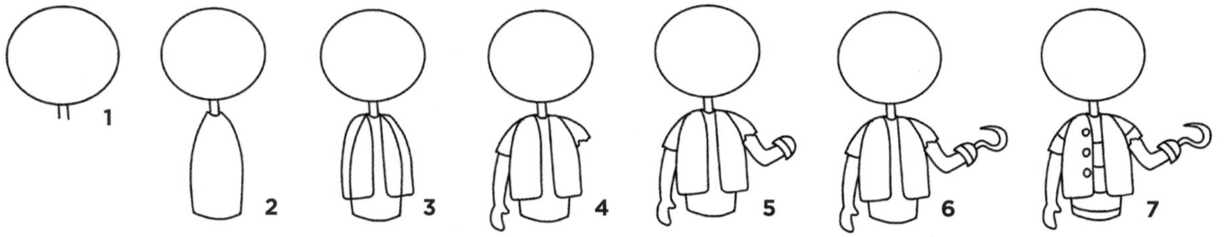

PIRATE WITH HOOK HAND

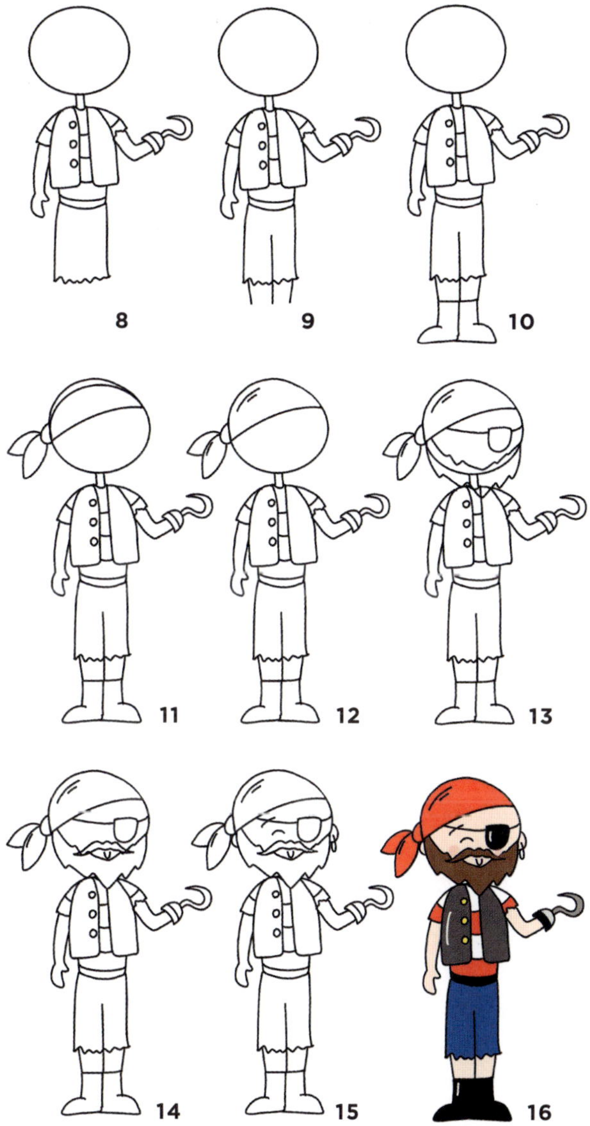

Not all pirates have peg legs, and some have hook hands! Here's another variation on the pirate doodle that will let you create another unique character. Start in the same way, with an oval head and a thin neck, as well as an upper body, vest and short sleeves. Give your pirate one arm, but on the other, use your hook doodle in place of a regular hand.

Add stripes to the shirt and buttons to the vest, and then draw a pair of shorts below. Sketch a pair of legs and boots. Instead of the typical hat, add the bandana doodle on top of his head, erasing overlapping lines. Draw a beard and mustache, again erasing extra lines, and give your pirate a face, including an eye patch, a smile and one eye. Finally, add an ear with a hoop earring. Then, finish your doodle by coloring your character.

practice here

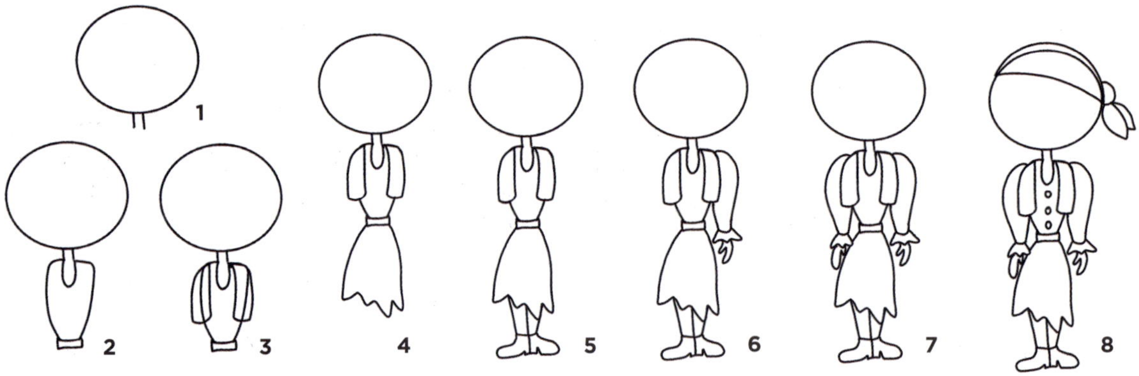

GIRL PIRATE

Let's draw a female pirate! Sketch an oval head with a thin neck, as well as a torso. Draw a belt below the upper body, and then add a vest on each side, erasing the overlapping lines. Sketch a skirt with a jagged hem, and a pair of legs with boots. Draw a puffy long sleeve on each side of the body, and a pair of hands. Sketch several round buttons in the center of the shirt. Give your pirate a bandana on top of her head, and then add polka dots. Draw hair, with detail lines to show texture, and add a pair of hoop earrings. Give your pirate a face, and then add color to complete the drawing.

Bonus: Try drawing all three pirates together, along with their ship!

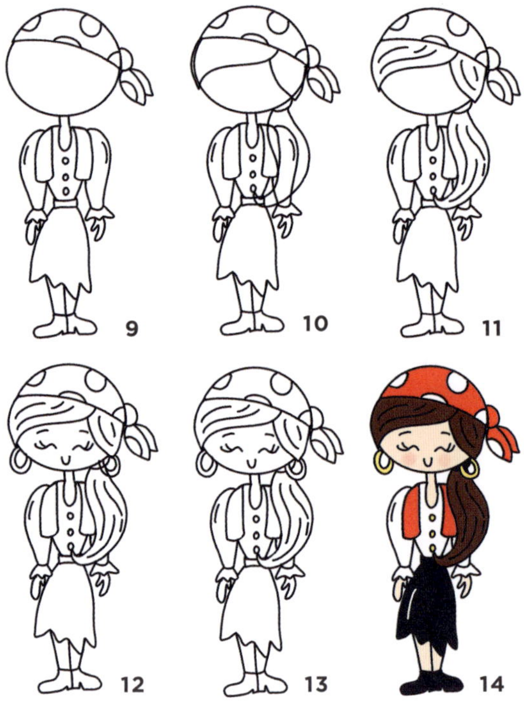

PIRATE SHIP

Let's sketch a ship for our pirates, starting with a long, very thin rectangle. Add a curving shape for the base of the ship, and then draw a cutout area in the top and erase the extra lines. Sketch three circles inside the main shape for portholes. Next, draw three long, thin rectangles extending up from the front, center and back of the ship.

Sketch a sail on each one, with the largest sail in the center. Erase any overlapping lines. Add a "crow's nest" on top of the center post, and then draw another curved rectangle on top with a flag attached. Finish your doodle by adding the skull and crossbones symbol to the largest sail. Color your ship, and then it's ready to sail the seven seas!

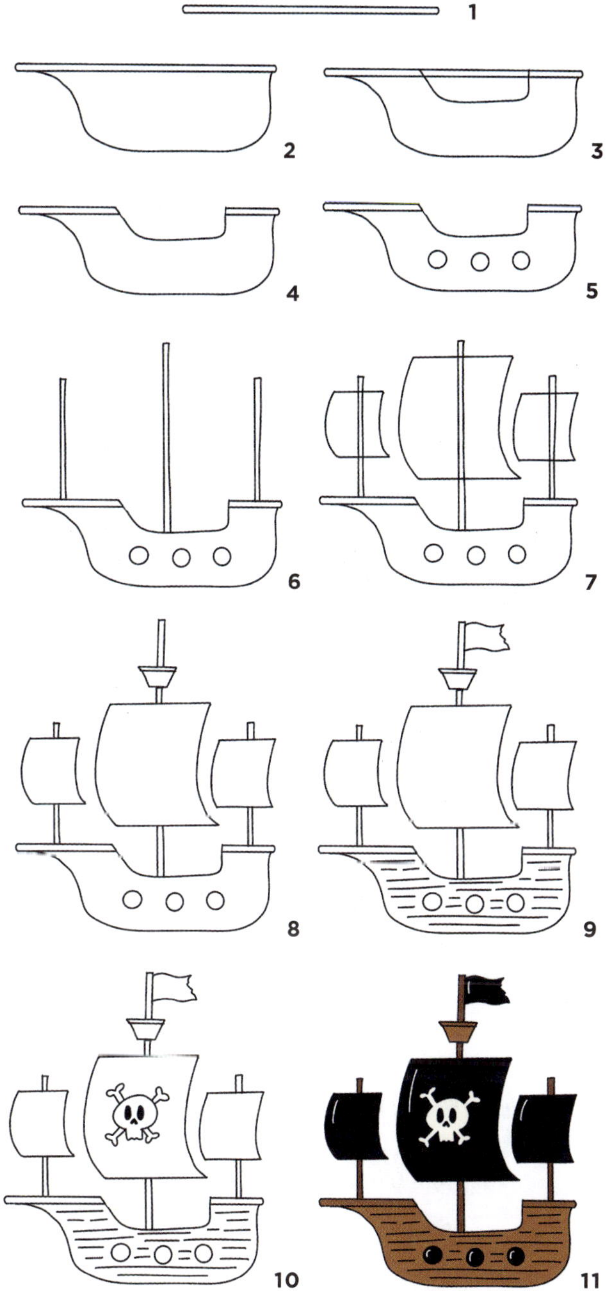

practice here

SHIP WHEEL

Help your pirates steer their ship with this wheel doodle. Start by drawing a pair of concentric circles. Then, use four intersecting lines to divide the circles into eight sections. Thicken the lines inside the circles by drawing a pair of lines around each one, and then erase the original lines. Draw rounded rectangles around the parts of the lines on the outside of the circles. Erase the original lines. Add three more concentric circles in the center of the wheel. Finally, add detail by drawing a few dots to represent hardware that holds the wheel together. Fill in your doodle with shades of brown.

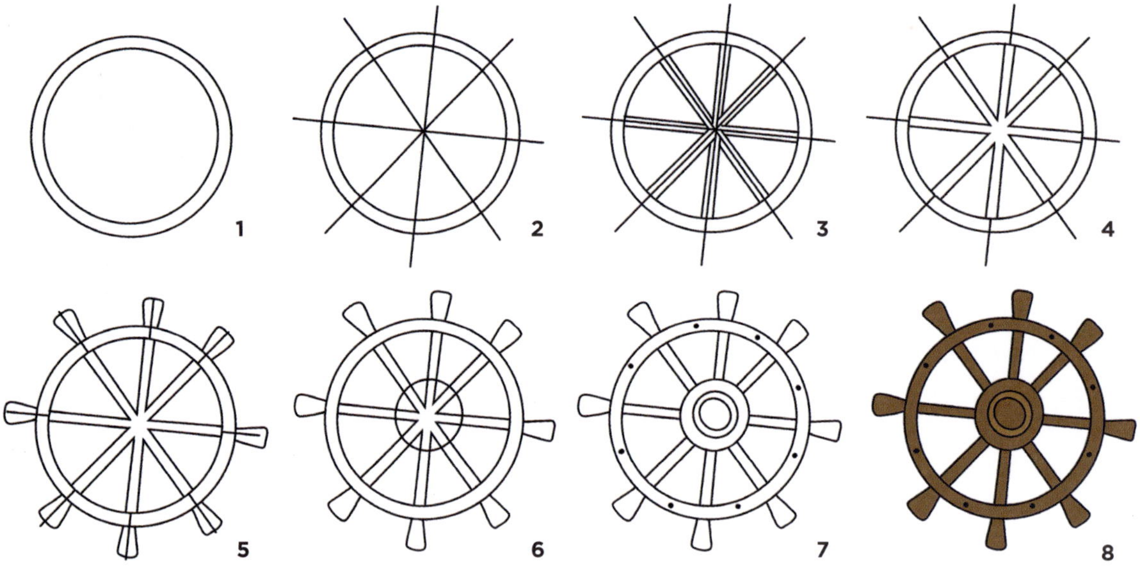

practice here

ANCHOR

Start your anchor drawing with a pair of long, vertical lines. Draw a pair of short, horizontal lines that intersect them to form a cross. Add a semicircle on the ends of the crossbar, and then erase the extra lines inside the cross. Draw two wide "u" shapes near the bottom, and then sketch an arrow on each end. Erase the inside lines again, and close off the bottom of the doodle. Add a circle on top, and erase overlapping lines. Draw a second, smaller circle inside the first one. Finally, color the anchor.

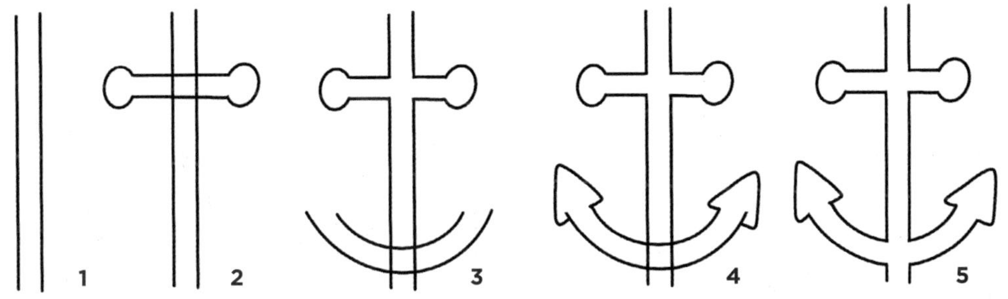

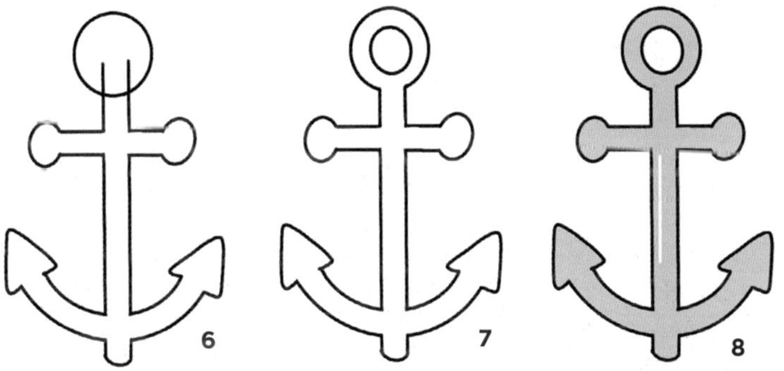

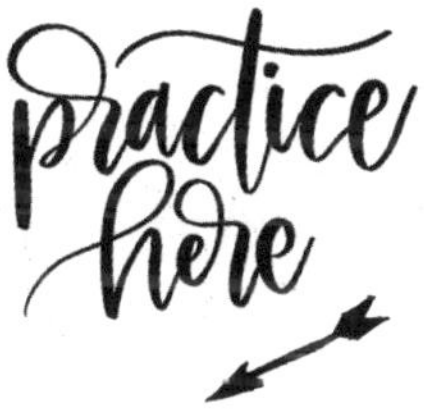

COMPASS

Sailors, including pirates, rely on a compass for guidance while at sea. To draw one, start with a pair of intersecting vertical and horizontal lines, and then draw an "x" over the spot where they meet. Draw a line from each end of the "x" to the end of each of the two closest longer lines. This will create a four-pointed cross. Then, draw four small "v" shapes, one between each pair of points. Divide each "v" in half. Then, sketch two concentric circles around the entire compass rose. Add letters for the directions, as well as a needle. Draw a rounded rectangle on top of the compass, and then draw two more concentric circles attached to it. Color your compass to complete the doodle.

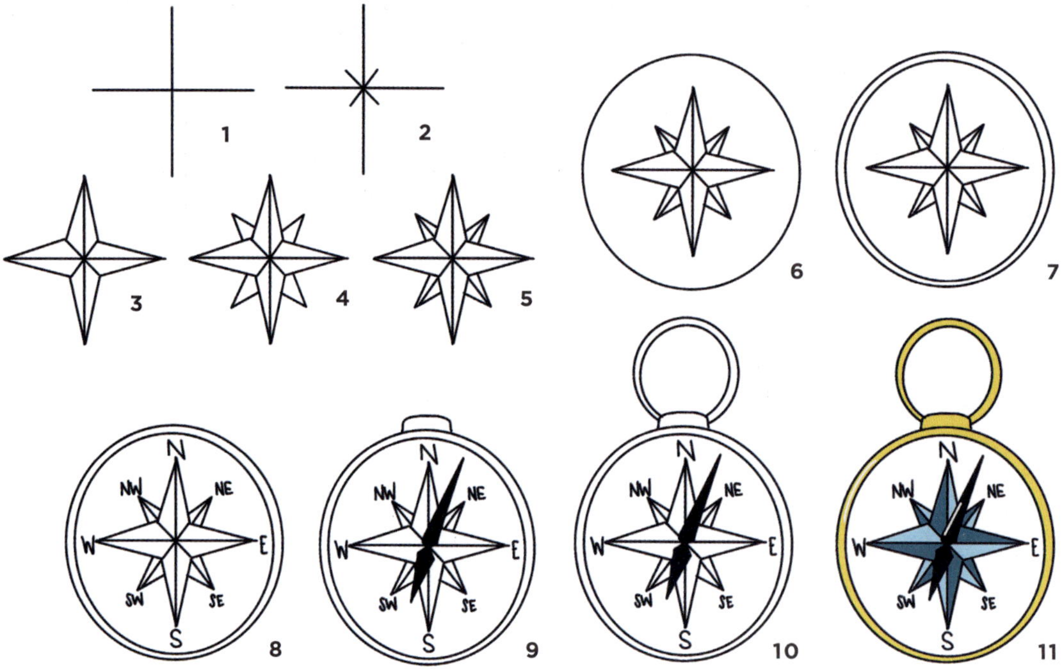

practice here

MAP

Help your pirates find their treasure with a special map. First, let's draw it rolled up, starting with a spiral. Then, draw a long line coming down from each side. Don't worry if these lines aren't perfectly straight. Connect them at the bottom, and then add a wavy line extending down from the end of the spiral. This will make it look like the edge of the map is ripped and worn. Finish your doodle by coloring it.

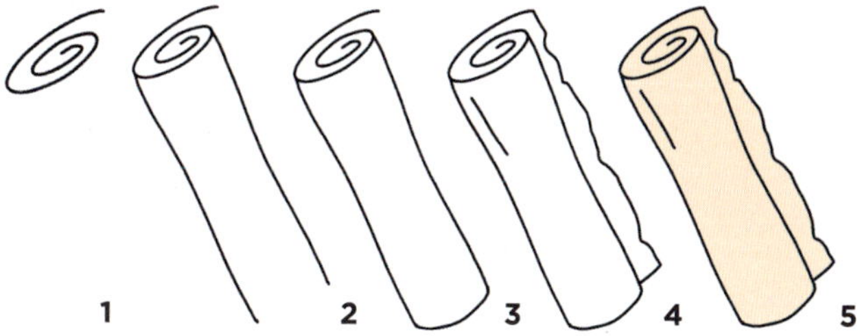

PIRATE FLAG

Draw a flag for your proud pirates, beginning with a pair of wavy, horizontal lines. Connect them on the left side with a vertical line, and then on the right side, draw a jagged line to show that the fabric has been tattered and torn. Add a rectangle flagpole, and then draw the skull and crossbones symbol. Finish your flag by coloring it. Traditionally, the background of a pirate flag is black, while the skull and crossbones are white.

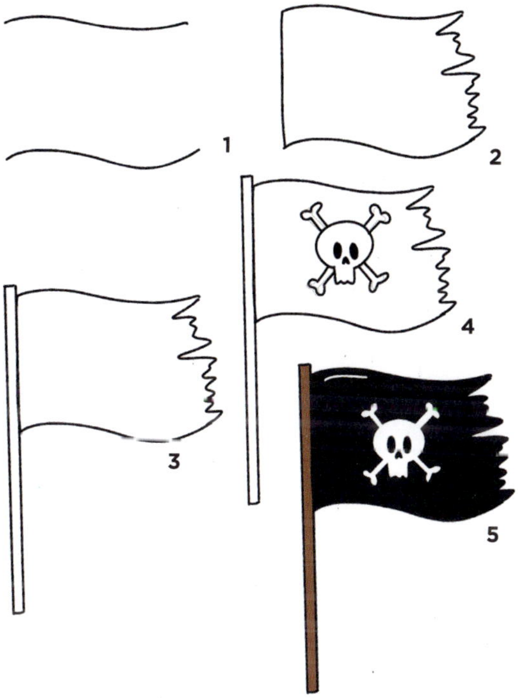

practice here

TREASURE MAP

Now, let's draw an open treasure map. Start with a line for the top of the map that curves in opposite directions on each end. Draw a pair of vertical lines extending down from the sides of the first curve, and connect them at the bottom. Then, draw a line extending down from the edge of the second curve. Add a short line connecting the end of the curve to the top of the map. This will give the illusion that the right side of the map is curled over.

Draw a line to create the bottom of the map. Then, draw several "u" shapes along the top and bottom, erasing the original lines in those spots to give the illusion that the map edges are ripped. All that's left to do is draw whatever symbols and landmarks you like on the map, like mountains, rivers, trees and lakes. Of course, don't forget to mark the treasure spot with a big "x"! Finish your map by adding color.

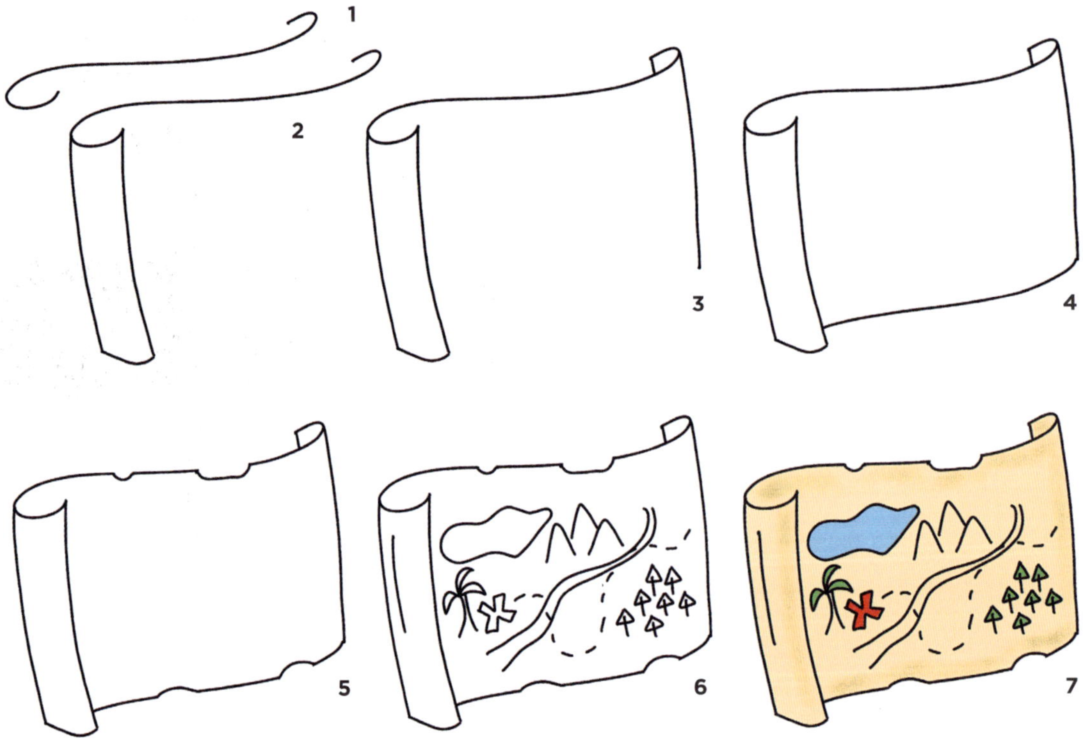

MESSAGE IN A BOTTLE

If you're lucky, you just might find a message (or a map!) in a bottle, floating on the sea. Create this doodle, starting with the sides of the bottle, which are closer together at the top than the bottom. Connect them at the base, and then draw an oval mouth at the top. For the message inside, use the rolled-up map doodle: a spiral with lines extending down from the sides and connected at the bottom. Don't forget the torn edge on the right side.

Next, sketch a rounded, rectangular cork at the top of the bottle, erasing the overlapping line, and add some dots inside for texture. Draw detail lines to indicate the bottle's curves. Finally, color your message in a bottle. I like to use a very light blue to represent the glass, but you can also leave it white.

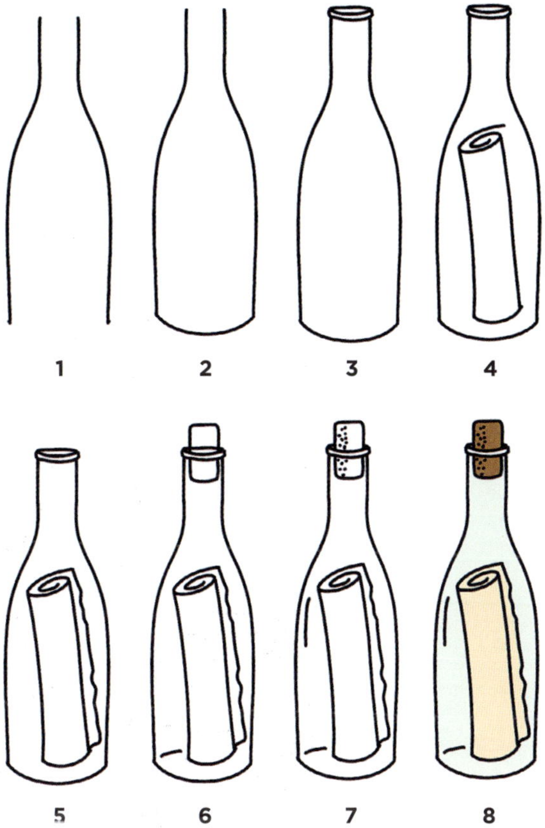

practice here

BARREL

To doodle a barrel, start with a pair of lines that curve toward each other to form the sides. Connect the lines at the bottom, and then draw an oval to connect the top. Add curving lines to create bands across the top, center and bottom of the barrel. Draw four curving lines to show the wooden texture, and erase the areas where they overlap the bands. Finally, color the barrel to finish your drawing.

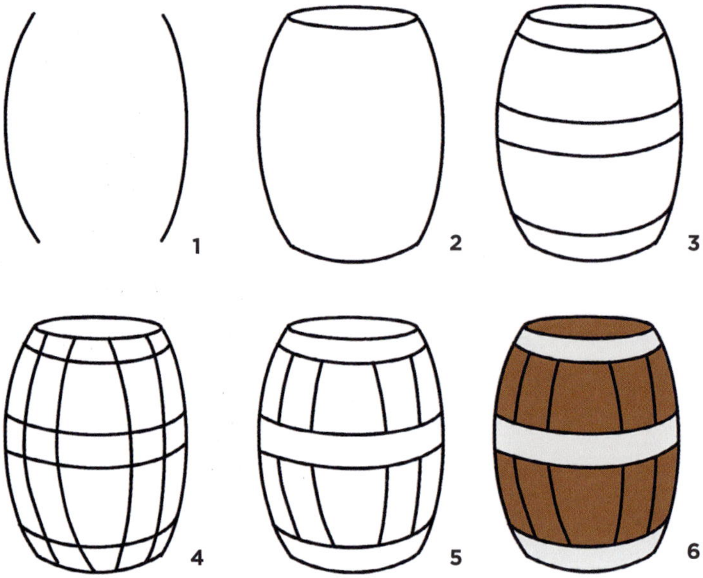

practice here

BOMB

The first step in drawing a bomb is to sketch a large circle. Next, draw a small, thin oval at the top, and a curving rectangle just below it. Add a fuse, drawing a shape that looks like a macaroni noodle. Erase the areas where your lines overlap. Sketch some small detail lines on the fuse to show a rope-like texture. Finally, color your doodle.

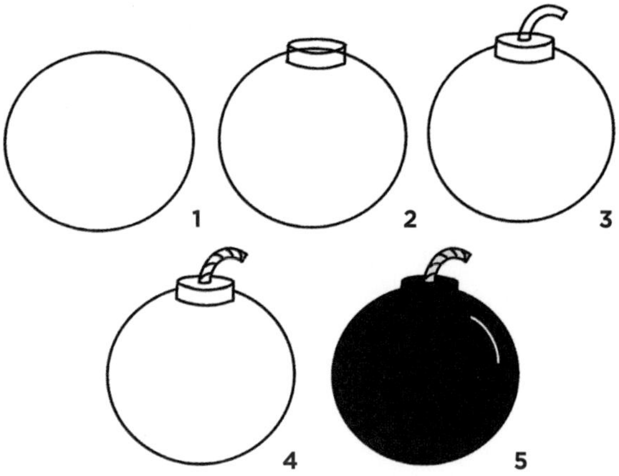

SPYGLASS

Let's doodle a spyglass together! First, draw an oval with a second, smaller oval inside. Then, sketch two diagonal lines extending from the ovals. Connect those lines, and then repeat, drawing two more sections of the spyglass, which get smaller each time. Finish with a rounded rectangle for the eyepiece, and then add color.

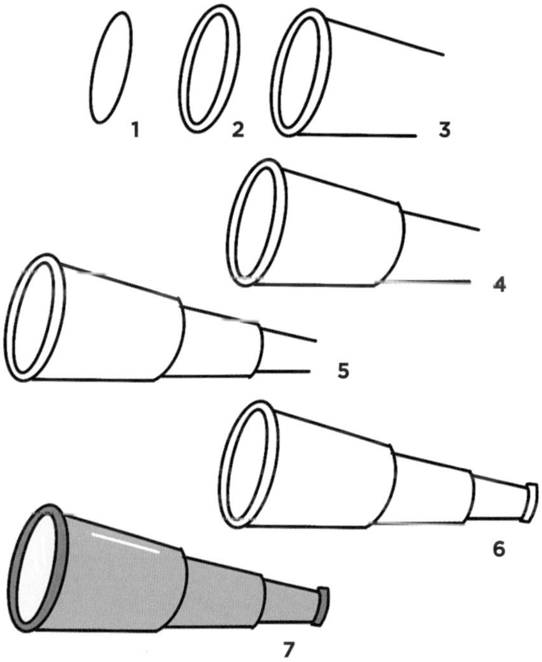

DIAMOND-CUT GEMSTONE

Treasures abound where pirates are found! In addition to gold coins, don't forget about precious gems. Sketch this treasure by drawing a "v" shape with a trapezoid on top. Add a "w" shape in the top section to divide it into five triangles. Draw lines from the two bottom points of the "w" to the bottom of the gem. Finally, choose a color for your gemstone, and add a white highlight line.

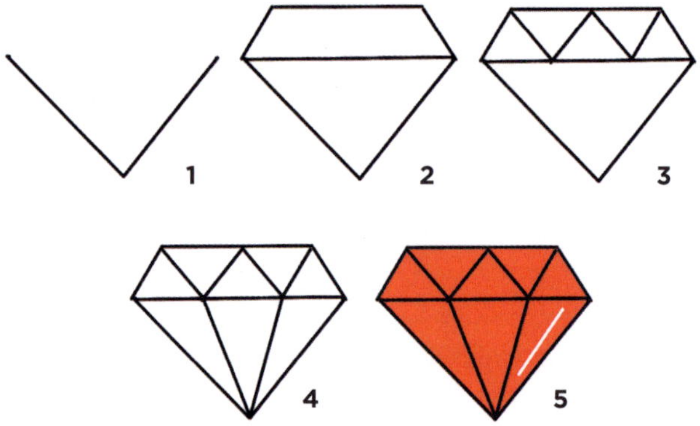

EMERALD-CUT GEMSTONE

To draw an emerald-cut stone, start with a rectangle. Draw a short, diagonal line in each corner, and then erase the corners. Then, sketch a smaller version of the same shape inside the original. Connect the corners of the inner shape to the outer ones using short lines. Finish your doodle by coloring your gemstone in any shade you like. Adding white highlight lines will help create the illusion that your gem is sparkling in the light.

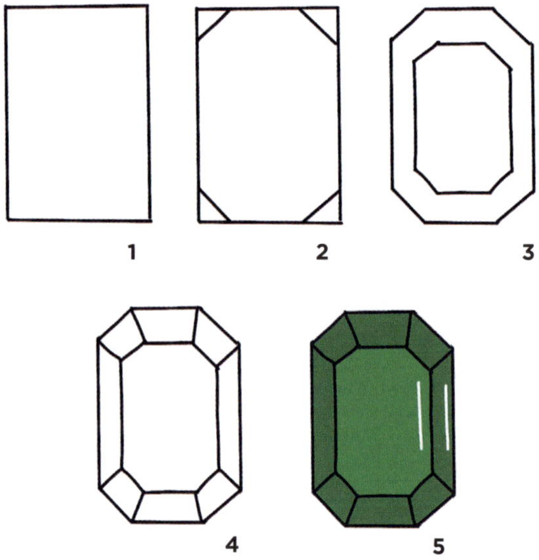

COIN

Of course, pirates always hope their treasure will contain plenty of gold coins! The first step in drawing a coin is to sketch an oval. Then, add a curving line below it to show the coin's side. Draw short, vertical detail lines to give the side texture. Add a smaller oval on the head of the coin. If you like, you can add an image, number or words inside the oval, or you can leave it as is. Finish your drawing by coloring your coin gold or silver.

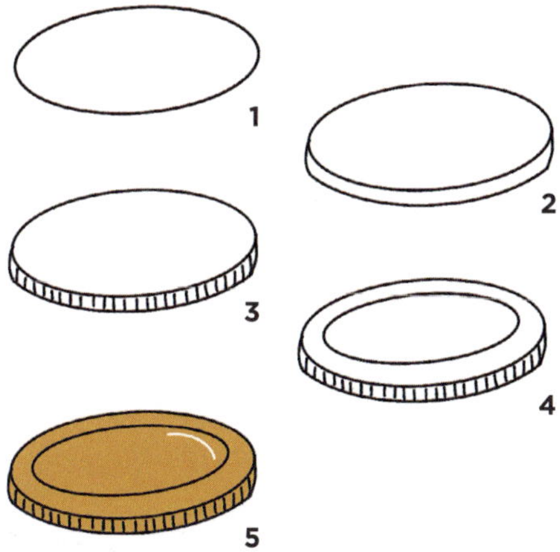

MONEY BAG

This bag is filled with gold coins, or so our pirates are hoping! Sketch it by drawing a "u" shape with a flat bottom. Connect the top with a few curving lines to form the rope that ties the bag shut. Then, draw a pair of diagonal lines extending in opposite directions, and connect them with a wavy oval to make the top of the bag. Add detail lines for texture, and don't forget to label the bag with a big dollar sign! Finish your doodle by adding color.

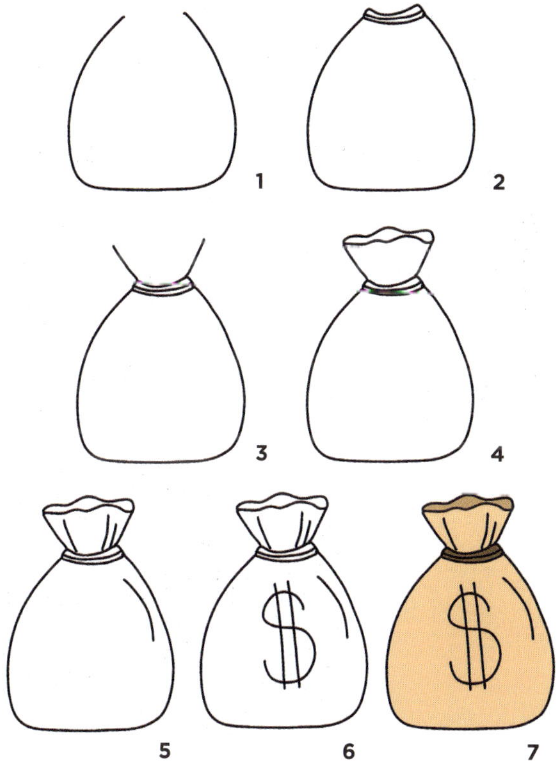

TREASURE CHEST

When your pirates find treasure, here's how to draw it! Start with a square that sits on a diagonal. Add a semicircle on top. Extend lines out to the side from the top and bottom of the square and the top of the semicircle to form the front of the chest. Connect them on the side to finish the basic outline. Sketch a smaller shape inside each of the four sections of the chest, and draw a rectangle with a keyhole inside. Draw a series of lines to show the wooden texture, and then color your treasure chest brown and gold.

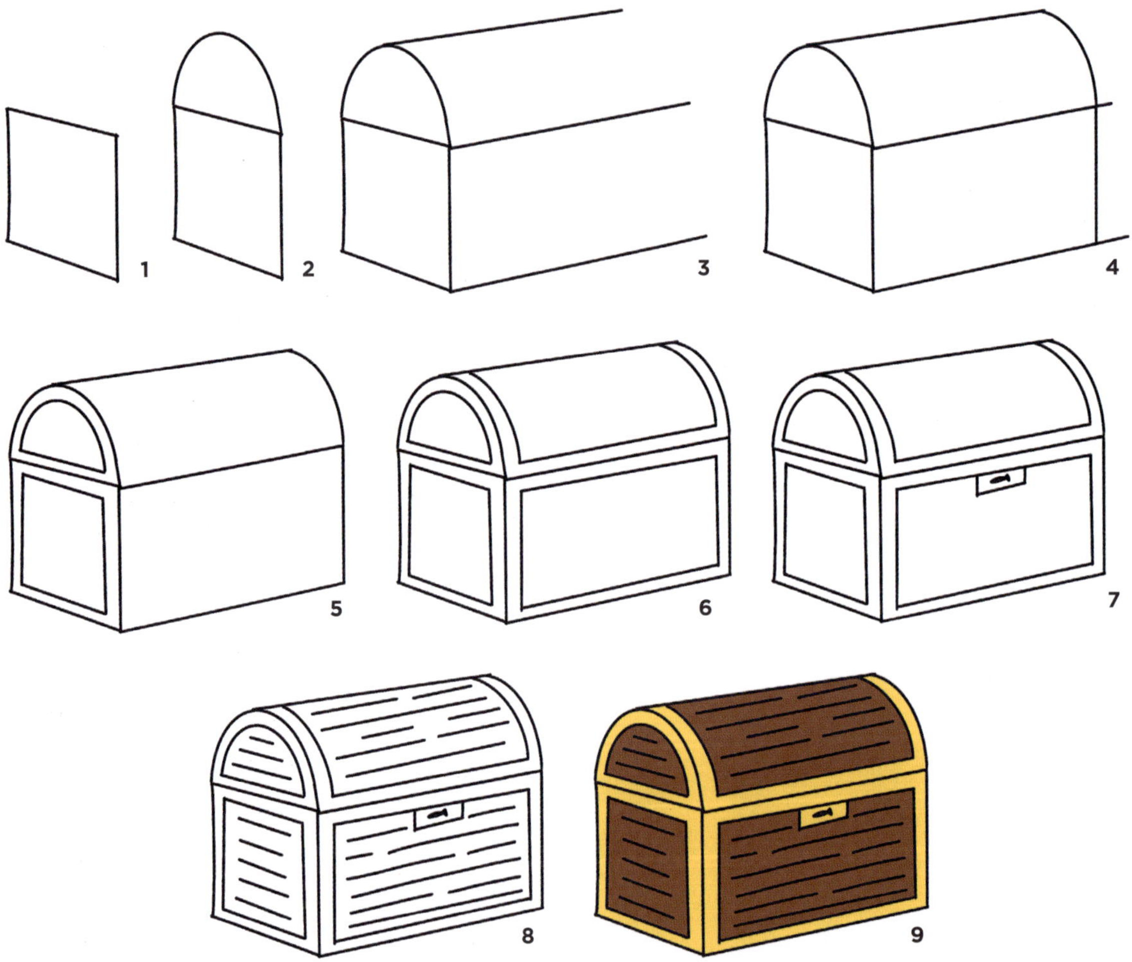

PALM TREE

To draw a palm tree, start with a pair of slightly curving lines that connect at the bottom to form the trunk. Next, sketch a pair of crescent-shaped branches. Draw two more branches, and then add three round coconuts, erasing any overlapping lines. For extra detail, sketch a line inside each branch, and a series of "w" shapes in the trunk to show texture. Finally, color your palm tree green and brown.

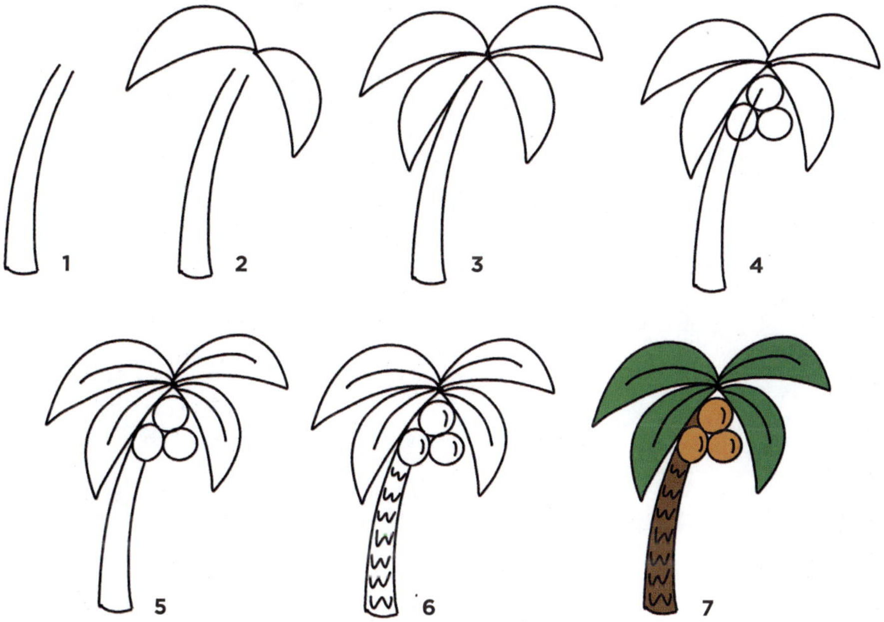

practice here

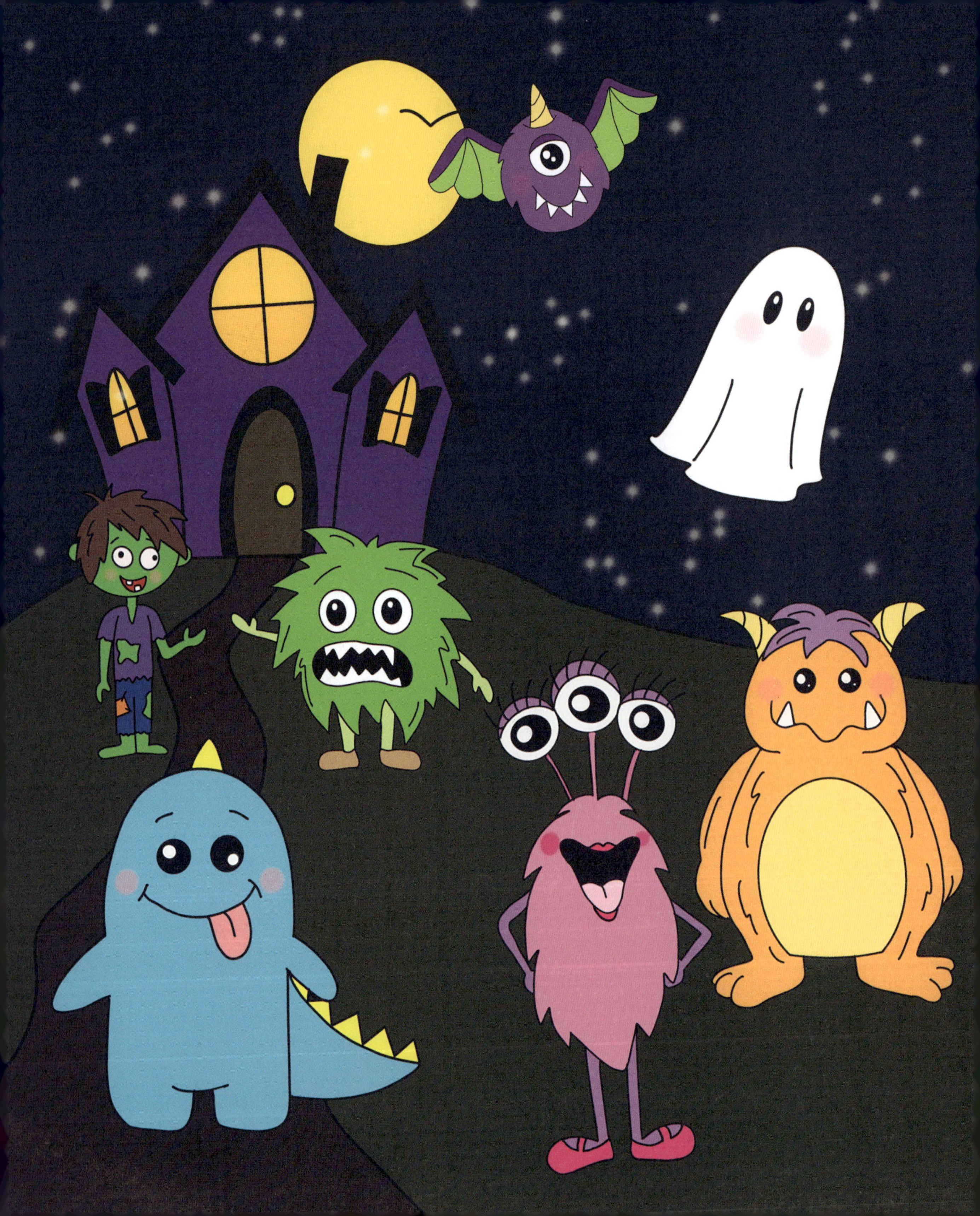

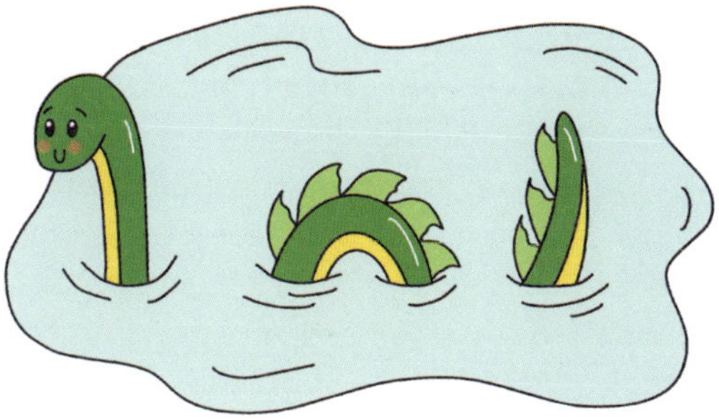

MONSTER'S *Lair*

Zombies, monsters and ghosts, oh my! In this chapter, we'll explore a variety of imaginary creatures than can be silly or spooky. As someone who doesn't like scary things myself, I've chosen to make all of these creatures friendly, with big smiles or funny expressions. However, when you create your doodles, you can give them whatever facial expressions and personalities you like. In this chapter, we'll learn to draw several variations of monsters, including famous ones like Frankenstein's monster, and mythical creatures like Yeti, Bigfoot and more. Grab your pencil and let's get started!

HORNED MONSTER

Monsters may be hairy, but they don't have to be scary! This friendly fellow just wants to say hello. Start drawing him by sketching a "c"-shaped head and a large "u"-shaped body. Add an oval-shaped belly and a pair of large arms. Give your monster feet with three toes, and erase the areas where the feet connect to the body. Sketch a pair of horns, and give your monster a face with eyes and a silly smile. Add two triangular teeth, and sketch detail lines on the horns. Draw a patch of hair on top of the monster's head, and erase any overlapping lines. Finally, add some zigzags on the body to show the fuzzy texture, and then color your monster.

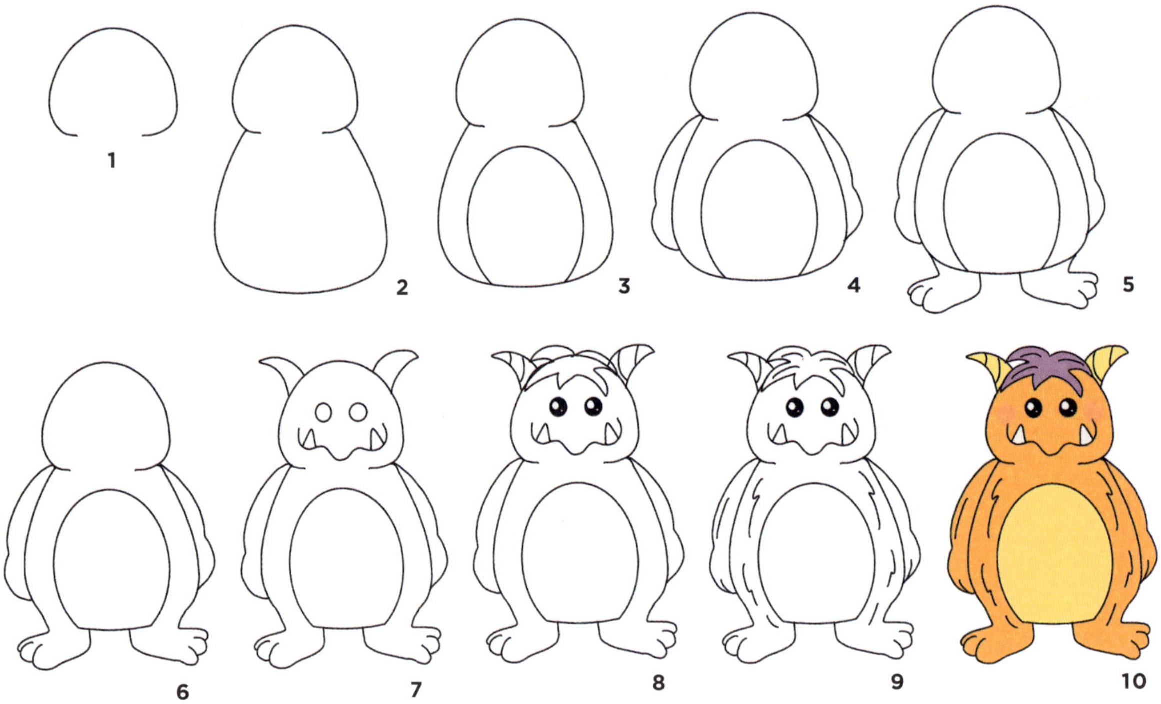

practice here

HAIRY MONSTER

This very hairy monster is more afraid of you than you are of him! To doodle him, use a series of zigzags to create a round body shape. Add a pair of large eyes inside, and draw an oval-shaped mouth. Sketch a row of sharp teeth on the top and bottom of the mouth. Color the inside of the mouth black, and then add eyebrows. Give your monster a pair of arms, as well as a pair of legs and shoes. Finish your doodle by coloring it in any way you like.

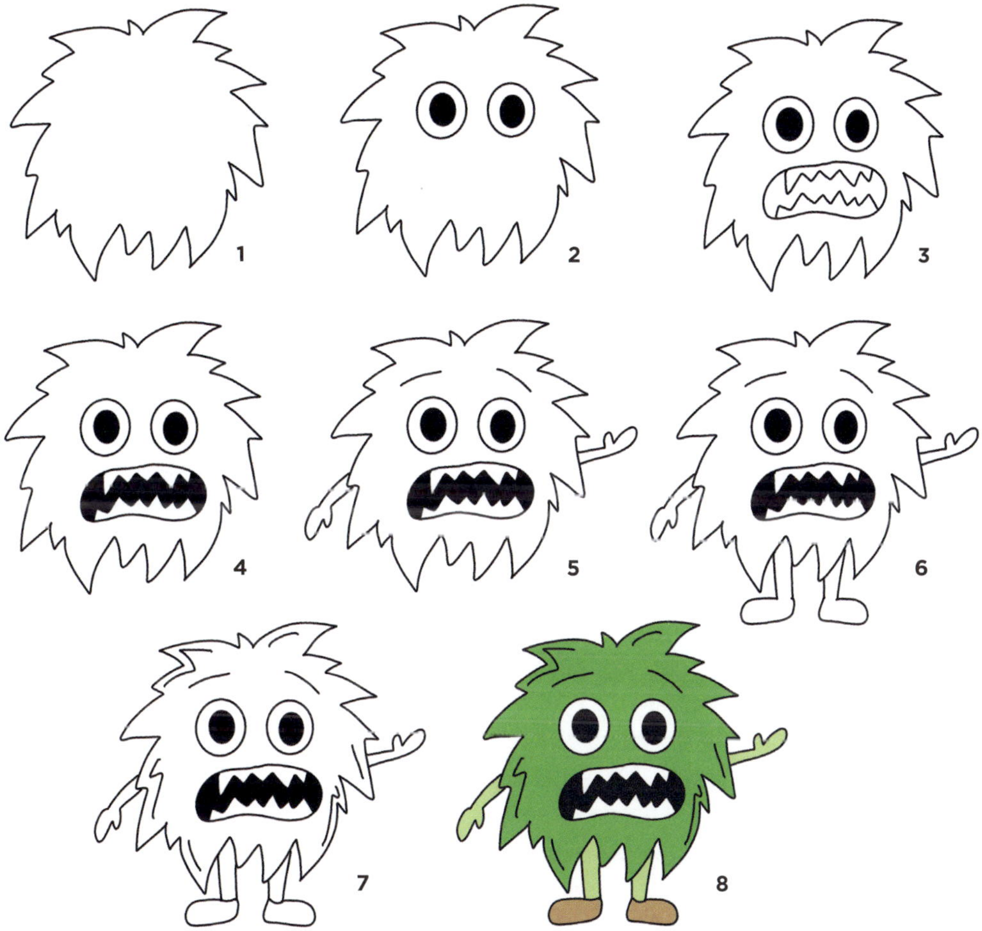

SPIKED MONSTER

Another type of monster that might live in your imagination is this one with spikes running down its back and tail. Draw an arch shape with two small, rounded arms. Add a pair of short legs and a thick, pointed tail. Sketch a triangle on top of the head and several more spikes running along the top of the tail. Then, give your monster a face with eyes, a large smile and a tongue. Bring your monster to life by adding your favorite colors.

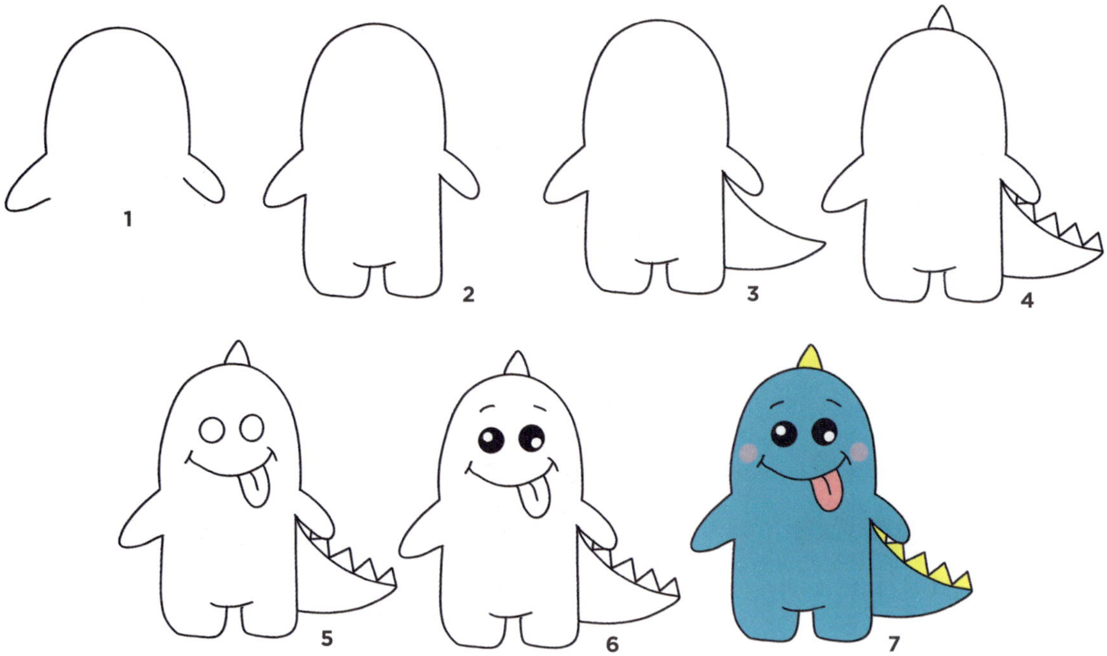

practice here

THREE-EYED MONSTER

This monster sees you . . . with all three of its eyes! Sketch three circles, and give each one a stem made of two parallel lines. Below them, add an oval-shaped body made from zigzag lines. Add a pair of thin arms and hands. Add a curving line near the top of each circle to create an eyelid, then draw a round black pupil inside the eye. Finally, use a white gel pen or paint pen to add a final circle inside the pupil as a highlight. Add a large mouth and tongue inside the body. Then, draw a pair of long, thin legs with rounded shoes. Finish your drawing by coloring your monster. Try making a girl monster by adding eyelashes to each of the large eyes!

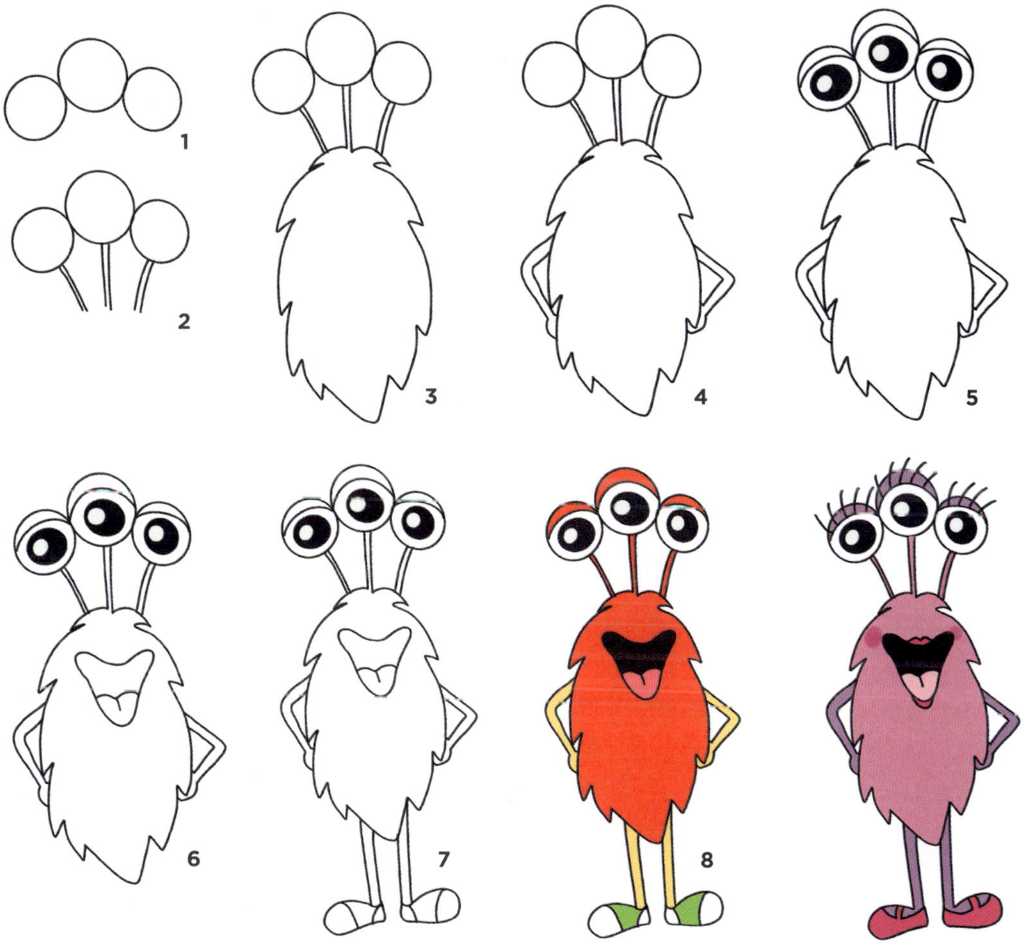

DUST BUNNY

Watch out for dust bunnies under the bed! To sketch these adorable little monsters, use a series of short, curving lines to form a fluffy circle for the body. Add a pair of large bunny ears with smaller ear shapes inside. Give your dust bunny feet made of three "u" shapes, and sketch a face with eyes and a smile. Then, all that's left to do is color your doodle.

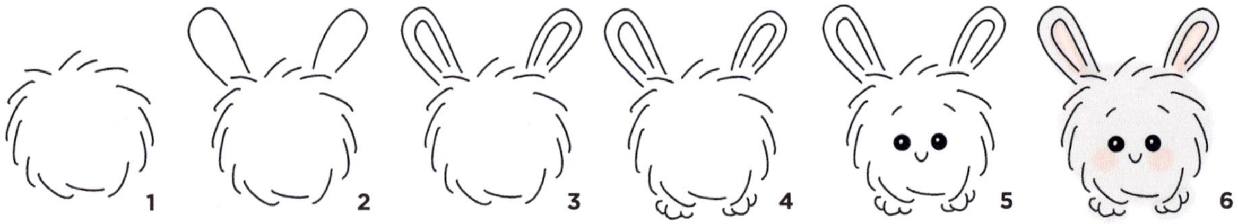

BED

If we're going to draw dust bunnies hiding under the bed, we should also learn to draw the bed itself. Start this doodle by sketching a headboard. Then, add a rounded rectangle in front of it, and erase the places where the lines overlap. Draw a long, thin rectangle underneath for the bed frame, and add two legs. Sketch details on the headboard, and then add two pillows. Finish your drawing by adding color.

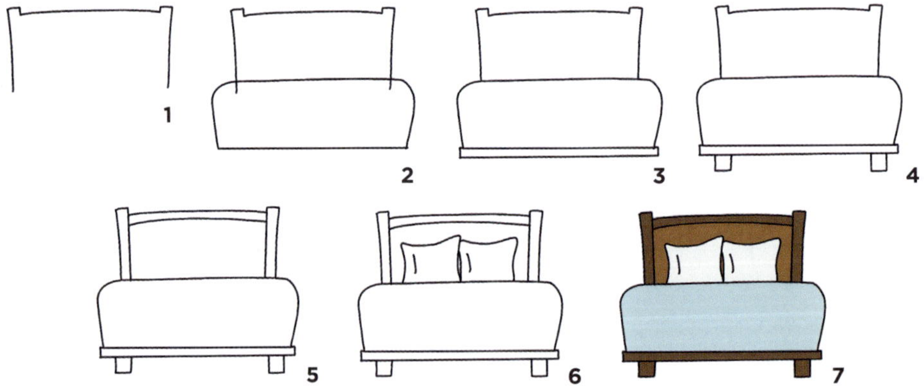

FLYING PURPLE PEOPLE EATER

It's a one-eyed, one-horned, flying purple people eater! To start drawing it, use jagged lines to sketch an oval body shape. Add a large, round circle for the eye, and draw an eyelid at the top. Add the inner part of the eye, and then draw a triangle-shaped horn on top of the head. Erase the areas where it overlaps the body. Sketch detail lines on the horn, and give your monster a large, toothy smile. Draw a pair of wings, and divide them into several sections. Finally, color your drawing, using purple, of course!

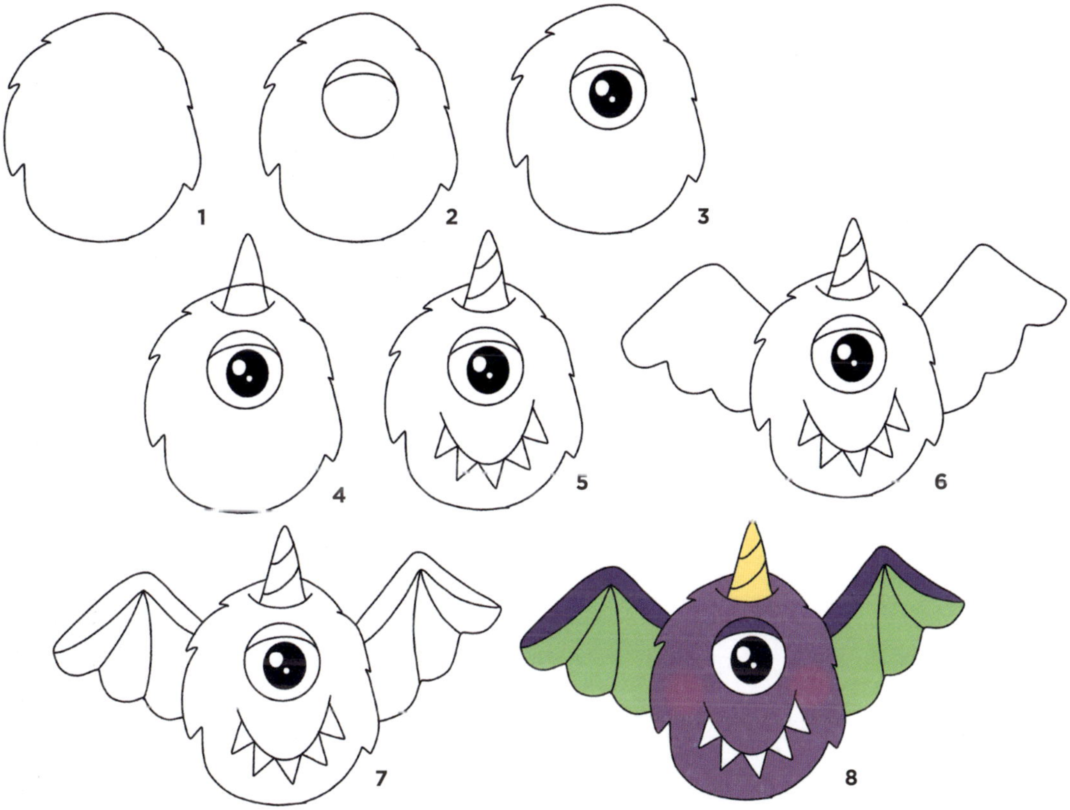

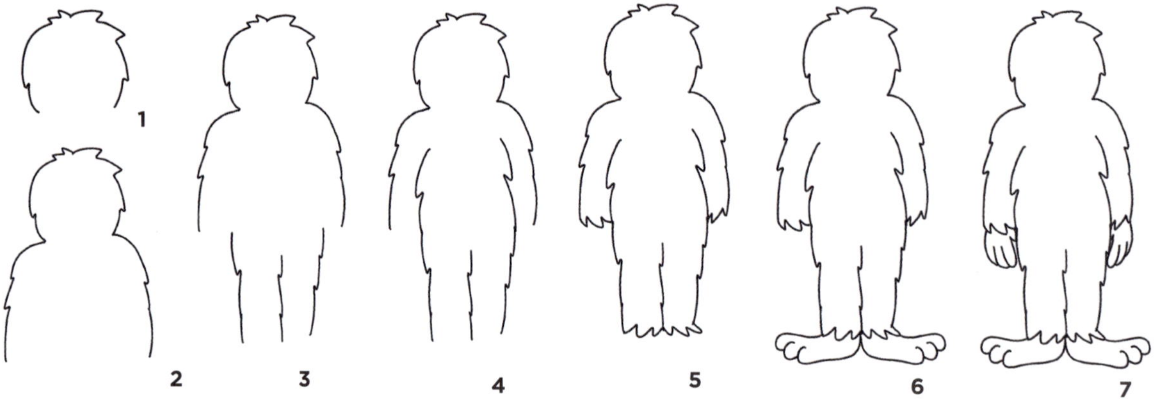

BIGFOOT

Bigfoot, also known as Sasquatch, is a very large, very hairy mythical creature that's said to inhabit the forests of the Pacific Northwest. To draw your own, start by using jagged lines to form the outline of a round head, shoulders and arms. Add a pair of legs and the sides of the body in the same style. Close off the arms and legs with a few zigzags.

Draw a large pair of feet with toes and large hands. Sketch a belly, and then draw an irregular shape inside the head area for the face. Add eyes, eyebrows, a nose and a smile. Then, draw texture lines throughout the body to indicate the shaggy fur. Finish your doodle by coloring it in various shades of brown.

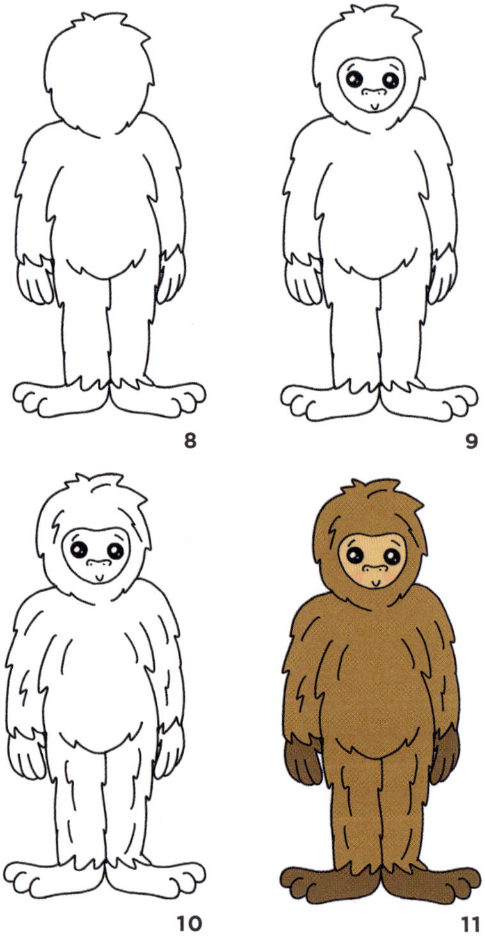

YETI

To draw the lovable abominable snowman, or Yeti, start with a jagged patch of hair, and then draw a wide "u" shape underneath it. Sketch a curved horn on each side of the head. Then, use curving zigzag lines to form a large body, and add a pair of feet at the bottom. Sketch a curve for the belly, and add arms with pointed fingers. Give your Yeti a smiling face, and draw detail lines on the horns. Add zigzag lines to give the body and head a furry texture. Finally, color the face and horns blue, while leaving (or coloring) the rest of the body white.

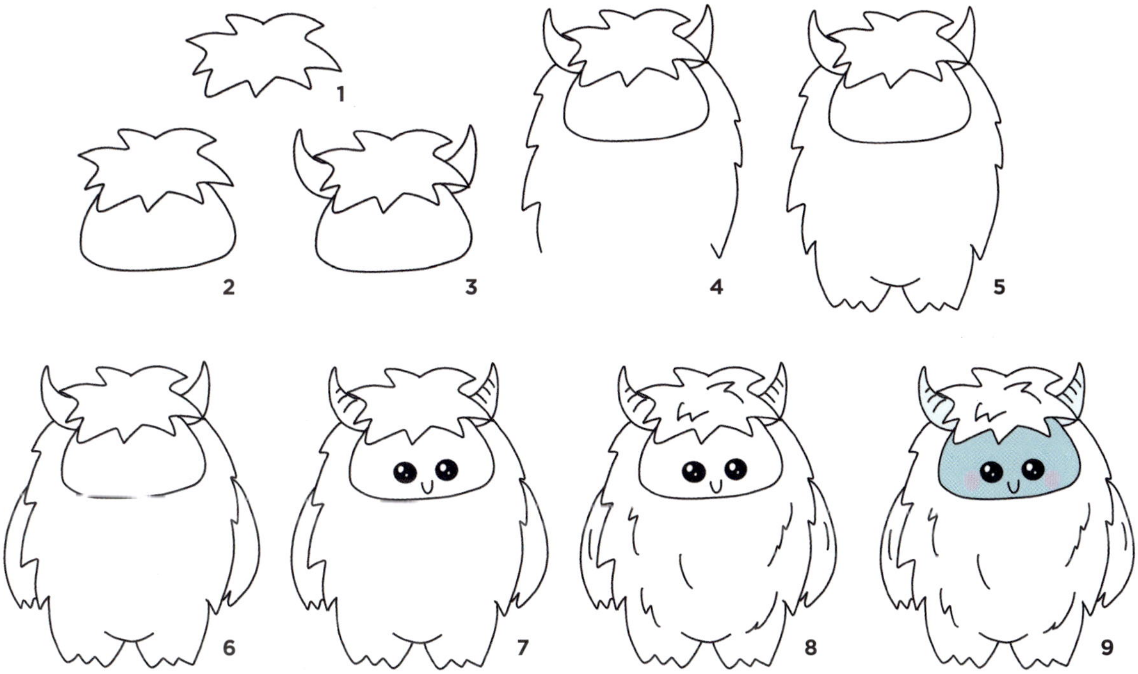

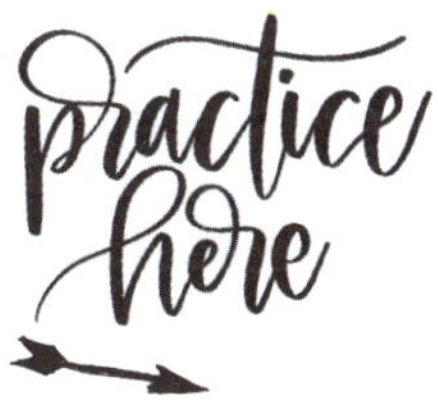

SEA MONSTER

The Loch Ness Monster isn't the only kind of sea monster in sailors' tales. Let's draw another variation together. Start with a curving line for the neck and back, and then form the front of the head, which curls up into a smile. Add a neck and belly, and then connect the belly and back with a long tail. Draw three fins, and erase the areas where the front fins overlap the body. Divide the lower section of the body from the upper part. Draw a simple face, and add a group of irregularly shaped spots on the back. Finish your sea monster by adding color.

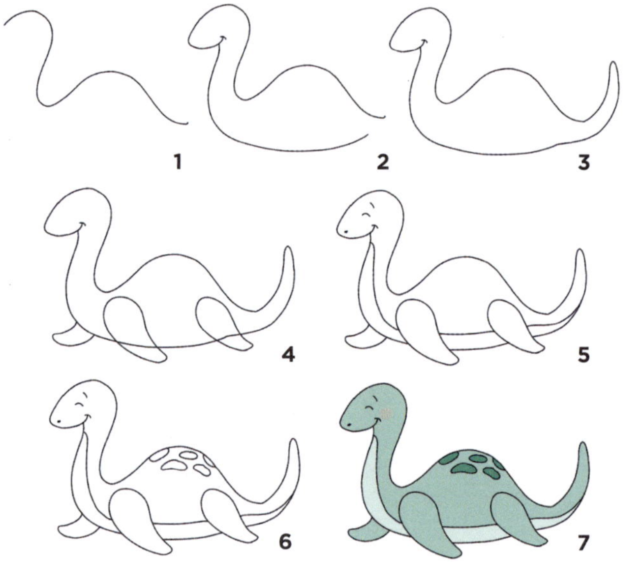

IGLOO

Let's give your Yeti a place to live by drawing him an igloo. First, sketch an arch and connect it at the bottom. Then, draw a smaller arch overlapping it. Divide the smaller shape with a curving line to add depth, and draw an arched opening. Erase the overlapping lines, and draw one more curving line inside the opening for dimension. Use curving lines to divide the entire igloo into bricks of ice. To color your doodle, use a very light blue or gray, or if you're drawing on a dark background, you can use a white gel pen.

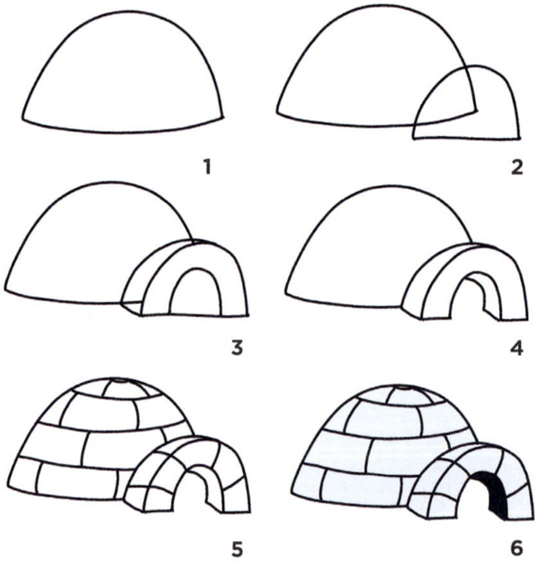

LOCH NESS MONSTER

Scottish folklore tells of a long-necked serpent-like monster in the Loch Ness. Even as recently as March 2024, photos of the unidentified creature have stirred up speculation. Here's how to doodle this sea monster, affectionately known as "Nessie." First, draw an upside-down "J" for the neck, an arch for the center part of the body and a tail, leaving space between the three shapes. Add the rest of the head and neck, as well as a smaller arch inside the larger one.

Draw curving lines under each section of the body to show that the rest is underwater. Sketch an irregular lake shape all around the monster. Divide each body section so that there's an upper and lower part. Draw jagged triangles on the arch and tail sections, and then add a face. Finally, color your doodle.

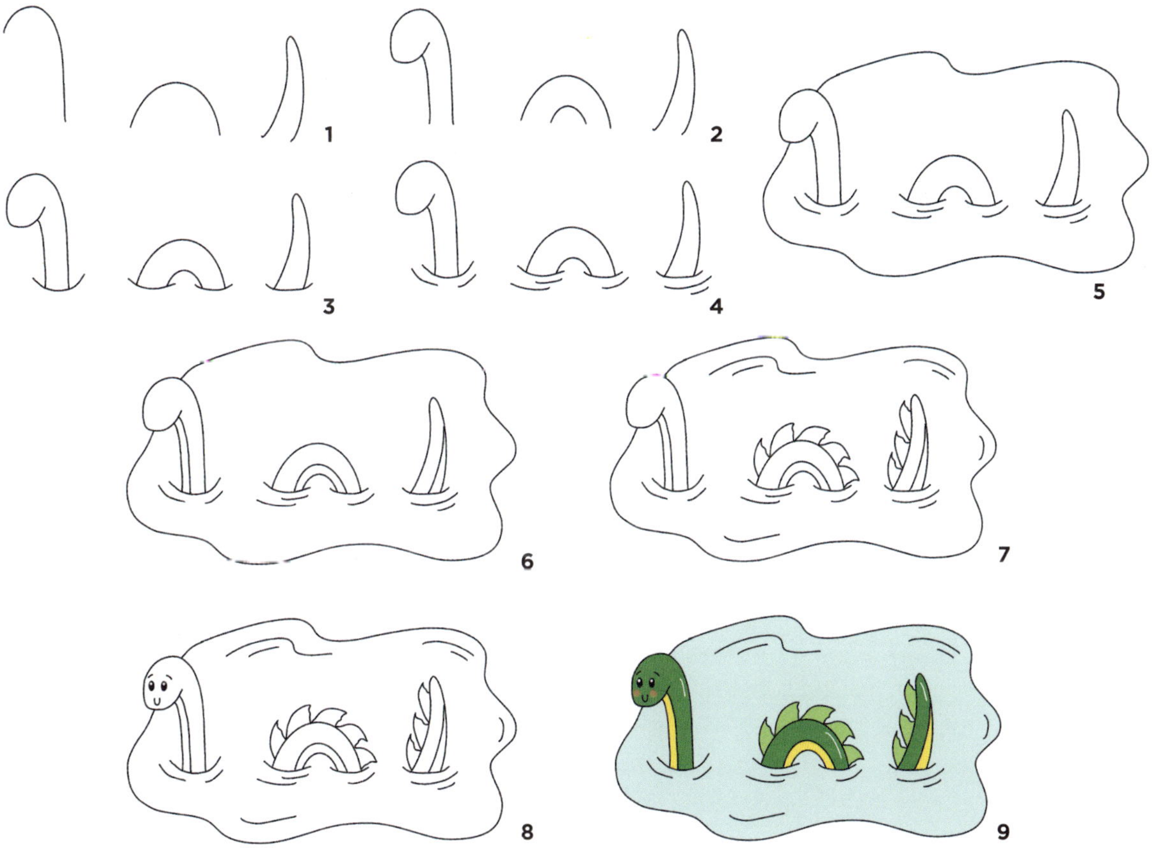

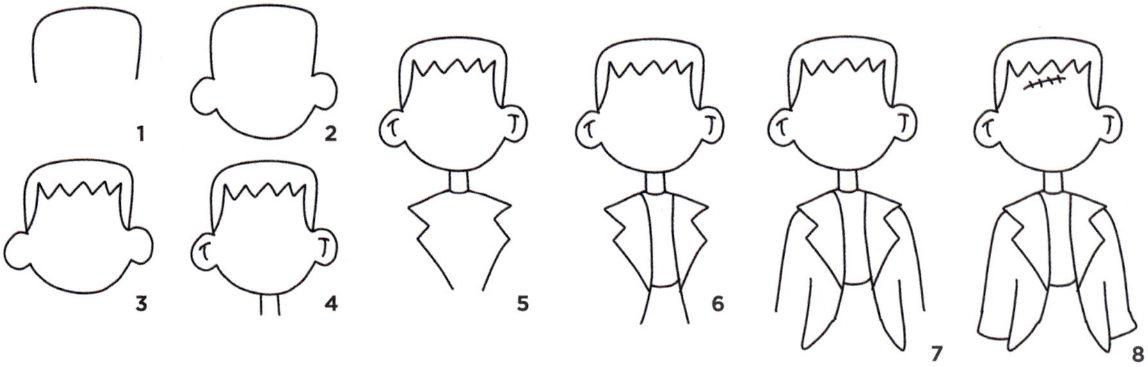

FRANKENSTEIN'S MONSTER

One of the most iconic monsters in pop culture comes from Mary Shelley's story *Frankenstein*. While people often refer to the monster as Frankenstein, technically it was the scientist that was named Frankenstein; the creature he created never actually had a name!

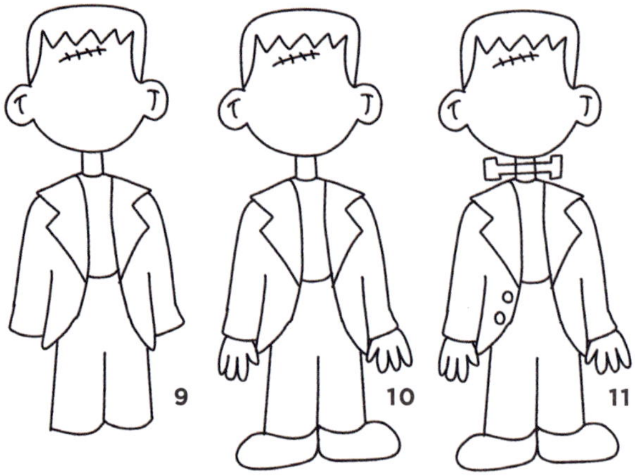

To draw your own version of Frankenstein's monster, start with the top of the head, which should be flat and somewhat square. Add a pair of ears, and connect them with a curve for the bottom of the face. Draw a zigzag hairline and "t"-shaped details in the ears.

Give your monster a neck, and then sketch the collar of his jacket. Add arms and the bottom of the jacket, and draw the infamous scar on the forehead. Sketch a pair of pants, along with hands and shoes. Draw buttons on the jacket and the bolt going through the monster's neck. Erase the overlapping lines. Then, give your monster eyes, eyebrows and a smile. Finish your doodle by adding color, making sure that the body is green.

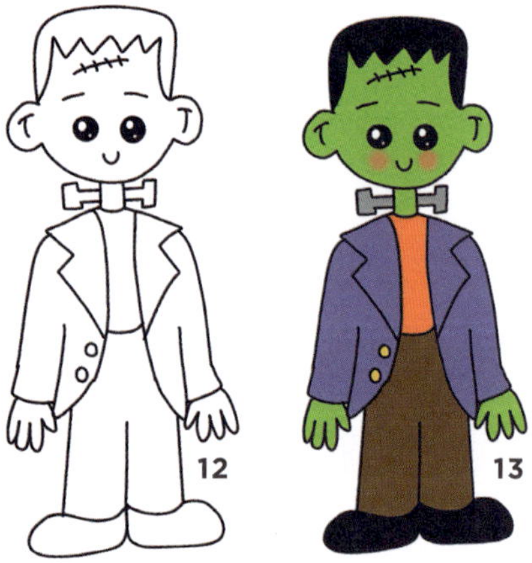

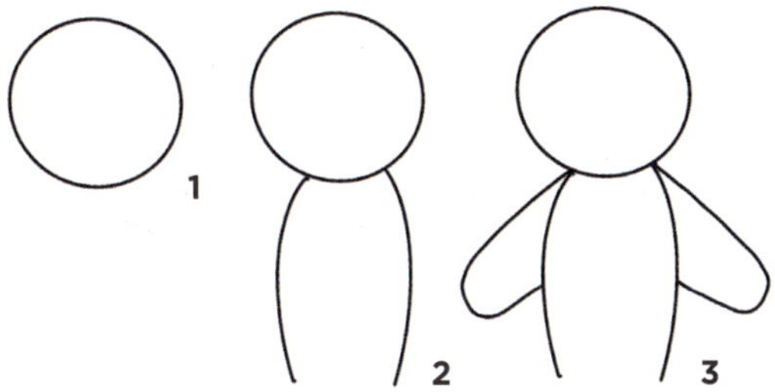

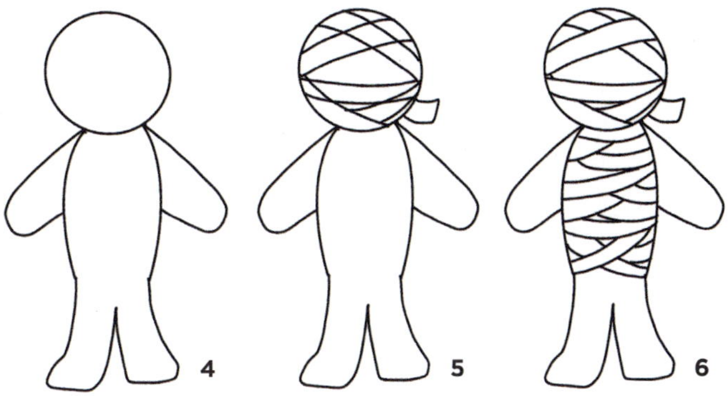

MUMMY

To doodle a mummy, start with a round head and two curving lines for the upper body. Add a pair of rounded arms and a pair of legs. Starting with the head, draw a series of curving lines that cross over each other to create the illusion of being wrapped with strips of linen. Erase overlapping lines. Leave an open space in the center of the face.

Continue the same technique, dividing the body, arms and legs into wrapped sections. Add a pair of eyes, and then sketch a few curving rectangles extending out from the body to show the ends of the strips. Leave your mummy white, except for the visible part of the face, or color it white with a gel or paint pen.

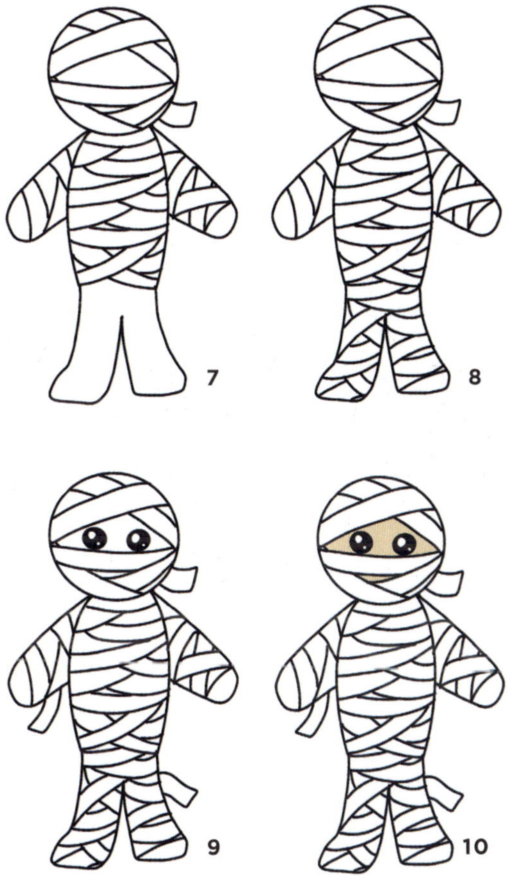

practice here

VAMPIRE

Start drawing a vampire by sketching an oval head and a thin neck. Next, add a bowtie and a jacket collar. Sketch the body of the jacket and the sleeves, adding hands. Then, draw a pair of pants with shoes at the bottom.

Draw a rounded triangle on each side of the neck with a curving line extending down from it to form the outline of the cape. Add lines for the front edges of the cape, as well as detail lines on the collar, and erase the areas where they overlap the body. Add center-parted hair with texture lines, and draw a simple face, including two sharp teeth. All that's left to do is color your vampire doodle.

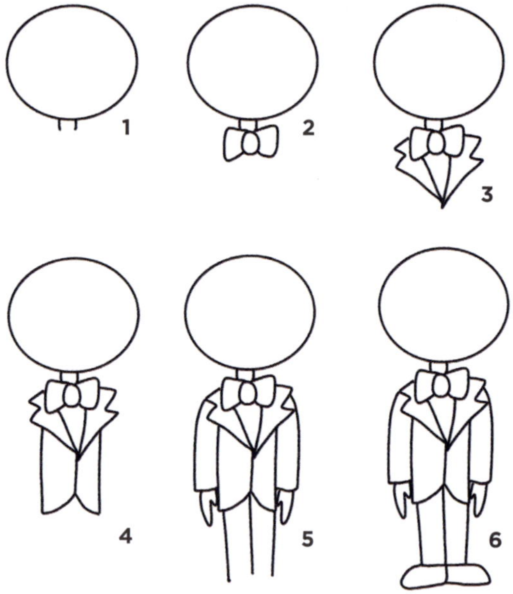

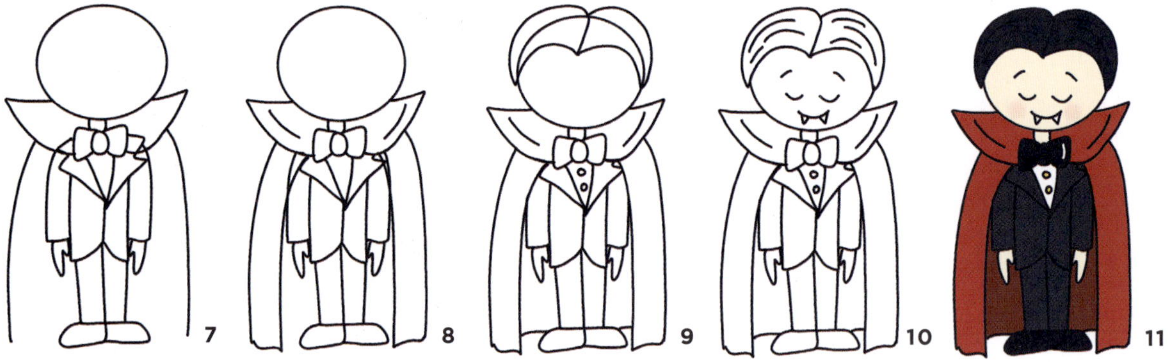

practice here

ZOMBIE

Hide your brains, and then draw a circle to doodle this zombie's head. Give him a thin neck, and then draw an upper body with a ragged short-sleeved shirt. Add a pair of pants, as well as arms and hands in any position you like. Draw patches and splotches of dirt on the clothing. Sketch a pair of feet, and then add unkempt hair outlined with jagged lines. Erase any overlapping areas, and then draw a few zigzag lines in the hair for texture. Give your zombie eyes and an open smile with just a few teeth. Finish your doodle by coloring the zombie green, and coloring the clothes and hair in any way you choose.

practice here

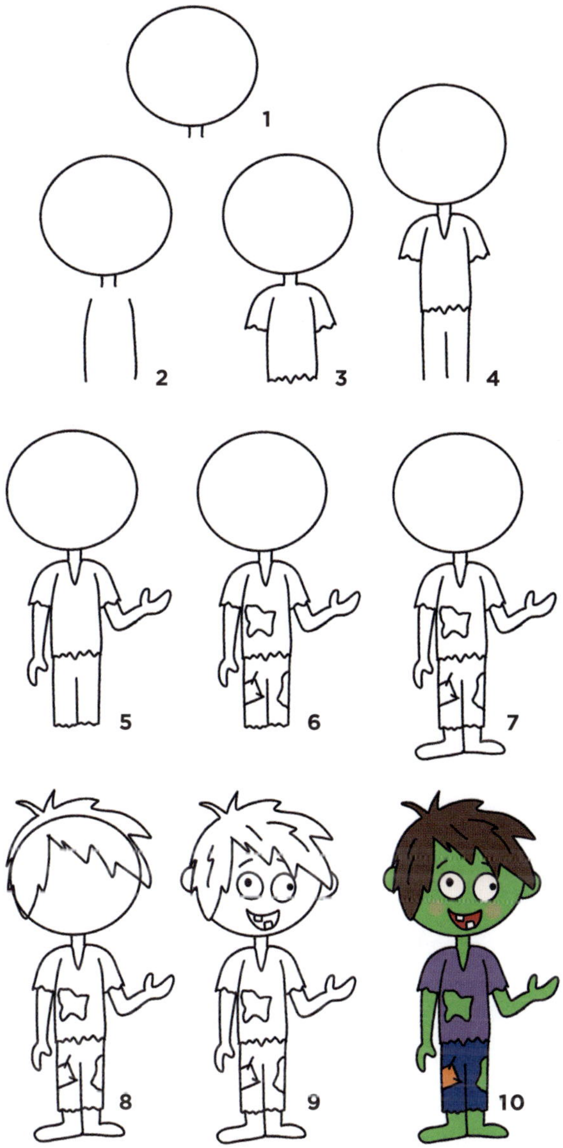

GHOST

To doodle a basic ghost, start with a tall arch, and then connect the bottom with a wavy line. Add detail lines inside the shape to show a flowing texture. Draw a pair of eyes, and then color your doodle. Since ghosts are typically thought of as being white or transparent, the only thing you really need to color is a pair of rosy cheeks, if you like. Of course, if you are drawing on dark paper, you can use a white paint pen or gel pen to color in your whole doodle and make it really pop.

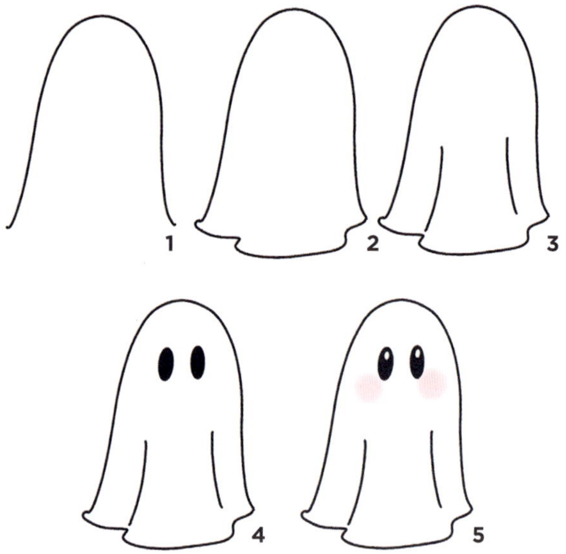

CLOSET

Since monsters are sometimes said to live in closets (don't worry, as I've never seen any evidence that this is true), let's learn to doodle a door you can add to your monster drawings. First, draw three sides of a rectangle, and then draw the same shape slightly larger around it.

Connect the corners to the original shape to make the door frame, and connect the frame at the bottom. Then, draw the door itself by sketching diagonal lines for the top and bottom and connecting them on the side. Add a doorknob, as well as a pair of hinges, erasing the areas where they overlap existing lines. Add color to finish your drawing.

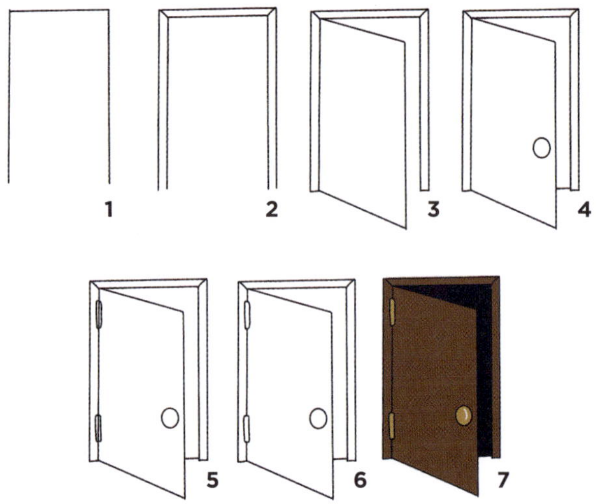

TROLL

You never know where you might stumble across a troll. Start this doodle with the boxy head shape and a pair of large, pointed ears. Divide the top section of the ears from the inner part. Add lines for the wide shoulders and short sleeves, and then draw curving lines for the thick upper body. Sketch a belt and a pair of large arms and hands. Add the bottom of the tunic and a large pair of feet with three toes. Draw a big nose inside the face area, along with eyes and a mouth. Sketch detail lines in the tunic and on the forehead for texture. Finish your drawing by coloring your troll.

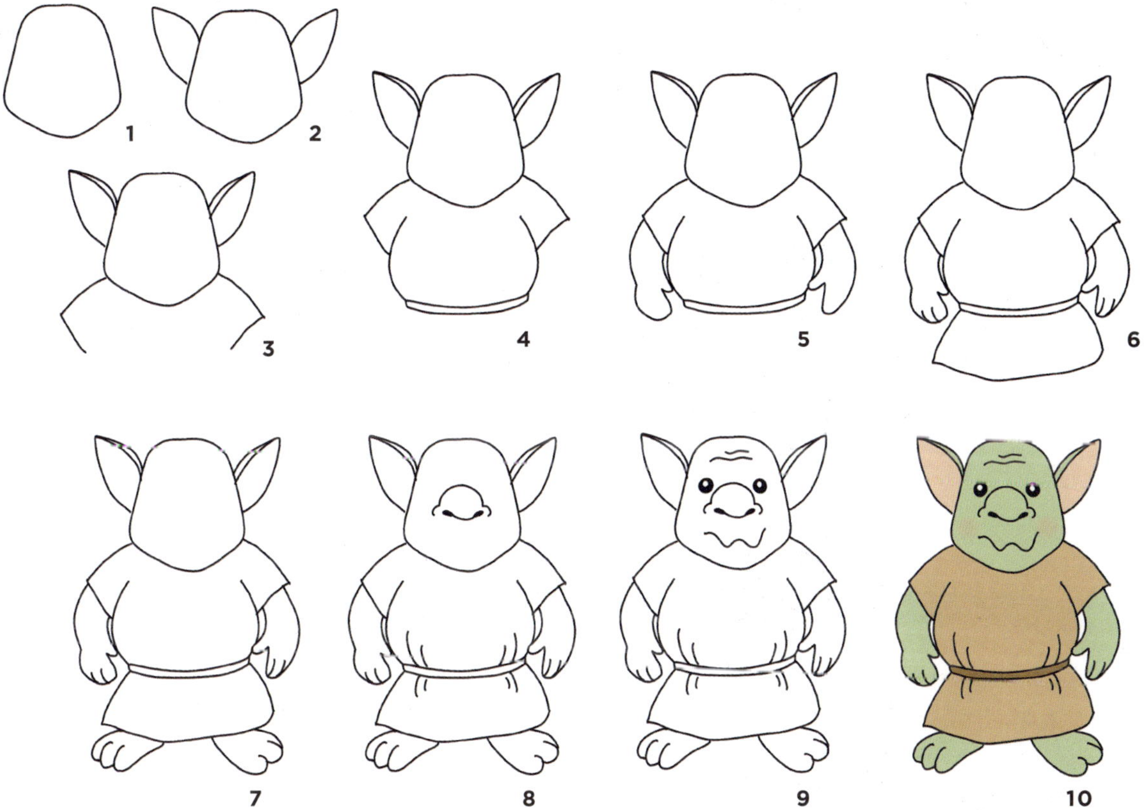

BAT

To doodle a bat, start with a round head and an oval-shaped body. Add a pair of pointed ears, and divide them into two sections. Draw two large wings, each with three scallops across the bottom. Use two straight lines to connect the scallops to the point at the top of the wing, dividing the wing into three sections. Add a face, as well as a pair of small feet made from three “u” shapes. Color your bat to complete the doodle. It’s even more fun to draw your bat hanging upside down from a tree or the ceiling!

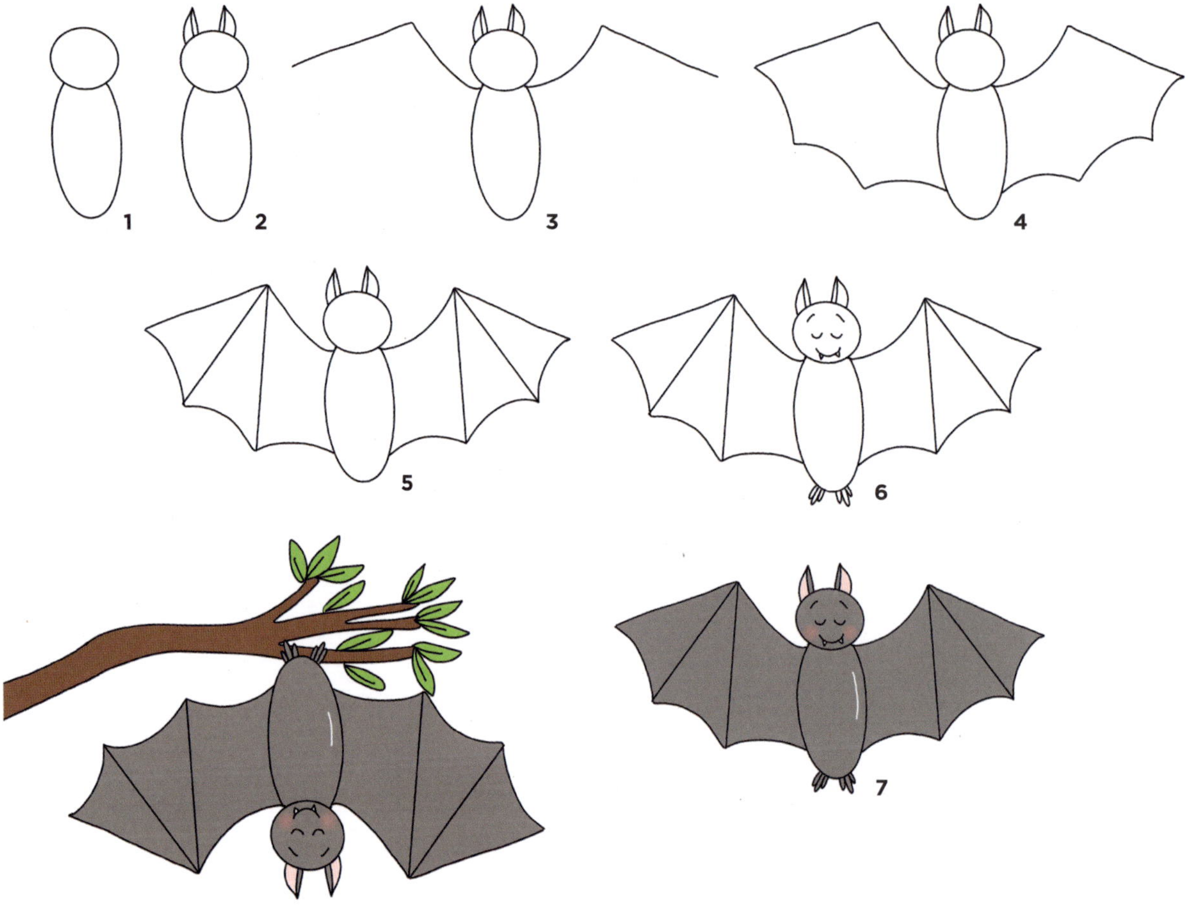

HAUNTED HOUSE

Let's finish off our adventures in the monster's lair by sketching a haunted house. Start this doodle by creating the basic house shape with a horizontal line and two curving vertical ones. Add a "v"-shaped roof and a crooked chimney. Draw another, smaller "house" shape on each side of the main one, letting the shapes curve outward. Erase the areas where the lines overlap.

Add an arched door and a round window to the main part of the house, and draw "v" shapes to thicken each of the three rooftops. Also, draw a second arch around the door shape. Sketch arch-shaped windows with shutters on each of the smaller house sections, and then finish your drawing by coloring it. If you like, you can set the mood by drawing a moon behind the house.

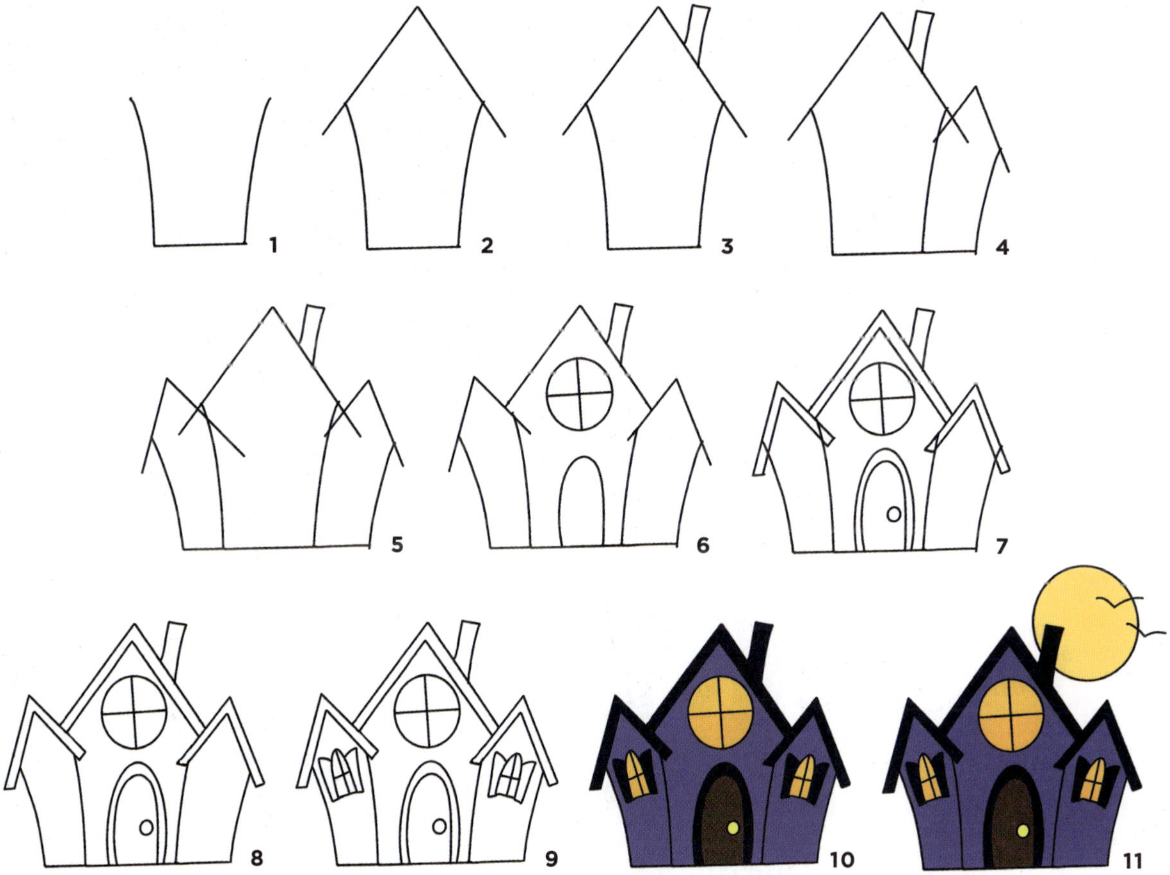

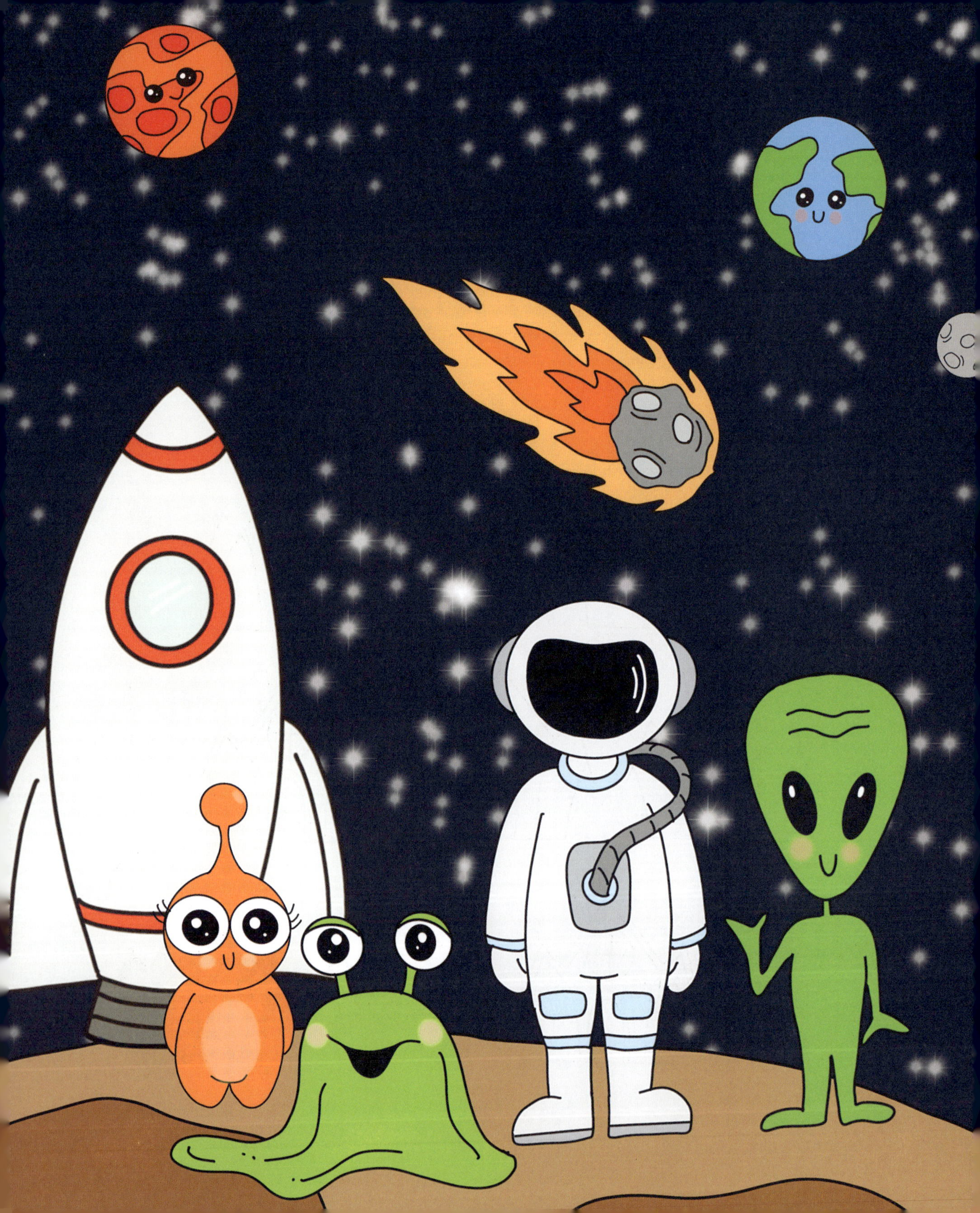

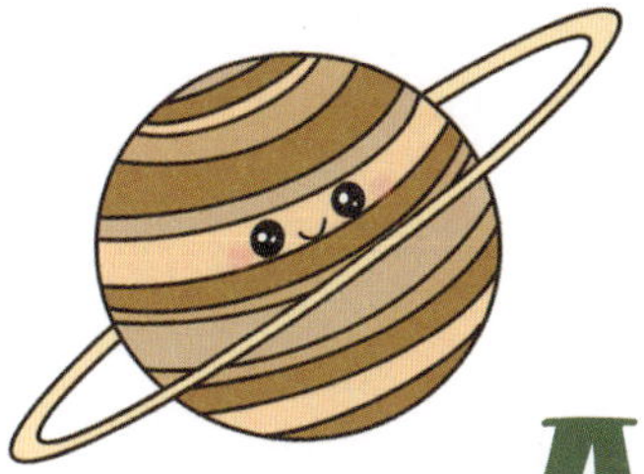

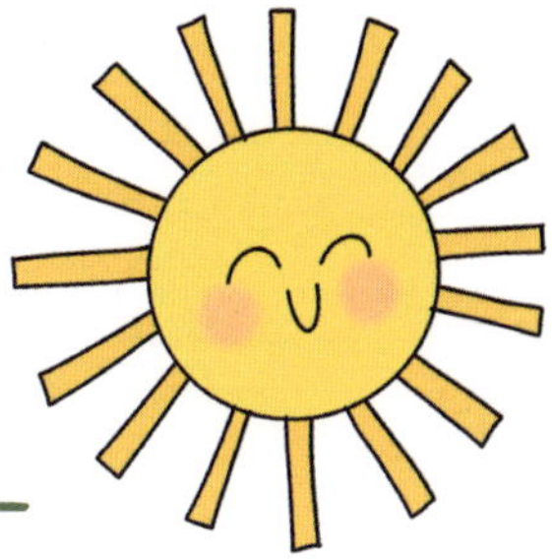

A PLANET Far, Far Away

Space is sometimes called "the final frontier," because while humans have explored most of the Earth, there's so much more beyond our planet that we have yet to discover! In this chapter, we'll be learning to doodle the planets that make up the Milky Way galaxy, as well as the sun, moon and stars. We'll also draw a variety of aliens and their spacecraft, an astronaut and a rocket. Grab your drawing supplies, and let's get ready to doodle our way through the universe. Who knows what kind of creatures you will encounter!

ALIEN

Let's start our journey to outer space by doodling a friendly alien. First, sketch a large head shaped like a rounded, upside-down triangle. Draw two ovals for eyes, and then add a smile. Sketch a thin neck, as well as wavy lines across the forehead for texture. Next, draw two lines for the sides of the body. Add legs and feet, and then draw arms with "v"-shaped hands. Finish your doodle by adding color. I chose green, but your alien can be any color (or combination of colors) you choose.

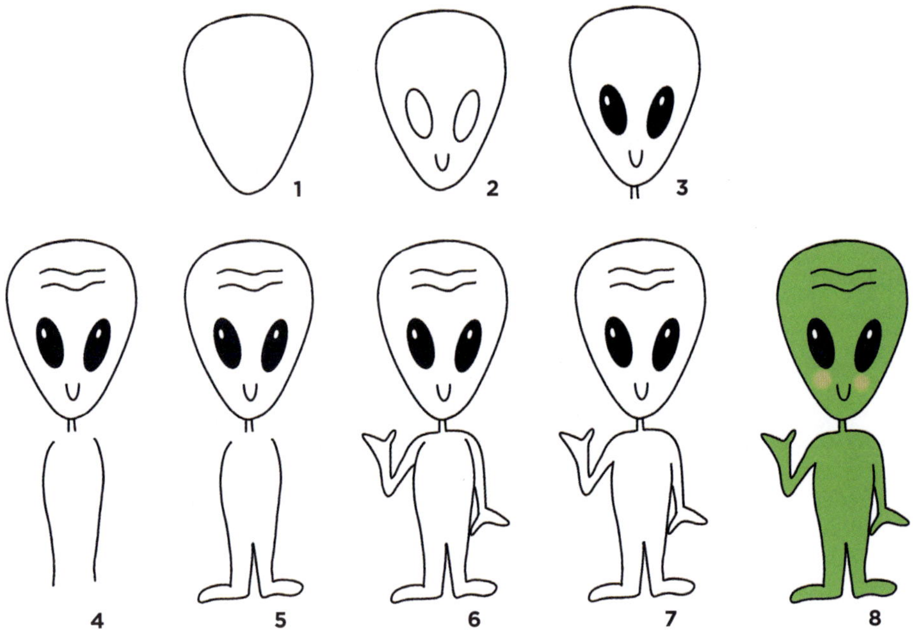

practice here

SLIMY ALIEN

Since we don't really know what aliens look like, there's plenty of opportunity to imagine different kinds of otherworldly creatures. This variation doesn't have a human-like body, and it's lots of fun to draw. Start with an arch shape, and then connect the bottom with a wavy line.

Draw a pair of circles above the body, and connect them to it with parallel lines. Draw smaller circles inside to create eyes, and add a mouth. Sketch curving lines inside the top of the eyes for eyelids, and draw detail lines to show movement in the body. Finally, add color to complete your alien.

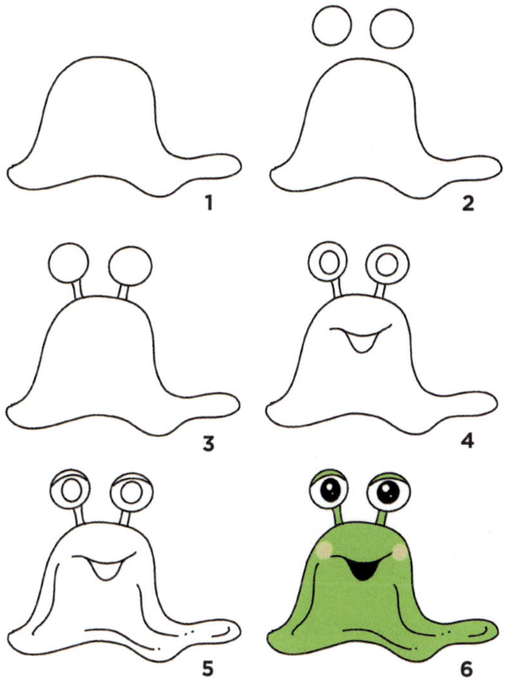

ANTENNAE ALIEN

Imagine one more kind of alien creature with me. This variation is plump and adorable and is sure to befriend any interplanetary visitors. Draw a round head, and then add a rounded "w" shape for the body and legs. Sketch a curving line for the bottom of the belly, and draw two rounded arms.

Make a circle above the head, and connect it to the top of the head with two curving lines. Erase the extra lines so you have just an outline left. Draw a pair of very large eyes made from concentric circles, and give your alien a smile; you can even add eyelashes if you like. Finish your drawing by adding color.

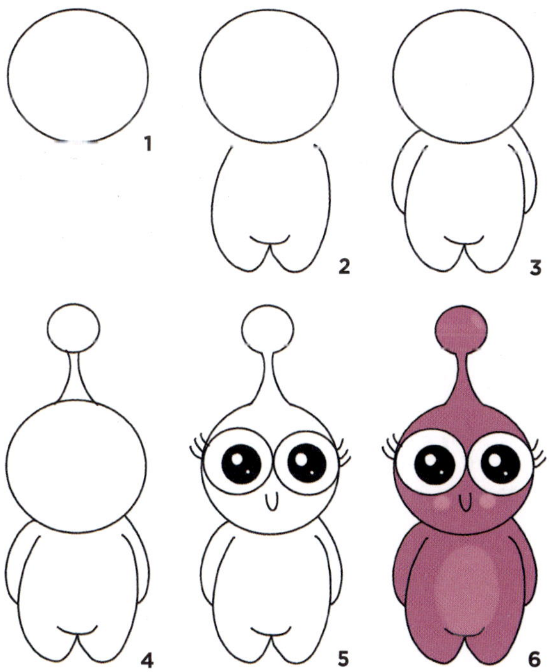

UFO

Let's help our aliens travel through space in their own UFO. Start by sketching an arch. Connect the bottom with a curve, and then draw a pair of diagonal lines extending out from the bottom corners. Connect those lines with another curve. Draw several circles inside the lower shape for lights, and add a stripe near the top.

Sketch an antenna, and then add a rounded rectangle on the bottom of the UFO. Draw some vertical texture lines on the base, as well as detail lines inside the arch shape. Finally, add curving lines on either side of the UFO to show movement and a few lines around the top of the antenna. Color your UFO using any color combination you choose.

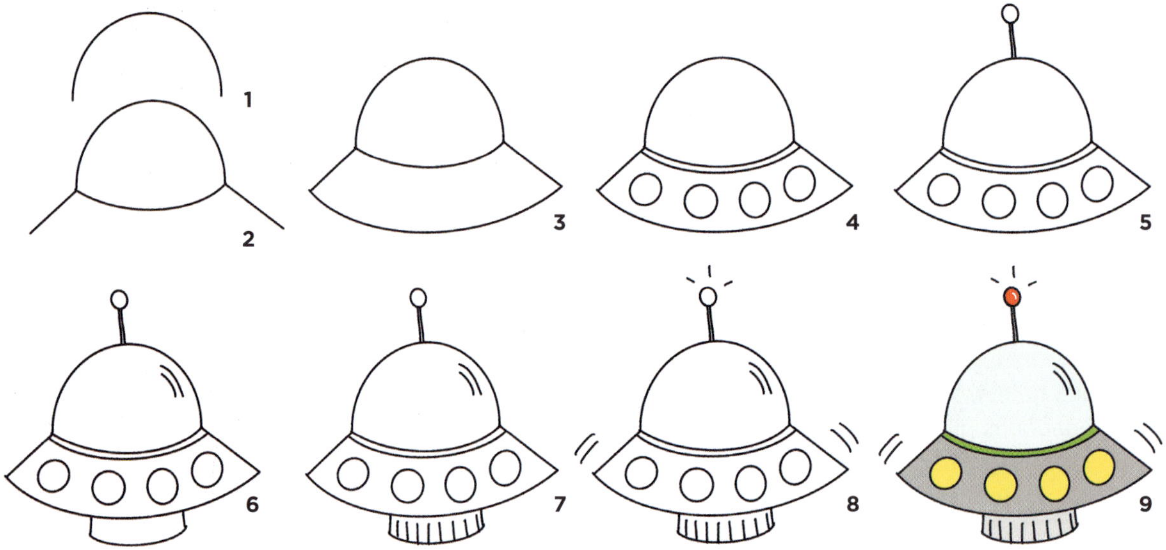

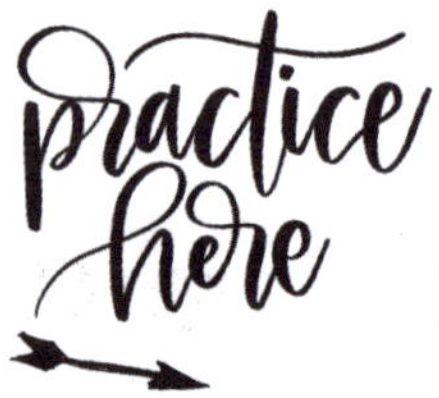

BEAMING UFO

Sometimes a doodle is all about perspective. For this variation on a UFO, we're going to draw it as though we are looking up at the spacecraft from below. Draw an arch with an oval underneath, erasing the overlapping lines. Add a double "c" shape inside the oval. Draw curving lines in the arch to show the reflection on the glass.

Sketch a pair of diagonal lines coming down from the "c" shapes to represent light. Between the lines, sketch a series of longer and shorter lines to indicate more rays of light coming out of the UFO. Draw lots of small circle shapes inside the oval. Finally, add a semicircle and a pair of antennae to show a little alien inside the spacecraft, and then color your doodle.

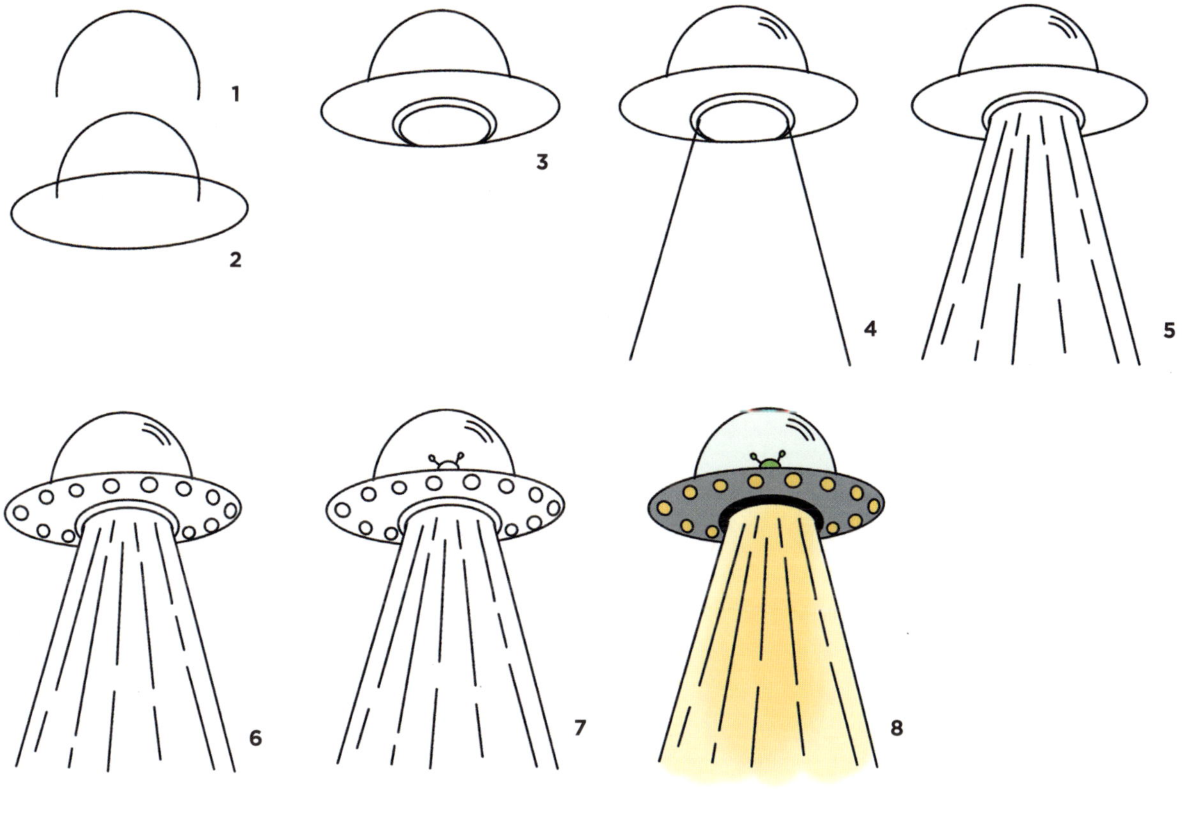

TRAPEZOID UFO

Here is one more variation of a UFO that you can add to your outer space drawings. Start with a pair of diagonal lines that point in toward each other. Connect the top with a curving line, and draw an oval at the bottom. Add a stripe at the top of the shape, and draw a series of ovals for windows or lights. Draw a "c" shape inside the bottom oval, and then sketch a pair of diagonal lines extending downward from it. Draw multiple longer and shorter lines inside the light beam to represent shining rays. Then, add color to your UFO.

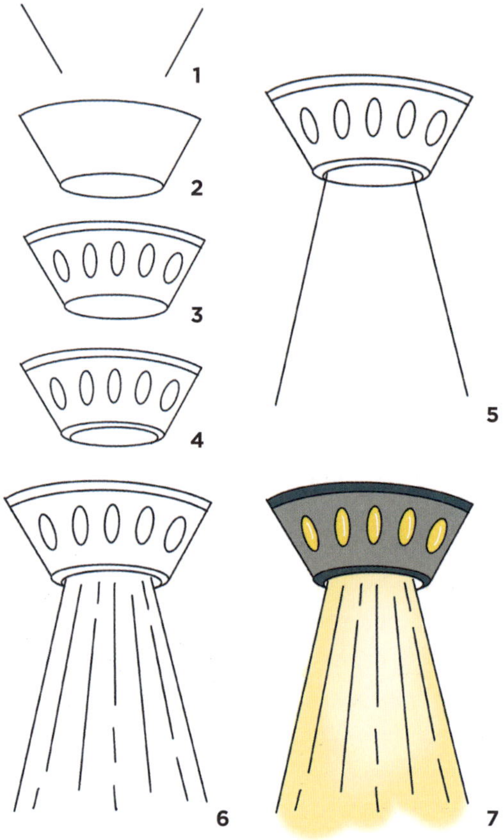

practice here

ASTRONAUT'S HELMET

To draw an astronaut's helmet, start with a circle, and then draw a backward "c" shape right below it. Add a semicircle on each side of the head. Next, draw a large visor in the center of the helmet. If you like, you can add a line with a circle for an antenna. Finally, color your helmet to complete the doodle.

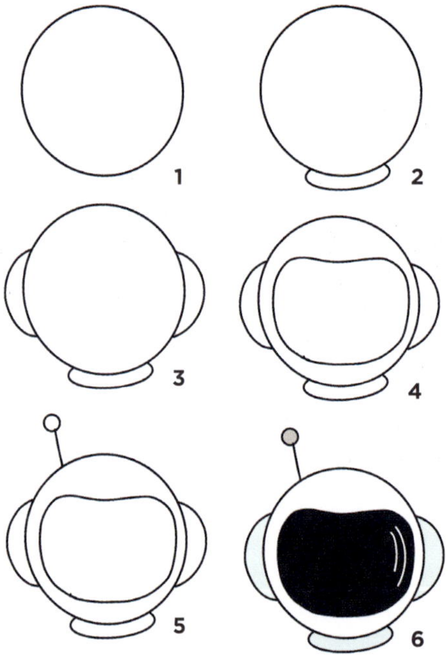

ASTRONAUT

Begin your astronaut by sketching the round helmet shape with semicircles on the sides. Add a double "c" shape below it, and then draw two lines for the sides of the body. Sketch a pair of arms, with stripes at the bottoms of the sleeves. Then, draw legs, with stripes at the bottoms to complete the basic space suit.

Draw a pair of gloves, and add the visor to the center of the helmet. Next, sketch a pair of boots. Add details to the suit, such as rounded rectangles on the knees and a rectangle with a circle for the oxygen hose attachment. Sketch the hose, erasing the places where it overlaps the space suit, and then add detail lines. Finish your doodle by adding color.

practice here

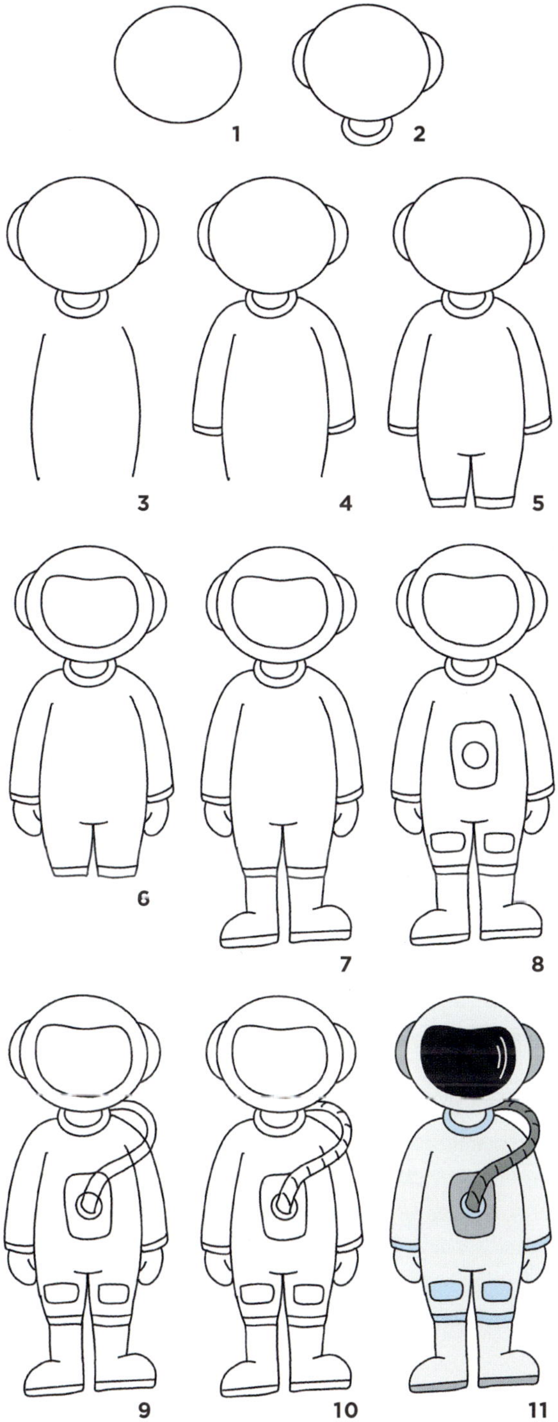

ROCKET

Blast off into outer space with this cute rocket doodle! Start with a pair of curving lines that touch at the top to form a point. Connect the lines at the bottom to create the body of the rocket. Add a wing on each side. Draw a curving line below the rocket and connect it to the body, adding several horizontal stripes. Sketch decorative lines on the upper and lower part of the rocket's body and a round window. Add detail lines to the wings, and sketch a jagged "v"-shaped flame with a smaller flame inside. Finish your doodle by coloring your rocket and flame.

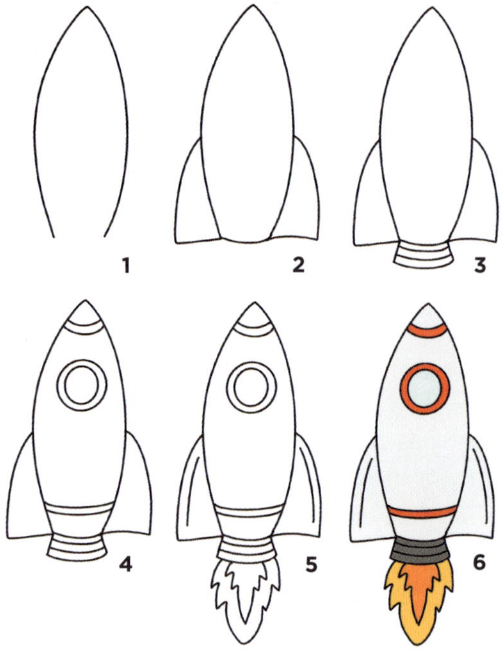

TELESCOPE

Keep your eye on the sky with this telescope drawing. First, draw an oval for the lens, with short lines extending from the top and bottom. Connect them with a curving line, and then draw a pair of longer lines that get slightly closer together as they extend. Connect those, and then make one more section of the telescope that is slightly thinner than the previous one. Add a band at the bottom, and then draw texture lines in the top section and the lens. Form a tripod by drawing three long, thin legs and connecting them with two thin rectangles. Finally, color your telescope.

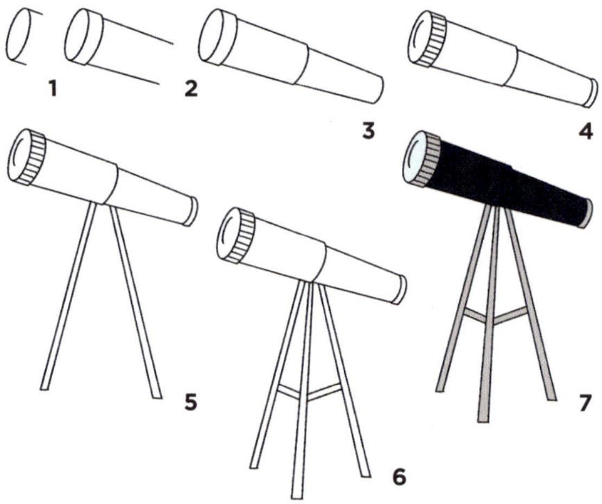

MERCURY

If you think it gets hot on Earth, try living on Mercury, the closest planet to the Sun! To doodle it, start with a small circle. Then, add texture by sketching a series of roundish shapes made from zigzag lines. If you'd like to bring the planet to life, you can add a simple face made of eyes and a smile. Color your doodle in light and dark gray, or using your favorite combination of colors.

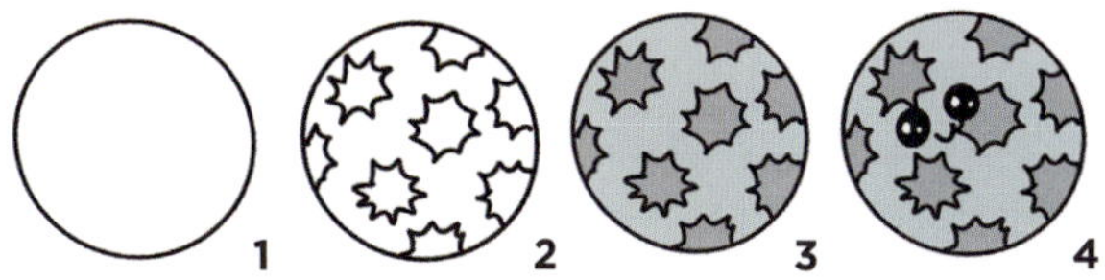

VENUS

To doodle Venus, one of the Earth's neighbors, draw a circle, and then cover the surface with a combination of wavy lines and spirals. You can leave it as is, or you can add a cartoon face, if you choose. Since Venus is often associated with women ("Women are from Venus, men are from Mars . . ."), I gave this particular planet eyelashes. Once your sketch is finished, all that's left to do is color it.

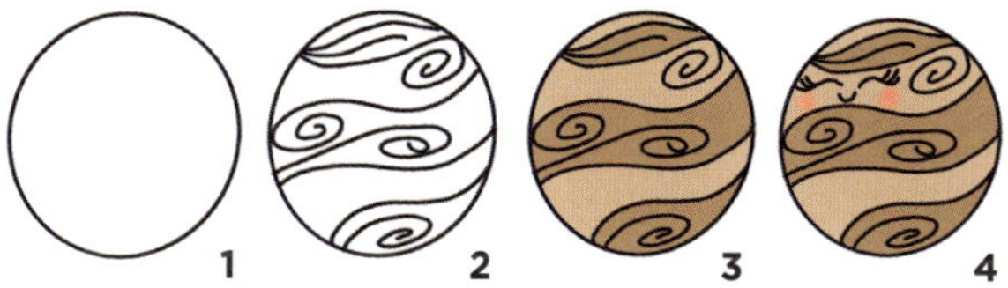

EARTH

It's time to draw our home planet: Earth! Sketch a circle, and then draw wavy shapes inside to indicate the land masses of some of the continents. Don't worry about being exact; it will still be very obvious what you're drawing. Add a face if you choose, and then color the oceans blue and the land masses green or brown.

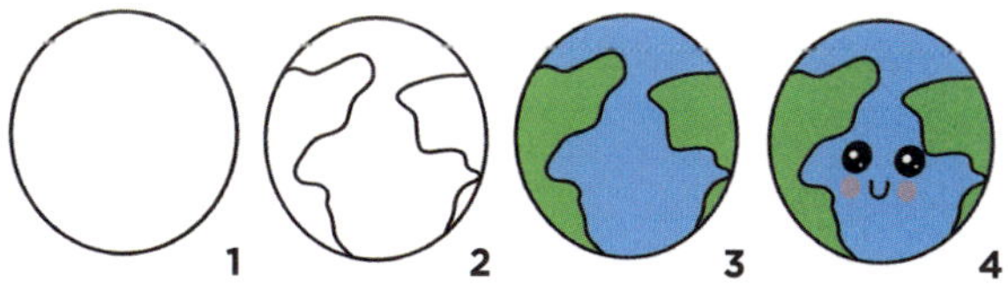

MARS

Mars is the Earth's closest neighbor, known as the "red planet." To doodle it, start with a circle, and then add several oval-shaped spots spread out around the surface. Next, add a few wavy lines running through the parts where there aren't any spots. Then, color your doodle using shades of red and orange. If you like, add eyes and a smile to give your planet a cheerful face.

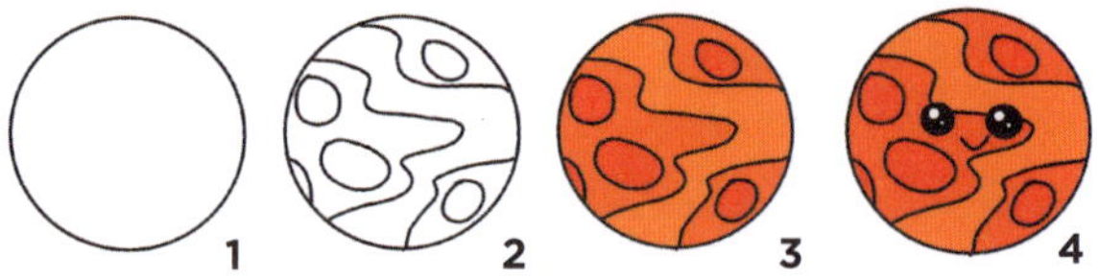

JUPITER

Let's learn to draw our solar system's largest planet, Jupiter. Sketch a large circle, and then divide it into many smaller sections using curved and wavy lines. Each section should be a different size. Choose several sections and add oval shapes inside. Add a face, if you like, and then color your planet in various shades of brown and gray.

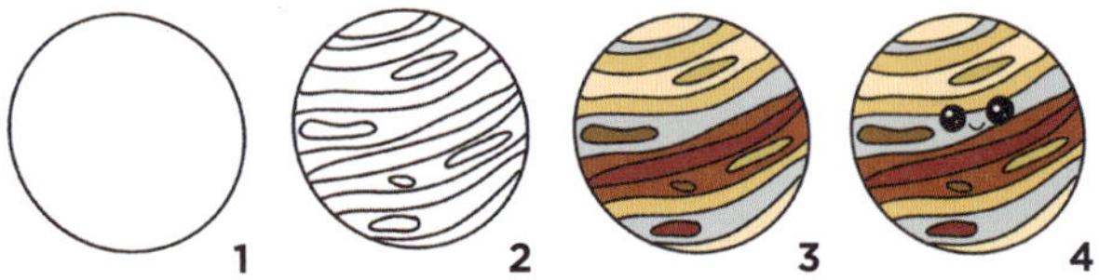

SATURN

Saturn is the second largest planet in the Milky Way, and is known for its large ring. To create this doodle, start with a large circle and use curving lines to divide it into many different sections. Don't worry about making the sections uniform; some should be smaller than others. Then, add two oval shapes around the planet to create the ring, erasing the spots where it overlaps the circle. Color your drawing using different shades of brown, and feel free to add a simple face.

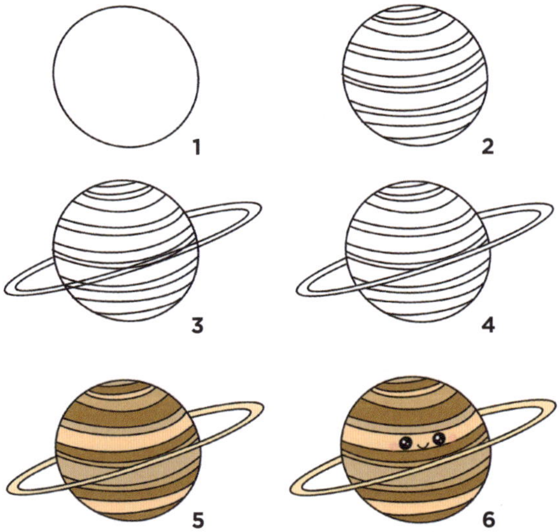

URANUS

The planet Uranus may be the butt of a few jokes, but it's also an important member of the Milky Way. To sketch it, draw a circle, and then add a ring around it. Erase the areas where the ring overlaps the planet. Color your doodle blue, and add a face if you like. I chose to make my planet wink, but you can use any combination of eyes and mouth to create your own favorite facial expression.

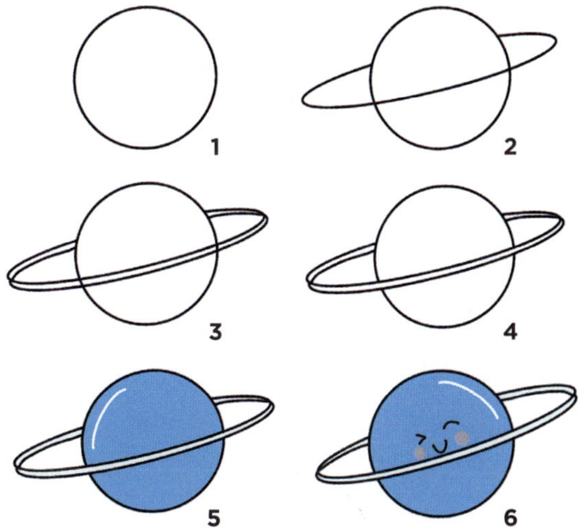

NEPTUNE

Neptune is the farthest planet from the Sun. To draw it, start with a circle, and then divide it into eight or more uneven sections using a series of wavy lines. Add a few oval shapes in the larger sections. Color your planet using various shades of blue. If you like, you can also add eyes, a smile and rosy cheeks to give your doodle a happy expression.

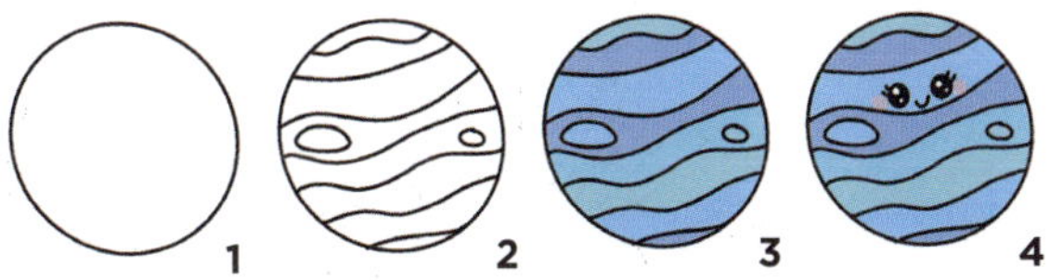

PLUTO

Pluto was considered the ninth planet in our solar system until 2006, when the International Astronomical Union (IAU) demoted it to a dwarf planet. Either way, it's still a fun doodle to create and to add to your outer space drawings. To sketch it, draw a circle, and then add a heart-shaped area in the bottom right. Color the heart section light brown, and the rest a darker shade of brown. Feel free to add a cute face.

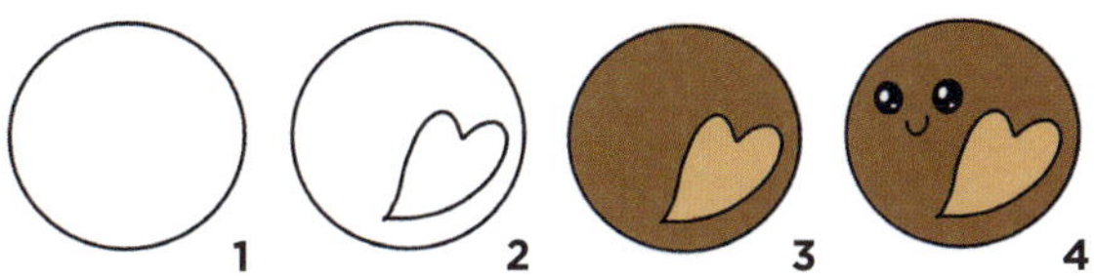

SUN

There are many ways to sketch the Sun, including just a simple circle. In the Rainbow Unicorn World chapter, we learned to draw it as a circle with zigzag rays around it (see page 19). Here's another easy variation, again starting with a basic circle center. To create rays, draw four, thin rectangles; one at the top, one at the bottom and one on each side. Then, draw three more thin rectangles in between each pair. This will give you sixteen rays. Finish your drawing by adding eyes and a smile, and then coloring the sun yellow.

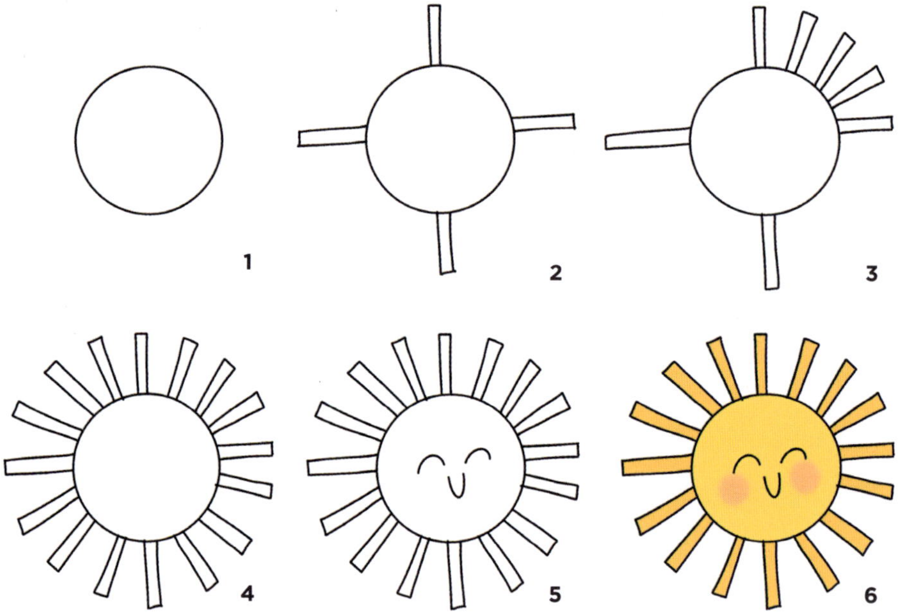

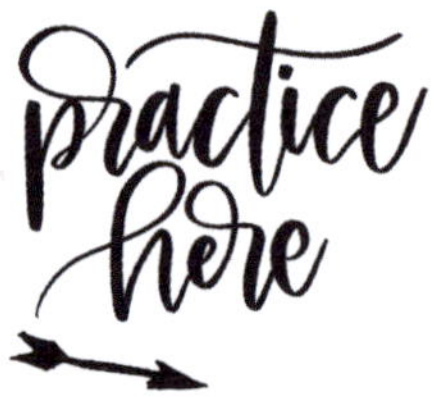

MOON

The Earth's moon goes through various stages during its monthly cycle, so there's more than one way we can draw it. One popular way is a crescent moon. Just sketch a basic crescent shape, made of two curving lines connected at the top and bottom to form points. Then, add color and a detail line to finish this simple doodle.

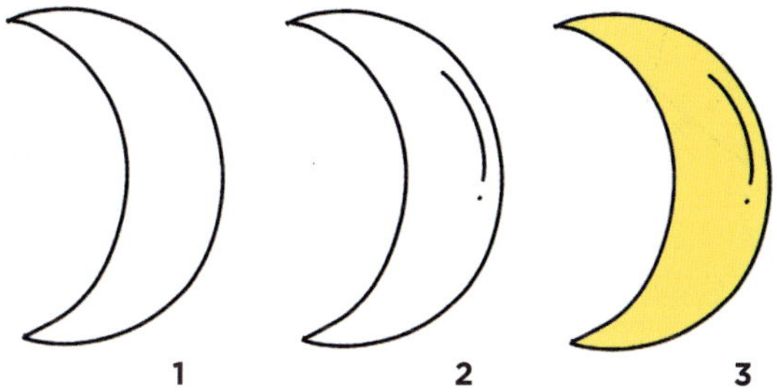

Another option is to draw the full moon. Start with a circle for the basic shape, and then add several "c" shapes inside to show the cratered texture of the moon's surface. Draw a few oval shapes on the surface as well, and then sketch some curving lines to finish creating the texture. Finish your doodle by coloring the moon.

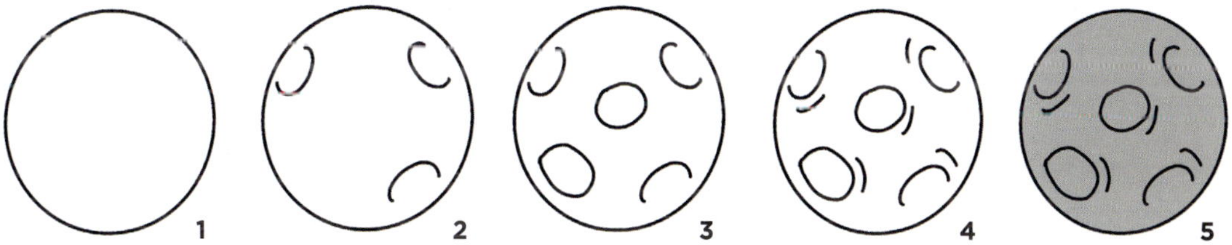

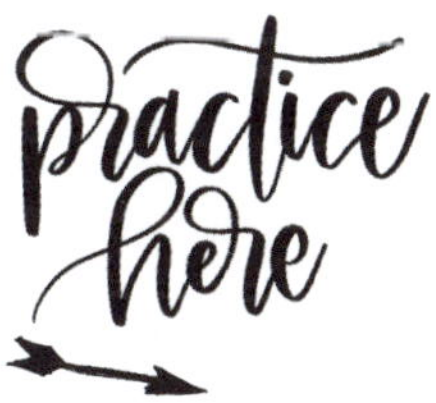

STARS

Just as there are many ways to draw the sun and moon, we can also draw various styles of stars. The simplest one is the basic five-pointed star. Simply sketch the star shape, and then erase all of the inside lines so that you're left with just an outline. Then, add color.

To create an eight-pointed star, start by drawing two long, thin "v" shapes that connect to one another. Then, draw another pair of "v"s on the left and right. This creates four points. Now, add smaller "v" shapes in between each pair of points. Erase the extra lines so that you're left with just the star's outline. Then, add color to finish your drawing.

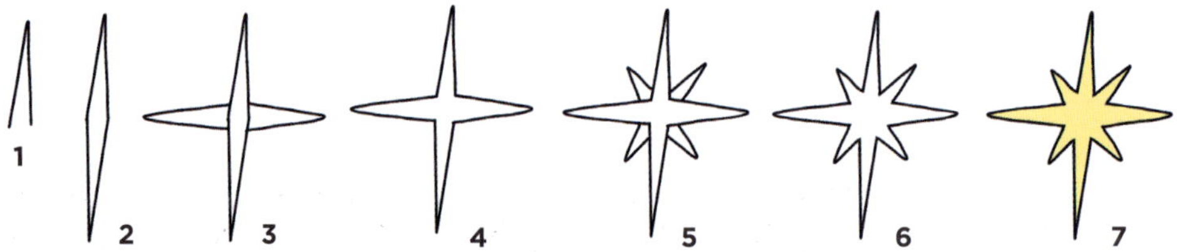

Another variation on a star is to simply draw a series of zigzags going around in a circle until they meet. This can be as large or small as you like, and you can keep the zigzags similar in size or vary them. Once your shape is sketched, you can add color to complete it.

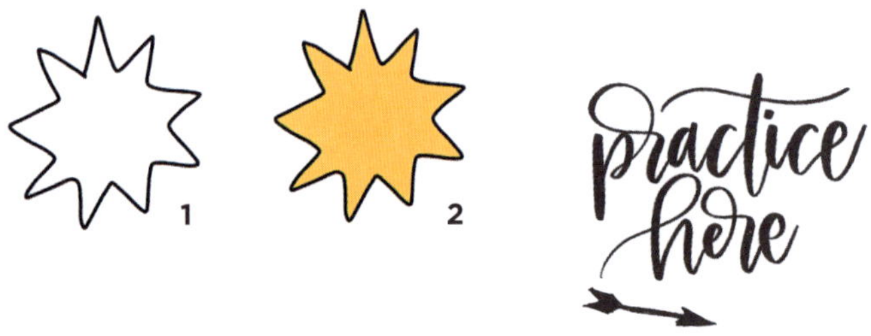

CONSTELLATIONS

Constellations, or formations of stars, are fun to add to drawings of the night sky. There are tons to choose from. We'll be drawing the Big Dipper and Little Dipper, but you can also do a search online for any constellation you like and use this technique to replicate it. One way to draw a constellation is by using simple dots to represent the stars. Once you know the pattern and arrangement of the stars, sketch your dots in those places. Then, all that's left to do is connect the dots with straight lines to form the picture of the constellation, which in this case is the Big Dipper.

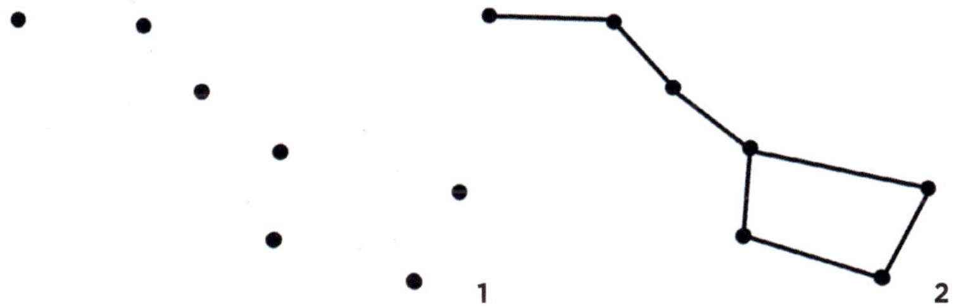

To take your constellation doodle to the next level, you can make some or all of the stars a little more detailed. Rather than just using dots, use small diamond shapes, open circles or any combination of the other star shapes we learned. As before, position them in the pattern of the constellation, and then connect the stars with straight lines to make the picture, as seen here for the Little Dipper. Since these star shapes are open, you can color them yellow or make them white against a dark sky.

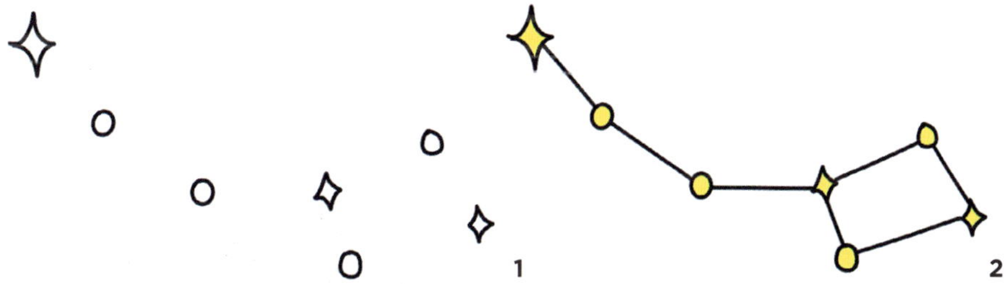

METEOR

Start your meteor doodle with an irregular round shape. Add several ovals and "c" shapes to the surface of the meteor for texture. Sketch a zigzag line starting below the meteor and extending above it to begin creating the shape of the flame. Add another zigzag line for the other side of the flaming tail. Then, add two smaller flame shapes inside the large one. Color your meteor gray with a red, orange and yellow tail.

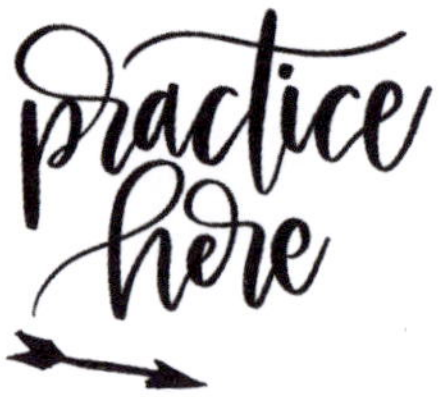

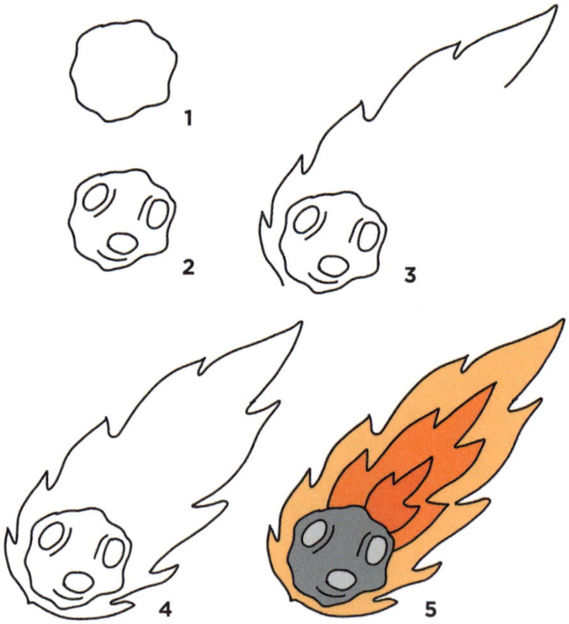

SHOOTING STAR

Make a wish on this shooting star! Draw a basic five-pointed star, erasing all the inside lines. Then, sketch a pair of curving lines that get gradually farther apart extending from one side of the star. Between them, add a series of detail lines, some longer than others, to indicate light trailing behind the star. Color your shooting star in any way you like, and feel free to give it a personality with eyes and a smile.

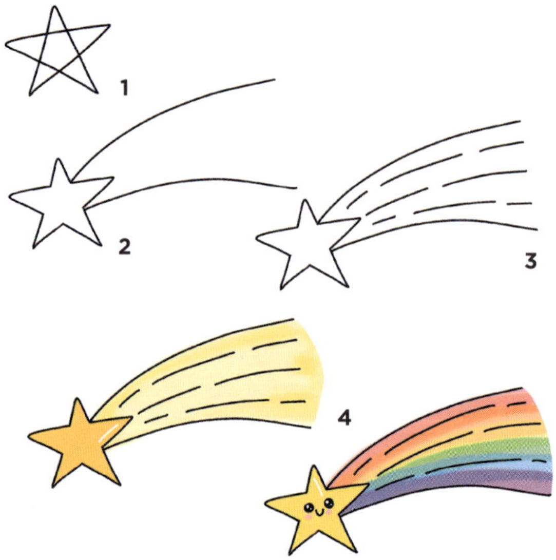

ACKNOWLEDGMENTS

Will and the Page Street Team: Thank you for partnering with me once again and allowing me to make a career of doing what I love. I don't take that for granted.

Sarah: You are the best editor a girl could ask for. We make a great team, and I am incredibly thankful for you.

Dan, Nathan and Noah: Thank you for your unfailing support and for putting up with my schedule while I promote one book and write another. I love you more than I can say.

Noah: Your input and ideas make me better. I so appreciate your creative feedback. I owe you dinner at Fratelli's . . . let's have a book party!

Mom and Dad: You have always believed in me, and your continued encouragement means the world. Love you forever.

The Holy Donut Club: Thank you for keeping me on my toes and being the bright spot in every week. Love you all. The donut doodle is for you.

You, dear reader: Without you, there would be no books. Thank you for your interest and your support. Let's keep making wonderful art together.

ABOUT THE AUTHOR

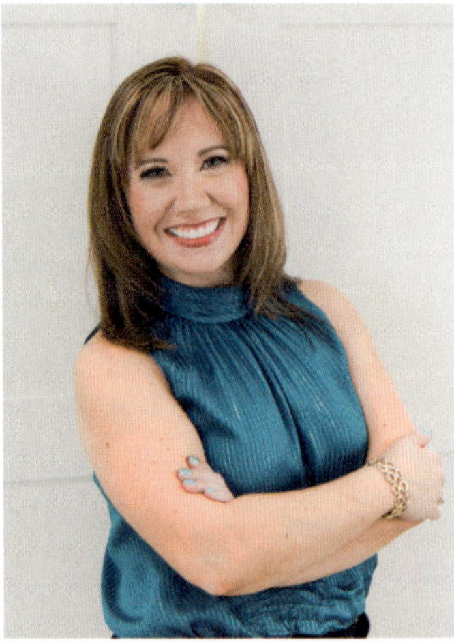

Amy Latta is an artist, illustrator and founder of the award-winning blog www.amylattacreations.com, where you'll find all kinds of creative projects anyone can make! She loves teaching virtual and in-person workshops, and regularly shares creative ideas on lifestyle television shows nationwide. Amy is happiest when crafting or teaching, and her passion is to help people discover that they can create beautiful things. Her work has been featured by Gap® Stores, Starbucks®, Tombow USA, Martha Stewart and more in a variety of professional collaborations. Amy lives in Maryland with her husband and two teenage sons.

INDEX